Shocking the Conscience of Humanity

Professor Margaret M. deGuzman is the James E. Beasley Professor of Law and Co-Director of the Institute for International Law and Public Policy at Temple University's Beasley School of Law. Her scholarship focuses on the role of international criminal law in the global legal order, with a particular emphasis on the work of the International Criminal Court (ICC). She has written extensively about international criminal law theory and practice, including topics ranging from the definition of crimes against humanity to crime selection and sentencing at international courts and tribunals. Before joining Temple Law School, Professor deGuzman practiced criminal defense in San Francisco, served a   ..dvisor to the Senegal delegation at the Rome Conference of the ICC, was a law clerk at the International Criminal Tribunal for Former Yugoslavia, and a Fulbright Scholar in Daru N'Diar, Senegal.

'Margaret M. deGuzman navigates perhaps the most difficult challenge confronting international criminal law: how to understand the gravity of the crimes under investigation and whether an international tribunal should be seized with their prosecution. Gravity is what elevates justice from the national to the international level, and the criteria for that ascent are fraught with peril. Professor deGuzman provides the roadmap, which reconceptualizes gravity as a function of values and goals centering on human dignity. Collective bodies of states must play a central role in establishing the goals while international jurists and scholars will find her remarkably lucid thinking indispensable in framing the arguments of the future.'

Ambassador David Scheffer, Northwestern University Pritzker School of Law

'In this important book Professor deGuzman rethinks 'gravity,' a term that despite its undertheorization animates much discussion of international criminal law. Of particular significance, she places human dignity at the center of her reconceptualization, and then calls for ongoing, pluralistic dialogue on how to prevent harms to this and other global values.'

Diane Marie Amann, University of Georgia School of Law

'From an insignificant afterthought at the Rome Conference where the International Criminal Court was created, 'gravity' has emerged as one of international criminal law's central conundrums. Margaret M. deGuzman's masterly and comprehensive presentation of the subject will frame the debate for many years.'

William A. Schabas, Middlesex University in London

'In this pathbreaking book, Professor deGuzman masterfully argues that gravity should be reframed to reflect and uphold the core universalist value of protecting human dignity. Shocking the Conscience of Humanity is an important book for anyone interested in the past, present, and future of international criminal justice.'

Charles C. Jalloh, Florida International University

Shocking the Conscience of Humanity

Gravity and the Legitimacy of International Criminal Law

MARGARET M. DEGUZMAN

OXFORD
UNIVERSITY PRESS

OXFORD
UNIVERSITY PRESS

Great Clarendon Street, Oxford, OX2 6DP,
United Kingdom

Oxford University Press is a department of the University of Oxford.
It furthers the University's objective of excellence in research, scholarship,
and education by publishing worldwide. Oxford is a registered trade mark of
Oxford University Press in the UK and in certain other countries

First published 2020
First published in paperback 2022

Published in the United States of America by Oxford University Press
198 Madison Avenue, New York, NY 10016, United States of America

British Library Cataloguing in Publication Data
Data available

Library of Congress Cataloging in Publication Data
Data available

ISBN 978-0-19-878615-3 (Hbk.)
ISBN 978-0-19-288697-2 (Pbk.)

To Anthony, for everything

Preface

As I began to consider the role of gravity in international criminal law, the United States was celebrating the election of its first African-American president, Barack Obama, whose administration espoused the values of global liberalism, including that of promoting human dignity through respect for human rights and international humanitarian law. Although the US government was far from perfect in respecting such values, its domestic and foreign policies were rooted in the country's longstanding commitment to rights and the rule of law. Globalism was seen as both a moral imperative and a way to promote US interests.

Much of the world took for granted the value of international cooperation in the promotion of human rights and humanitarian law. The European Union made human rights a high priority, and there was a thriving human rights regime in Latin America. In the Middle East, the Arab Spring opened new spaces for democratic governance, and the African Union's Constitutive Act authorized intervention to prevent war crimes, crimes against humanity, and genocide—the "core international crimes." At the 2005 World Summit, states unanimously endorsed the Responsibility to Protect doctrine, agreeing to act to prevent the core international crimes, including by military force in some circumstances.

These broad commitments to globalism manifested in strong support for the International Criminal Court (ICC). By 2016, over 120 states had joined the ICC, including most of Western Europe, Africa, and the Americas, as well some states in Asia. This high level of support exceeded the expectations of many of the lawyers, diplomats, and activists who helped to create the Court. Although some of the world's most powerful and populous states—including the United States, Russia, China, and India—remained outside of the regime, even those states did not generally seek to undermine the Court's work. On the contrary, the Obama Administration adopted a policy of constructive engagement with the ICC, providing important logistical and technical support to the Court.

Much has changed in the past few years. The current US administration has repeatedly abrogated the United States' commitment to human rights and the rule of law. The US president has declared his approval of water boarding "and a hell of a lot worse." He has espoused racist, sexist, and xenophobic values, likely contributing to a rise in hate crimes and other rights violations, many of which have gone unaddressed by his administration. The administration's immigration policies include systematic violations of the rights of migrants, including asylum seekers. Its foreign policy has focused on promoting US political and economic interests, regardless of the effect on rights or the rule of law around the world.

Basic human rights are also under assault outside of the United States. Ethno-nationalism is on the rise in Europe, and humanitarian tragedies abound in Africa, Asia, and Latin America. Russia has annexed Crimea. The Syrian conflict is in its second decade, and Myanmar is accused of perpetrating genocide against the Rohingya. Even the ICC is under attack. The United States has banned ICC personnel from entering the country, and has threatened to arrest them and seize their assets. The African Union has urged states to consider leaving the Court. Burundi and the Philippines have withdrawn from the regime, and South Africa and Kenya have considered doing so.

Against this backdrop, some of this book's claims may appear overly optimistic or even naïve. A central premise of the book is that a global community exists, with shared values and a common interest in enforcing those values. The book argues that an essential function of international criminal law, and especially of the ICC, is to promote the global community's values and goals. Moreover, the book endorses a broad range of potential global values and goals rooted in the promotion of human dignity.

I remain committed to the book's global cosmopolitan claims. I also acknowledge that the current political climate impedes progress toward a stronger global justice community. Yet the importance of the international criminal justice project is greater than ever. With global values under assault, it is vital for global institutions to speak on behalf of people who value the protection and promotion of human dignity.

It is also important to be realistic about what the ICC and other international criminal justice institutions can accomplish, and to avoid charging them with failings that are beyond their control. For example, the ICC cannot address crimes committed on the territory and by the nationals of non-party states without a Security Council referral. Most of the crimes committed in Syria are therefore outside of the ICC's jurisdiction, as are many crimes committed by nationals of the United States, China, and Russia. The ICC does not have the resources to prosecute more than a handful of cases each year, and therefore cannot address the needs of many victims in situations that come before the Court.

Such weaknesses do not negate the ICC's legitimacy. There will always be costs associated with creating institutions to act on behalf of a global community that is not fully united, and might never be so. But a flawed institution for pursuing justice is better than none at all, and the ICC has an important role to play in the global legal order. The Court should continue to identify and express global norms, such as the prohibitions against sexual and gender-based violence and the use of child soldiers, thereby signaling their importance to the world. In this way, the ICC can help to build the global justice community, and to promote the foundational norm of respect for human dignity.

Acknowledgements

A host of friends and colleagues helped me to develop the ideas in this book over the years, through conversations and by reading and commenting on draft articles on the topic. Among them, I want to especially thank Diane Amann, Jane Baron, Elena Baylis, Ziv Bohrer, Pamela Bookman, Alejandro Chehtman, Shahram Dana, Mark Drumbl, Jeffrey Dunoff, Fabricio Guariglia, Jonathan Hafetz, Rebecca Hamilton, Hurst Hannum, Adil Haque, Kevin Jon Heller, David Hoffman, Jean Galbraith, Duncan Hollis, Laura Little, David Luban, Milan Markovic, Saira Mohamed, Valerie Oosterveld, Sarah Nouwen, Lauren Ouziel, Mark Pollack, Jaya Ramji-Nogales, Rachel Rebouche, Darryl Robinson, Barrie Sander, James Shellenberger, Peter Spiro, Beth Van Schaack, Milena Sterio, Sergey Vasiliev, and David Zaring. I am also grateful to Gregory Mandel for his helpful mentoring when he was Associate Dean for Research at Temple Law School, and for his support as Dean. All of my work is inspired by that of the late Cherif Bassiouni, a friend and mentor.

For their insightful comments on draft chapters, I particularly thank Nancy Combs, Richard Greenstein, Barbora Hola, and Jenia Turner. I am especially indebted to my friend Rod Rastan at the Office of the Prosecutor of the International Criminal Court. Despite his busy schedule, Rod takes the time to read drafts of much of my work, including parts of this book, and provides very helpful comments and corrections from the perspective of a scholar-practitioner. My deepest gratitude goes to my brilliant friend and colleague, Craig Green, who read the entire manuscript over a weekend and gave me incredibly helpful substantive comments and meticulous edits. Finally, I am eternally grateful to my teacher, mentor, colleague, Ph.D. supervisor, and friend, Bill Schabas, who helped me to develop the ideas in the book and encouraged me through many years of research and writing.

Many smart and industrious Temple Law students provided research assistance at various stages of this, and related projects including Clementa Amazan, Jeffrey Azarva, Edwin Bogert, Connor Brooks, Caroline Conrad, Megan Cribbs, Danielle DerOhannesian, Marie-Theres DiFillippo, Brian Farrell, Keith Greenwald, Karen Hoffman, Catherine Houseman, Zane Johnson, Tim Kelly, Manish Kurien, David Layne, Kelsey Lee, Benjamin Magid, Douglas Maloney, Lauren Marsh, Samuel Mills, Tony Rock, Michelle Tabach, Anna Trenga, Charles Williams, Mike Witsch, Kevin Yoegel. I thank you from the bottom of my heart. My special thanks go to three students who worked extra hard to help me finish the manuscript: Steven Galinat, Kathleen Killian, and Courtney Kurz. For excellent administrative support, I am deeply indebted to Roshonda Scipio, Caitlin Harrington, and Josette

Oakley Finnegan. I also thank Temple Law School's research librarians for their invaluable help.

My parents, Jane and Dennis McAuliffe, both brilliant academics, instilled in me a deep love of learning from a young age, and continue to support my work and life in so many ways. I can't thank you enough. Special thanks go to my mother who edited parts of the book, and whose trailblazing work as a scholar of Islam and college president inspires everything I do. Thanks to my sister Katie McAuliffe, also an academic, whose work on morality informs my thinking about punishment, and to my siblings, Jamie and Light, for their inspiration and support. Many friends supported me through the challenges of recent years. Special thanks go to Jordan Bastien, Katie Capecchi, Durga Devi, Melissa Dymond, Lakshmi Hettihewa, Nikki Eldridge Marcus, Gitte Peng, Gayatri Bridget Rauch, and Lisa Turner.

Above all, I am grateful to my husband Anthony, whose love and support sustain me every day, and to our children, Elena, Lydia, Evie, Rosie, and Vivian, who bring joy and adventure into my life.

Table of Contents

Table of Cases and Documents

INTERNATIONAL CRIMINAL TRIBUNAL
FOR RWANDA DECISIONS

INTERNATIONAL CRIMINAL TRIBUNAL FOR
THE FORMER YUGOSLAVIA DECISIONS

SPECIAL COURT FOR SIERRA LEONE DECISIONS

EXTRAORDINARY CHAMBERS IN THE COURTS
OF CAMBODIA DECISIONS

OTHER INTERNATIONAL AND NATIONAL COURT DECISIONS

UNITED NATIONS DOCUMENTS

General Assembly

Security Council

TREATIES AND OTHER INTERNATIONAL DOCUMENTS

List of Abbreviations

ACHR	American Convention on Human Rights
ECCC	Extraordinary Chambers in the Courts of Cambodia
ECHR	European Convention on Human Rights
ICC	International Criminal Court
ICCPR	International Covenant on Civil and Political Rights
ICRC	International Committee of the Red Cross
ICTY	International Criminal Tribunal for the Former Yugoslavia
ICTR	International Criminal Tribunal for Rwanda
IDF	Israeli Defense Forces
ILC	International Law Commission
IMT	International Military Tribunal at Nuremberg
IMTFE	International Military Tribunal for the Far East
JCE	Joint Criminal Enterprise
LGBTQ	Lesbian, gay, bisexual, transgender, and questioning (or queer)
LRA	Lord's Resistance Army (Uganda)
OTP	Office of the Prosecutor
SCSL	Special Court for Sierra Leone
STL	Special Tribunal for Lebanon
TWAIL	Third World Approaches to International Law
UDHR	Universal Declaration of Human Rights

Introduction

Each day brings news of tragedies around the world: a gunman kills dozens in a European capital; a hospital is destroyed in a Central American conflict zone; a rebel group kidnaps children in an African civil war; a cyberattack shuts down government services in an Asian nation; a racist kills black worshipers in a North American church; a police officer tortures suspected drug dealers in a South American city. Increasingly, the world reacts to such events by insisting on criminal prosecution of the perpetrators, either in a national court with jurisdiction or in an international court. Yet unresolved questions remain about which crimes are legitimate subjects of international adjudication, how international trials ought to be conducted, and what punishments are appropriate for those convicted. Many responses to such questions, whether in legal documents, political statements, or popular media, invoke the concept of gravity: the idea that certain crimes are so serious as to merit special treatment. After World War II, Robert Jackson justified prosecuting German defendants in the newly created Nuremberg Tribunal by appealing to the extreme gravity of their crimes; the Security Council relied on the gravity of the crimes in the Former Yugoslavia and Rwanda in establishing *ad hoc* international criminal tribunals; and states around the world cited "unimaginable atrocities that deeply shock the conscience of humanity" as the reason to establish a permanent international criminal court with jurisdiction that extends even to nationals of non-consenting states. International criminal law's institutions and supporters invoke gravity to justify situation and case selection, modified standards of proof, restrictions on defendants' rights, and harsh punishments, among other decisions.

Yet what it takes to "shock the conscience of humanity" and thus justify special rules of jurisdiction, process, and punishment remains unclear. Scholars, international lawyers, and the general public often assume the answer is largely quantitative: crimes are especially grave when they cause massive suffering. This contributes to the widespread belief that international criminal law's purview is limited to crimes on the scale of the Holocaust, ethnic cleansing in the Former Yugoslavia, and the Rwandan genocide. Yet international criminal courts and tribunals increasingly are claiming authority to adjudicate a wide range of crimes. This disconnect between the popular understanding of gravity and the reality of international criminal law threatens the legitimacy of the international criminal law regime.

Shocking the Conscience of Humanity. Margaret M. deGuzman, Oxford University Press (2020). © Margaret M. deGuzman. DOI: 10.1093/oso/9780198786153.001.0001

Although the regime's primary actors, especially its prosecutors and judges, have sought to explain gravity in qualitative as well as quantitative terms, their efforts have failed to yield an understanding of the term sufficient to bolster the legitimacy of their decisions. Most efforts to explain gravity simply list factors, making little or no effort to justify the choice of factors, or the priorities assigned among them. The factors most commonly cited are the scale, nature, manner of commission, and impact of the crimes. This factor-based approach to gravity is so malleable that it can be used to justify most outcomes. Usually, at least one of the factors can be said to render a crime grave. Often, the number of victims is highlighted to justify gravity claims; but when a crime affects few victims, a decision-maker can usually point to one or more aspects of the nature of the crime, the way it was committed, or the impact of the crime on society to justify a claim that the crime is grave. This approach fails adequately to justify gravity-based decisions because the factors are not rooted in regime values and goals.

A related problem is that decision-makers typically frame the gravity inquiry as a threshold above which decisions are said to be justified. Thus, when a crime is declared to be *sufficiently* grave it is said to merit international proscription, international adjudication, and various deviations from procedural norms that often disadvantage defendants. Such claims exacerbate the problem of relying on an undertheorized justification by creating categories to which the justification is said to apply. They thus entrench the deficient justification in the regime's substantive and procedural norms.

This book examines the role that the concept of gravity plays in determining the legitimacy of international criminal law. It uses the term "legitimacy" to mean justified authority, and analyzes regime legitimacy largely from a normative perspective, with occasional references to the concept of sociological legitimacy. A regime's normative legitimacy derives from both legal and moral norms; and its sociological legitimacy is a function of the perceptions of relevant audiences about the extent to which its exercises of authority are justified. Supporters of international criminal law, as well as regime decision-makers, rely heavily on the concept of gravity to support the regime's normative and sociological legitimacy. However, because the concept has little agreed content, its use sometimes undermines, rather than bolsters, the regime's legitimacy.

After exposing the pernicious effects on the regime's legitimacy of its heavy reliance on the undertheorized concept of gravity, the book proposes a method to address the problem. It argues that gravity should be reframed as a function of the values and goals that ought to guide decision-makers in each context in which the concept is used. Instead of relying on factors that are said to be inherent components of gravity, decision-makers should explain their selection of gravity factors, and the priorities they allocate among them, by reference to the values they seek to promote and the goals they seek to achieve in each context in which they seek to rely on gravity as a justification.

Two aspects of this prescription bear mention at the outset. First, because gravity is at the heart of efforts to justify international criminal law, a theory of how gravity can best promote the regime's legitimacy essentially requires a theory of international criminal law. Critiquing current vague uses of gravity and demonstrating their detrimental effects on the regime is relatively easy; developing a theory of legitimate global prescription, adjudication, defenses, and sentencing is not. Thus, although the chapters on each of these subjects seek to contribute productively to the emerging theoretical literature on international criminal law, they also leave substantial aspects of the issues for future development.

Second, the proposed reconceptualization of gravity as a function of values and goals could be understood as an implicit rejection of gravity as a guiding principle in international criminal law. Readers may wonder whether decision-makers should simply explain their decisions by referencing the relevant values and goals directly, rather than through the mediating concept of gravity. I do not advocate this radical step for two reasons: first, gravity is too deeply entrenched in the fabric of international criminal law for such a proposal to be practical. The discourse of international criminal law will not easily abandon the practice of calling genocide the "crime of crimes" or of referring to the International Criminal Court (ICC) as an institution created to adjudicate crimes that shock humanity's conscience. Second, gravity can be a useful short-hand to summarize a complex set of value judgments. Although gravity should not be used in ways that obscure values, as it often is at present, once relevant value judgments are made, it can helpfully summarize them for purposes of efficient communication. It is, like justice, a concept that must be imbued with values to play a useful role in the world, but remains helpful for describing conclusions once the necessary analysis is performed.

To make concrete the difference between the way gravity is currently used—as a justification independent of values and goals—and the proposed goal-dependent approach, consider the following hypothetical situation: a state has just emerged from a years-long conflict in which both sides committed large-scale and systematic crimes against civilians. Peace was achieved via a blanket amnesty, and the state's social, economic, and political systems are just starting to recover. A leader of one of the armed groups has been captured and sent to the ICC, which has jurisdiction because he is a national of a state party. The ICC Prosecutor and judges must now decide whether and how to adjudicate and, if he is convicted, what punishment to impose. Gravity will play an important role in each of these decisions.

Applying the current goal-independent approach to gravity, the Prosecutor and judges are likely to cite various factors, including, in particular, the scale of the crimes, to explain why the situation is sufficiently grave to be admissible before the ICC; that is, why it meets the gravity threshold. If the defendant raises the national amnesty as a defense, the Prosecutor will probably argue that international crimes, as a category, are so grave that amnesties do not apply; and the judges may agree. The judges will again list gravity factors in justifying the sentence they impose on the defendant. Although some of these decisions may mention the ICC's goals, they will almost certainly not assess gravity as a function of those goals, but will instead treat it as a stand-alone justification.

The approach to gravity advocated in this book would require decision-makers to engage in a deeper inquiry into the values and goals that the Court ought to pursue in each decisional context. With regard to the decision whether the ICC ought to adjudicate the situation, decision-makers would have to explain both how adjudication of the situation would help achieve the institution's most important goals, and why institutional resources are best used to adjudicate this situation, rather than a different one. Moreover, even if the situation is sufficiently grave in both of these senses, it should not be adjudicated unless such adjudication would produce a net benefit to the world. The importance of adjudicating for purposes of achieving the ICC's goals should be weighed against any countervailing values or goals, particularly those of the national community most affected by the crimes. For instance, if adjudicating the situation presents a relatively small chance of preventing future crimes, and there is a high likelihood it will reignite the conflict or otherwise destabilize the state or region, the situation might be grave, but adjudication would nonetheless be illegitimate.

With regard to whether the ICC ought to respect the national amnesty, gravity would again be a function of the importance of adjudication in terms of achieving the ICC's goals, and that value would be balanced against competing values—those associated with respecting the national preference for amnesty, including sovereignty interests. Instead of prohibiting amnesties categorically for all "international crimes" the court would determine whether adjudication or respecting the amnesty produces a greater net benefit to the world. If the defendant were a particularly powerful leader, the ICC might decide that adjudication of such a case is especially important to preventing future crimes by powerful leaders; whereas for a lower-ranking defendant it might be better to respect the amnesty to promote future peace processes. Finally, in determining the defendant's sentence, the court would assess gravity as a function of the ICC's punishment goals: it would seek to impose a sentence that provides a net benefit by punishing the defendant no more than necessary to promote global norms and deter future crimes.

Because the book advocates reconceptualizing gravity as a function of values and goals, it also seeks to uncover some of the values and goals that ought to be part of the analysis in each decisional context. The first step in this process is to determine which community's values and goals ought to be privileged. The book argues that international criminal law is essentially a tool of the global community, which is made up of all people in the world. As such, gravity should be understood in relation to that community's values and goals.

With regard to the difficult question of how to ascertain the global community's values and goals, the book suggests a process and offers some substantive ideas. The process is a dialogic one whereby regime actors explain their decisions as clearly and transparently as possible, thereby facilitating responses from constituent communities. They then incorporate feedback into subsequent decisions, and the process continues. Over time, this dialogue elucidates global values, thereby contributing to the development of the global justice community.

Although the book espouses the application of universal values, it argues that no person or group has unique insight into the nature of those values; and, as such, a global dialogue is crucial to discovering them. Moreover, it is important to ensure the robust participation of all segments of the global community in this dialogue, particularly those that are marginalized from political, economic, and other power sources. Throughout, the book highlights ways in which international criminal courts and tribunals, particularly the ICC, are already engaged in this process. Although the ICC's Prosecutor and judges rarely articulate the relationship between gravity and values as explicitly as this book suggests they should, their actions sometimes illuminate the values and goals they believe the institution ought to pursue.

Finally, the book suggests some of the global values and goals that ought to underpin exercises of authority by the international criminal law regime. It argues that the central value that animates international criminal law is that of protecting human dignity. As such, global prescriptive authority can be justified for a wide range of crimes that harm human dignity. However, in a world of limited resources, the global community must identify priorities. Moreover, the goal of preventing harm to human dignity sometimes comes into conflict with the goals of other communities, and priorities must be established in this context also. Gravity analysis can help with both of these tasks, if it is reconceptualized in the ways the book suggests.

The book espouses a range of values and goals for the global community. For instance, it argues that international courts, in particular the ICC, ought to privilege the goal of preventing harms to human dignity through deterrence and the expression of global norms. Such institutions are well-suited to this task by virtue of their broad reach and global stature. When the ICC issues convictions for the recruitment and use of child soldiers, for instance, it sends a strong message that such conduct is condemned by the global community. On the other hand, the book rejects retribution as a goal on the grounds that it is not a globally shared value.

The book's central argument—that undertheorized uses of gravity to justify decisions threaten the regime's legitimacy—assumes a long-term legitimacy horizon. In the shorter term, such undertheorization can yield benefits to the regime.[1] This was particularly true in the regime's earliest days when the ambiguity surrounding the concept of gravity encouraged support for the regime by states with different visions of how it would operate. For instance, some of the state representatives

---

[1] Cass Sunstein has explained how ambiguity can promote agreement in his article, 'Incompletely Theorized Agreements' (1995) 108 Harv. L. Rev. 1733, 1737.

involved in creating the ICC appear to have envisioned the Court's authority as restricted to crimes on the scale of the Holocaust and the Rwandan genocide, while others wanted the Court's reach to extend even to small-scale war crimes and relatively isolated acts of terrorism. By declaring the Court's jurisdiction to include only "the most serious crimes of concern to the international community as a whole," without defining the idea of seriousness, the Rome Statute's drafters satisfied both constituencies.

However, as the international criminal law regime develops, the uncertainty surrounding gravity increasingly threatens the regime's longer-term legitimacy. At the micro level, it promotes criticism of regime decisions. For instance, when the Prosecutor of the ICC invokes insufficient gravity as a justification for deciding not to investigate crimes, gravity's malleability leads some commentators to suspect it is being used to mask improper motives. Perhaps more importantly, by obscuring disagreement, undertheorized uses of gravity discourage the dialogue about global values and goals that is necessary to build the global justice community. The international criminal law regime cannot grow and flourish without developing greater consensus around its motivating values and central goals.

In arguing that gravity ought to be reconceptualized to enhance the regime's legitimacy, the book does not purport to address the full range of factors that impact upon such legitimacy. A complete assessment of regime legitimacy must take account of the inequities of the international system within which the regime operates. Defining gravity in terms of global values will not make it easier for the ICC to pursue defendants from powerful states, nor will it change the veto power at the Security Council that keeps certain areas of the world outside the Court's reach. The unequal application of law that results from the unequal distribution of power and wealth in the world is surely the greatest impediment to the legitimacy of international criminal law. Yet the book assumes, as do many supporters of international criminal law, that a flawed global justice regime is better than none at all. It therefore argues that, although gravity's reconceptualization will not resolve all challenges to the regime's legitimacy, it will bolster that legitimacy by helping to build the global community.

The book's first chapter frames the argument. It defines the concept of legitimacy, and explains how gravity affects the legitimacy of the international criminal law regime. The chapter also elucidates and justifies the book's reliance on the concept of global community, and provides preliminary thoughts about the kinds of global values and goals that ought to undergird gravity decisions. Chapter 2 describes the evolution of gravity in the development of international criminal law's legal and moral norms. It shows that the regime's strong reliance on gravity is more a matter of historical circumstance than of moral necessity. International criminal law could have developed to address crimes like drug trafficking that cross borders, or crimes like piracy that are committed outside any state's territory. Instead, due to the historical context in which it evolved, international criminal law came to rely for its legitimacy on the idea that it addresses particularly serious crimes.

The next three chapters assess gravity's role in justifying global authority over crimes, criminal process, and punishment. Chapter 3 explores the relationship between gravity and global prescriptive authority—the authority to identify conduct that ought to be globally proscribed. Global prescriptive authority is exercised when states draft treaties prohibiting crimes and elaborate criminal prohibitions in court Statutes, as well as when courts interpret such prohibitions. The chapter surveys the principal theories of international crimes and shows that virtually all of them rely significantly on a gravity threshold above which international prescriptive authority is justified. In light of the ambiguity surrounding the concept of gravity, this reliance has meant that no clear and coherent theory of international prescriptive authority has emerged, which in turn threatens the legitimacy of international criminal law.

After demonstrating how gravity has impeded the development of a coherent moral theory of global prescriptive authority, Chapter 3 advocates a theory that links such authority to the moral values at stake in labeling a crime "international." It argues that the real value at the heart of global criminal prescriptive authority is that of human dignity—the same value that underpins the international human rights regime. Criminal law is universally considered an important tool for the protection of human dignity through crime prevention; and international criminal law seeks to extend that protection to all humans.

The basic goal of international criminal law, therefore, is to protect human dignity at the global level to the greatest extent possible. As such, it ought to have a very broad *potential* reach. To the extent a gravity threshold is needed it should serve only to exclude crimes that are arguably beyond the purview of criminal sanction altogether. In other words, virtually any kind of conduct that meaningfully jeopardizes human dignity should be a potential subject of international prescriptive authority because all such conduct is a matter of concern to the global community.

Nonetheless, given the limited resources devoted to international criminal law, the regime's institutions must establish priorities among goals. Properly understood, gravity can help to establish which crimes best align with global community priorities at a given time. In sum, although gravity provides only a minimal threshold for legitimate global prescriptive authority, it can be defined in a way that helps to justify the global community's prescriptive choices, and that thus bolsters the regime's legitimacy.

Chapter 4 turns to global adjudicative authority—the global community's right to create adjudicative institutions, and for those institutions to adjudicate crimes. It argues that such authority is justified when two conditions are met. First, there must be a globally shared norm proscribing the conduct and subjecting violators to criminal sanction; and, second, the global community's adjudicative goals must be sufficiently important to outweigh any countervailing goals, particularly those of relevant national communities. Additionally, to best promote the regime's legitimacy, the situations and cases adjudicated must be those that achieve the global community's most important goals most efficiently. Chapter 4 explains how gravity's reconceptualization can help to ensure these conditions are met.

Chapters 5 and 6 turn to questions about gravity's role in relation to defendants' rights, defenses, and sentencing. Chapter 5 demonstrates that courts sometimes cite gravity to justify restricting defendants' rights and defenses without adequately balancing the competing values and goals at stake. By reconceptualizing gravity as a function of global goals and values, the concept can support a more productive approach to such decisions. Chapter 6 argues that gravity's inconsistent and unexplained use in sentencing detracts from the legitimacy of sentencing decisions; and that a better approach would be to more clearly link gravity to the punishment goals being pursued in each case. Additionally, international courts should resist any impulse to impose harsh sentences based on unsupported claims about the categorical gravity of international crimes.

The book's concluding chapter stresses the need for an inclusive dialogic process to surface the most appropriate values and goals for the global community. It suggests that the process of unmasking the choices that are currently obscured by vague references to the gravity of international crimes may initially expose the regime to new legitimacy challenges. In the long term, however, it is an important step toward a strongly legitimate international criminal law regime. Communities are held together by shared values. The global community must decide what it values for its institutions to be in a position strongly to reflect and implement those values.

1

Legitimacy, Gravity, and Global Community

This chapter provides a theoretical framework for the book's central argument that the concept of gravity should be reconceived as a function of values and goals to promote the legitimacy of international criminal law. It does so by: (1) explaining how the book uses the concept of legitimacy; (2) describing the pervasive goal-independent approach to gravity as a justification for regime decisions, and explaining the proposed reconceptualization; (3) elaborating a theory of international criminal law as both a tool, and constructor, of the global justice community; and (4) suggesting some of the global values and goals that ought to guide regime decisions.

I. Legitimacy in International Criminal Law

The term "legitimacy" has a long pedigree in international relations and political science; and more recently it has gained currency in international legal theory. Given these varied contexts, it is not surprising that the term is subject to many diverse interpretations and uses.[1] Unfortunately, legal scholars sometimes employ the term without precision, diminishing its analytic value and leading some to suggest the concept may be too imprecise to serve as a useful conceptual tool.[2] Yet, the "explosion of interest" in legitimacy among scholars of international law and international relations in the past two decades suggests the concept can provide important insights.[3] To ensure the usefulness of legitimacy analysis it is important to be clear at the outset about how the term is being used.

---

[1] For a discussion of the various uses of legitimacy, see Daniel Bodansky, 'Legitimacy in International Law and International Relations' in Jeffrey L. Dunoff and Mark A. Pollack (eds.), *Interdisciplinary Perspectives on International Law and International Relations: The State of the Art* (Cambridge University Press 2013) 321.

[2] Nigel Purvis, 'Critical Legal Studies in Public International Law' (1991) 32 Harv. Intl. L.J. 81, 112 (stating that "Debates about the alternative characteristics of legitimacy—their normative and political origins—are destined to the same indeterminacy as other international legal debates."). Martti Koskenniemi goes so far as to argue that legitimacy rhetoric can be detrimental to the international legal order. See 'Miserable Comforters: International Relations as New Natural Law' (2009) 15 Eur. J. Intl. Relations 395, 409 (arguing that the point of legitimacy is to avoid normative substance and "to uphold a *semblance* of substance").

[3] Bodansky, 'Legitimacy in International Law' (n. 1) 321.

Shocking the Conscience of Humanity. Margaret M. deGuzman, Oxford University Press (2020). © Margaret M. deGuzman.
DOI: 10.1093/oso/9780198786153.001.0001

In this book, the term legitimacy means "justified authority."[4] Legitimacy in this sense is often applied to governments, but can relate to any institution that governs.[5] To "govern" here means to seek to compel actors outside the regime to comply with regime decisions for reasons other than rational persuasion or forcible coercion.[6] International criminal courts, as well as national courts adjudicating international crimes, seek to compel political actors to cooperate, victims to participate, and, ultimately, to encourage norm compliance around the world. The stronger their legitimacy, the greater their ability to achieve these goals.

Although legitimacy is sometimes treated as binary—institutions or decisions are labeled "legitimate" or "illegitimate"—it is often more useful to assess it along a continuum. Institutions and decisions are more or less legitimate depending on the extent to which they meet whatever criteria are employed for making the legitimacy determination. Analysis of the extent of an institution's or decision's legitimacy can contribute productively to efforts to increase support for the institution, and to promote reform. In contrast, binary legitimacy evaluations are most useful in deciding whether an institution or decision deserves any support at all, a less common question.

An important distinction among the uses of the term "legitimacy" is between normative and sociological variants.[7] Normative legitimacy addresses the bases upon which authority is justified. An institution's authority, or that of a decision within the institution, can be justified in terms of legal or moral norms, or both. Sociological legitimacy, on the other hand, concerns the perceptions of relevant audiences that the authority is justified. A decision or institution is sociologically legitimate when people believe it is normatively justified.

The three kinds of legitimacy—moral, legal, and sociological—are interrelated.[8] The normative legitimacy of a legal institution or decision often derives from a combination of moral and legal norms, since the latter tend to be rooted in the former. Likewise, legal norms shape social perceptions about morality, and perceptions of morality both shape and are shaped by legal norms. In an excellent article about legitimacy in international law, Chris Thomas wrote: "International law

---

[4] Daniel Bodansky, 'The Legitimacy of International Governance: A Coming Challenge for International Environmental Law?' (1999) 93 AJIL 596, 601.

[5] Ibid. 596 ("The legitimacy of domestic government has been a central focus of political theory since at least the time of Hobbes and Locke.").

[6] Ibid. 600. See also Richard H. Fallon, Jr., 'Legitimacy and the Constitution' (2005) 118 Harvard L. Rev. 1787, 1795.

[7] This distinction is sometimes given other labels, including *de jure* and *de facto* legitimacy. Christopher A. Thomas, 'The Uses and Abuses of Legitimacy in International Law' (2014) 34 OJLS 729, 734. Sociological legitimacy is sometimes called "descriptive" legitimacy. Ibid.

[8] In fact, scholars sometimes conflate the various types of legitimacy either by failing to specify what kind of legitimacy they mean, or by engaging in analysis that elides the differences. See, e.g., Hitomi Takemura, 'Reconsidering the Meaning and Actuality of the Legitimacy of the International Criminal Court' (2012) 4 Amsterdam L.F. 3, 5 (equating sociological legitimacy with substantive legitimacy, and asserting that it has moral dimensions).

embodies, normalizes and enforces particular conceptions of the world. It informs our understandings of what is moral even as it is shaped by such understandings."[9] Thus, while it is analytically useful to distinguish among the three types of legitimacy, it is also important to remember the overlaps among them. For instance, while relevant audiences may believe that an institution is acting in accordance with appropriate legal and moral norms even when it is not doing so, such belief is much more likely when it is based in reality.

In this book, legitimacy is primarily used as a normative concept. The central question addressed is whether, and to what extent, the concept of gravity helps to justify the institutions of international criminal law and the decisions they make, as a legal and moral matter. When the term legitimacy is used without qualifier herein, it refers to a combination of legal and moral legitimacy. At other times, moral or legal sources of justification are specifically referenced. This is not intended to signal a strong distinction between law and morality, or indeed to take any position on the centuries-old debate about the relationship between them. Rather, the goal is simply to highlight the particular influence of law or morality in helping to justify international criminal law's authority in a given context.[10]

Although not a central focus, the book sometimes refers to the likely impact of gravity-based decisions on perceptions that the authority of international criminal law's institutions is justified—the regime's sociological legitimacy. For instance, Chapter 3 discusses the impact on perceptions of regime legitimacy of the failure to adopt clear definitions of crimes that results in part from reliance on gravity. However, this aspect of legitimacy is not a strong focus of the book for two reasons. First, sociological legitimacy is an empirically measurable phenomenon. At least in theory, it is possible to ascertain the extent to which people around the world perceive the institutions and decisions of international criminal law to be legitimate. However, this empirical data is not currently available, and commentary on international criminal law's sociological legitimacy is thus necessarily speculative.[11]

Second, my goal in writing this book is to help promote the normative legitimacy of the international criminal law regime. Generally, increased normative legitimacy also improves sociological legitimacy. Notably, the converse is not true—improved perceptions of legitimacy will not necessarily bolster the regime's normative legitimacy. When perceptions of legitimacy are discussed, it is generally to highlight the view of a particularly important audience, such as the states parties to the ICC's Rome Statute. The perceptions of states parties will help to determine

---

[9] Thomas (n. 7) 740.

[10] I disagree with Nigel Purvis' argument that legitimacy theories "reflect a positivist or naturalist first premise." Purvis (n. 2).

[11] In Bodansky's literature review, he notes the importance of developing an empirical approach to sociological legitimacy, describing much of the existing writing on the topic as "informed speculation." Bodansky, 'Legitimacy in International Law' (n. 1) 337.

the ICC's continued survival, without which questions of legitimacy are clearly irrelevant.

In addition to specifying the *kind* of legitimacy at issue, legitimacy analysis is most useful when it specifies the *objects, subjects,* and *bases* for the legitimacy claims made.[12] This book's overarching legitimacy object is the international criminal law regime. It seeks to explain how the regime's reliance on the concept of gravity affects its legitimacy. A "regime" is comprised of "principles, norms, rules, and decision-making procedures,"[13] as well as institutions and actors within those institutions. To understand the effect of gravity on the regime's legitimacy, the book examines the concept's role in several normative and decisional contexts. It thus disaggregates its overarching object into norms and decisions that affect the legitimacy of the system.[14] Chapter 3 assesses gravity's impact on the legitimacy of norms of international criminality; Chapter 4 looks at its role in legitimizing decisions to exercise international and universal adjudicative authority; Chapter 5 examines norms related to defendants' rights and defenses; and Chapter 6 considers gravity's role in the legitimacy of international sentencing decisions.

The subjects of this book's legitimacy analysis are the communities the regime seeks—and should seek—to serve. It argues that international criminal law's institutions, whether supra-national courts or national courts exercising universal jurisdiction, should focus on the perceptions, goals, and values of at least two kinds of communities: the global community and the national communities most affected by the crimes the institutions address. Regional communities may also be emerging as constituents of international—or perhaps more accurately "regional criminal law"—but this development is so nascent that it must await future study.[15] For now, the international criminal law regime's normative legitimacy depends largely on the extent to which it appropriately addresses the goals and values of the global community.

The degree to which an international criminal law institution should emphasize global as opposed to local goals and values depends on the nature of the institution. For instance, the book argues that the ICC should focus primarily on building the global community. But the same is not obviously true of *ad hoc* and hybrid courts and tribunals. Indeed, an argument can be made that the latter institutions should place greater weight on the needs of affected national communities.[16] That said, all

---

[12] See Thomas (n. 7) 746–52.

[13] Stephen D. Krasner, 'Structural Causes and Regime Consequences: Regimes as Intervening Variables' (1982) 36 Intl. Org. 185, 186.

[14] Thomas (n. 7) 746.

[15] In particular, the African Union is considering adding a criminal chamber to the African Court on Human and Peoples' Rights. African Union, 'Protocol on the Statute of the African Court of Justice and Human Rights' (adopted July 1, 2008). For a review of the proposed court and its implications for international criminal law, see Charles C. Jalloh et al. (eds.), *The African Court of Justice and Human and Peoples' Rights in Context* (Cambridge University Press 2019).

[16] Because this book's focus is primarily on global institutions, it does not propose a theory of community for *ad hoc* and hybrid institutions.

institutions associated with the international criminal law regime should respect minimum global standards. Thus, for instance, a hybrid court might appropriately impose a higher punishment than would an international court in order to respect local punishment norms; but it should not apply the death penalty, which is contrary to global human rights norms.

The book employs different bases or criteria for determining legitimacy in the various contexts it addresses. Since the focus is on normative legitimacy, it refers primarily to criteria based in law and morality. Some of the criteria it employs can be categorized as procedural, while others are substantive.[17] One of the most important criteria the book employs is effectiveness: the requirement that a regime's institutions pursue appropriate goals in a reasonably efficient manner.[18] As Allen Buchanan and Robert Keohane argue, "If an institution cannot effectively perform the functions invoked to justify its existence, then this insufficiency undermines its claim to the right to rule."[19] Effectiveness is often considered to be a descriptive rather than a normative quality: a regime can be effective even in the pursuit of immoral objectives. In contrast, this book argues that an institution's legitimacy depends on its effectively pursuing normatively appropriate goals. Normatively appropriate values and goals are those that enable the institution to have a net positive impact on the world. An institution, or regime, cannot be said to have a right to rule unless its cumulative impact over time is a positive one. This does not mean that the institution must be making a positive contribution at each moment; rather, the analysis requires a long-term view.

International criminal law's central contribution to the wellbeing of the world is to promote the value of human dignity. The book argues that in making decisions about the exercise of global prescriptive and adjudicative authority the regime should reflect that central value. To do so, the regime should develop and articulate clear goals. These goals should include, in particular, preventing crimes through norm expression and deterring crime through punishment. If the regime reflects

---

[17] The analysis thus spans a divide in the literature between proper procedures and appropriate substantive norms as legitimizing forces. Thomas Franck, *The Power of Legitimacy Among Nations* (Oxford University Press 1990) 17.

[18] Yuval Shany, 'Assessing the Effectiveness of International Courts: A Global-Based Approach' (2012) 106 AJIL 225, 230. The direction of influence between legitimacy and effectiveness is not always clear in the literature. For instance, some commentators assert that sociological legitimacy is a potential basis of effectiveness because "the more an institution is perceived as legitimate, the more stable and effective it is likely to be." Bodansky, 'Legitimacy of International Governance' (n. 4) 603. Others consider effectiveness a source of legitimacy. See, e.g., G.C.A. Junne, 'International Organizations in a Period of Globalization: New (problems of) Legitimacy' in Jean-Marc Coicaud and Veijo Heiskanen (eds.), *The Legitimacy of International Organizations* (United Nations University Press 2011) 191. However, as Yuval Shany demonstrates, legitimacy and effectiveness are mutual influencers. See 'Stronger Together: Legitimacy and Effectiveness of International Courts as Potentially Mutually Reinforcing Notions' in Nienke Grossmanm et al., *Legitimacy and International Courts* (Cambridge University Press 2018) 11–13.

[19] Allen Buchanan and Robert O. Keohane, 'The Legitimacy of Global Governance Institutions' 20 Ethics & Intl. Affairs 405, 422.

the value of promoting human dignity, and efficiently pursues goals related to that value, it should have strong normative legitimacy, all other things being equal. The next section thus argues that gravity ought to be understood in relation to global community goals, rather than as a goal-independent threshold.

II. Gravity as a Function of Community Goals

International criminal law's decision-makers use gravity in various contexts, including decisions to: (1) prohibit conduct in a treaty, court Statute, or through judicial interpretation; (2) establish a criminal court and adjudicate particular situations and cases; (3) limit the rights and defenses of criminal defendants; and (4) impose punishments. In each of these contexts, gravity remains an undertheorized concept.

When decision-makers have sought to explain what gravity means, they have usually adopted a factor-based approach that is largely independent of institutional goals.[20] The most comprehensive efforts in this regard have come from the ICC's Office of the Prosecutor and judges. The Rome Statute of the ICC requires the Court to deem "inadmissible" cases that are "not of sufficient gravity to justify further action by the Court." This provision has been labeled the "gravity threshold." The ICC's Prosecutor and judges are required to consider the gravity threshold in determining whether to admit cases, as well as whether to investigate situations involving one or more potential cases.[21] The Office of the Prosecutor (OTP) has issued policy papers elaborating on the gravity threshold;[22] and the Court's decisions interpreting the threshold have largely echoed those policies. The Rome Statute also elaborates the concept of gravity somewhat in the sentencing context,[23] and the Court's sentencing jurisprudence supplies limited additional insight.[24]

The ICC's policies and jurisprudence, like those of other international criminal courts, largely depict gravity as a judgment that is independent of institutional goals—one that is ascertainable through the objective application of quantitative

---

[20] An important exception is the ICC Office of the Prosecutor's case selection policy, which implicitly asserts institutional goals in its elaboration of the gravity factors. See ICC-OTP, 'Policy Paper on Case Selection and Prioritisation' (September 15, 2016), available at https://www.icc-cpi.int/itemsDocuments/20160915_OTP-Policy_Case-Selection_Eng.pdf (last accessed on November 25, 2019); ICC-OTP, 'Policy Paper on Preliminary Examinations' (November 2013), available at https://www.icc-cpi.int/iccdocs/otp/OTP-Policy_Paper_Preliminary_Examinations_2013-ENG.pdf (last accessed on November 25, 2019). The Policy Paper is discussed in Chapter 4, section I.A.

[21] Rome Statute of the International Criminal Court (adopted July 17, 1998, entered into force July 1, 2001) art. 53.

[22] ICC-OTP, 'Policy Paper on Case Selection and Prioritisation' (n. 20); ICC-OTP, 'Policy Paper on Preliminary Examinations' (n. 20).

[23] See, e.g., Rome Statute (n. 21) art. 78(1) ("In determining the sentence, the Court shall, in accordance with the Rules of Procedure and Evidence, take into account such factors as the gravity of the crime and the individual circumstances of the convicted person.").

[24] For discussion, see Chapter 6, section I.

and qualitative criteria. With respect to the quantitative aspect of gravity, there is almost uniform agreement that counting victims is not an adequate measure. Beyond this, however, there is very little discussion, let alone agreement, about how to measure the quantitative aspect of gravity. The qualitative aspect tends to be articulated in relation to three factors: the nature of the crimes, the manner of their commission, and the impact of the crimes.[25] Another factor that is sometimes considered under the heading of gravity, and sometimes independently, is the degree of culpability of the accused. This is usually determined by examining the position of the accused in the hierarchy of authority and their role in planning the crime. To ascertain the gravity of a crime or situation of criminality, such factors are considered using a "totality of the circumstances" analysis.

In addition to treating gravity as a factor-based, goal-independent judgment, the policies and practices of international criminal law often obscure an important difference between two types of gravity judgments: absolute and relative. Absolute gravity is an abstract determination of weight: a case or situation has a certain importance irrespective of that of other cases or situations. The Rome Statute's gravity threshold requires an absolute gravity judgment: a situation or case is either grave enough to meet the threshold or is not. Relative gravity, on the other hand, requires a comparison between the situation or case under consideration and other comparable situations or cases to determine their relative importance.

Decision-makers sometimes frame gravity judgments as threshold claims when they ought to be simple claims about importance. The ICC Prosecutor has asserted, for instance, that a situation fails to meet the Rome Statute's gravity threshold because it is less serious than other situations before the Court. Such a statement conflates absolute and relative gravity. To explain why a situation meets the gravity threshold, the Prosecutor must provide some sense of what that threshold entails and how the particular situation qualifies. Whether other situations are more or less grave is irrelevant for this purpose. The Prosecutor might choose not to pursue a situation on the basis of its low gravity relative to other situations, but she must justify her authority to make such a decision—something that has not occurred to date.[26]

Conclusions about the gravity threshold that draw on relative gravity as a justification thus lack normative foundation because they are goal-independent; and

---

[25] See, e.g., ICC-OTP, 'Regulations of the Office of the Prosecutor' (April 23, 2009) ICC-BD/05-01-09 reg. 29(2), available at https://www.icc-cpi.int/NR/rdonlyres/FFF97111-ECD6-40B5-9CDA-792BCBE1E695/280253/ICCBD050109ENG.pdf (last accessed on November 25, 2019); *Situation in the Republic of Kenya* (Decision Pursuant to Article 15 of the Rome Statute on the Authorization of an Investigation into the Situation in the Republic of Kenya) ICC-01/09-19-Corr (March 31, 2010) para. 62), available at https://www.refworld.org/cases,ICC,4bc2fe372.html (last accessed on November 25, 2019). While these factors have been formally adopted at the ICC, other international courts and tribunals have cited similar criteria. See, e.g., *Prosecutor v. Jankovic* (Decision on Referral of Case under Rule 11*bis*) IT-96-23/2-PT (July 22, 2005) paras. 18–19 (considering such factors as the nature of the crimes, their temporal and geographical scope, and the number of victims affected in assessing gravity).

[26] These issues are elaborated in Chapter 4, section I.

they also compound the problem by imbuing the threshold with unjustified content. When a situation is said not to meet the threshold because it is not as grave as another situation, the supposedly graver situation becomes an indicator of the location of the gravity threshold, and the less grave situation creates a class below the threshold. Thereafter, future situations with characteristics like those of the less grave situation will presumably also not meet the threshold; and, although the graver situation may be well above what was originally intended for the threshold, decision-makers will likely use it as a reference point, thereby raising the bar. And all of this will have occurred without consideration of the values and goals the institution was intended to promote.

The risk to regime legitimacy of such unsupported gravity thresholds increases when they are used to explain why particular actions are not merely justified, but required. International criminal law's decision-makers frequently assert that once a crime or situation of criminality reaches a gravity threshold, certain consequences are mandated, including criminal adjudication, restrictions on defendants' rights, disallowance of particular defenses, and harsh sentences. When such categorical claims become entrenched in the regime's substantive and operational norms, they seriously threaten its legitimacy.

The current goal-independent, often threshold-based, method of assessing gravity to justify decisions threatens the regime's legitimacy because it is largely unmoored from moral values. To assert that an international court should adjudicate a situation because it involves harm to many people or because it shocks the world is to avoid the real work of justification: explaining the values that support an action, including why those values ought to be privileged over any competing values. It may be important to adjudicate a situation involving widespread harm to deter similar crimes in the future; but it may be more important to adjudicate a different situation involving more limited harm when the values at stake are in greater need of global attention. Without considering the benefits of adjudicating each situation, it is difficult to make a strongly legitimate decision about how to allocate resources.

The values used to justify actions can be deontological or utilitarian in nature. This book adopts utilitarian values, arguing that international criminal law's actions are only justified if they promote good in the world that is greater than any harm they cause. It rejects the retributive idea that punishment is a good in itself. Indeed, as elaborated in Chapter 6's discussion of punishment, retribution should generally be excluded from the purposes of global justice because it is not a globally-shared value. Moreover, even if international adjudication could be justified by the deontological value of inflicting retribution on wrong-doers, this would not solve the problem of defining gravity because there is no universally agreed method for aligning degrees of crime seriousness with degrees of punishment.

If international criminal law's legitimacy is contingent on the regime providing benefits to the world, the regime's decisions must be motivated by the particular benefits it seeks—and should seek—to achieve. That is to say, the regime's decisions should be justified by reference to its values and goals. Because gravity is the linchpin of many of the regime's important decisions, it should be reconceptualized as a function of regime values and goals.

This reconceptualization might be interpreted as rendering gravity redundant—perhaps decision-makers could simply reference regime values and goals directly in justifying decisions. But there are good reasons to retain the concept as an important driver of outcomes in international criminal law. First, the concept of gravity is so deeply entrenched in the discourse of international criminal law that any effort to excise it is unlikely to gain traction. As explained more fully in Chapter 2, although its meaning has always been ambiguous and contested, the concept of gravity has a history in international criminal law that goes back at least to the writings of Grotius. Gravity is also enshrined in the regime's legal documents. Most importantly, gravity is required in several provisions of the Rome Statute, a document adopted after many years of negotiation that is unlikely to be revised anytime soon. Additionally, using the concept as a vessel for values and goals provides efficiency benefits. Once the necessary analysis is conducted and explained, gravity provides a short-hand referent to the underlying complexities. Indeed, the use of gravity as a referent to values and goals both implies and prompts a degree of coherence among them that is beneficial to the regime's legitimacy.[27]

A goal-dependent conception of gravity would require decision-makers both to identify the values and goals they seek to advance through a given decision, and to explain how the decision would promote those goals. Decision-makers would still consider the kinds of factors discussed earlier, but rather than doing so in a vacuum, they would explain how the factors selected, and any priority accorded among them, relate to the values and goals they believe the institution ought to pursue. For instance, a prosecutor deciding whether to prosecute a particular situation or case might cite as her central goal the expression of global condemnation of a particular kind of crime perpetrated in the situation or case. She might select this goal because the crime in question is under-prosecuted around the world, and thus worthy of particular attention. On this basis, she might privilege the nature of the crime in determining its gravity for purposes of justifying her selection. Rather than considering abstractly all of the various factors that might be said to increase the gravity of a crime, therefore, she would focus on the aspects of the nature of the crime that make it particularly important for the global community to express its condemnation.

Likewise, a judge seeking to determine an appropriate sentence would be guided by the institutions' primary goals of punishment in determining which aspects of gravity to emphasize. A focus on general deterrence, for instance, would require

---

[27]   I am grateful to Craig Green for pointing out this benefit.

more attention to factors related to averting potential future crimes than to aspects of a case reflecting the particular defendant's moral culpability. In determining the appropriate jurisdictional scope of a new tribunal, political actors would be guided by the goals and priorities of the institution. If the institution's central mission were to address the suffering of a particular victimized community, the factors that would most contribute to the seriousness of the crimes for purposes of jurisdictional scope would be those related to victim suffering, such as the quantity of harm, the breadth of geographic scope, and the impact of the crimes on the community. In contrast, if the institution's central goal were to promote global crime prevention, its jurisdictional scope would reflect the kinds of cases for which such prevention is most necessary, and for which the institution is most likely to effectuate global prevention.

Clarifying both the nature of gravity as a goal-dependent judgment, and its role in threshold, absolute, and relative value determinations should contribute to the legitimacy of the international criminal law regime. As explained earlier, a regime's legitimacy requires it to reflect morally appropriate values and to pursue morally appropriate goals. Analysis and explanation of those values and goals is one way to ensure that result. The next section explains how the international criminal law regime ought to identify its goals and values.

III. Global Community: A Discursive Project

If the international criminal law regime's legitimacy can be enhanced through decisions based on community values and goals rather than claims of goal-independent gravity, decision-makers must know which community's goals to apply. The primary communities of interest for international criminal law are the global community and the national communities most affected by the crimes at issue. Many commentators have written about the importance of giving voice to the affected national communities—particularly the victims of crimes;[28] but the idea that a global community exists and that its goals ought to be considered is more controversial. At one extreme in the debate are those who deny the existence of a global community in any meaningful sense;[29] and at the other are those who proclaim the beginnings of a world federation. The latter camp includes, for instance, Quincy Wright who claimed as early as 1947 that:

---

[28] See, e.g., Luke Moffett, 'Meaningful and Effective? Considering Victims' Interests Through Participation at the International Criminal Court' (2015) 26 Crim. L.F. 1, 260 (describing reasons for the inclusion of victims' interests in international criminal mechanisms).

[29] For discussion, see Charles de Visscher, *Theory and Reality in Public International Law* (Princeton University Press 1957) 92 (asserting that "[i]t is ... pure illusion to expect from the mere arrangement of inter-State relations the establishment of a community order .... There will be no international community so long as the political ends of the State overshadow the human ends of power.").

[R]egularly enforced world criminal law applicable to individuals necessarily makes inroads upon national sovereignty and tends to change the foundations of the international community from a balance of power among sovereign states to a universal federation directly controlling individuals in all countries on matters covered by international law.[30]

This book takes a middle-ground position, arguing that international criminal law's institutions, doctrines, and norms reflect the existence of a global justice community, even as they help to constitute that community.[31]

"Global community" is used here to refer to the community of all persons in the world—humanity. Like national communities, the global community is in important respects "imagined."[32] We belong to communities—multiple, overlapping communities—because we view ourselves as sharing a history, values, goals, and perhaps a future together.[33] Increasingly, the fact of global interconnectedness encourages all people in the world to view themselves as linked by common bonds of humanity.[34] Exposure to worldwide media and social networks, as well as global economic and environmental concerns, make it more difficult for people, even in remote parts of the globe, to view themselves as entirely separate from their fellow humans. Structures such as the United Nations, the International Monetary Fund and the World Bank reinforce these perceptions of shared interests.[35] Akira Iriye writes that the world is developing:

transnational networks that are based upon a global consciousness, the idea that there is a wider world over and above separate states and national societies, and that individuals and groups, no matter where they are, share certain interests and concerns in that wider world. [36]

---

[30] Quincy Wright, 'The Law of the Nuremberg Trial' (1947) 41 AJIL 38, 47.

[31] For a similar view, see Bruno Simma and Andrea L. Paulus, 'The "International Community": Facing the Challenge of Globalization' (1998) 9 Eur. J. Intl. L. 266, 274 (arguing that a more highly institutionalized international society is emerging that is capable of adopting prescriptions, enforcing them to a certain extent, and shaping common values).

[32] Benedict Anderson, *Imagined Communities: Reflection on the Origin and Spread of Nationalism* (Verso 1991).

[33] See, e.g., David McMillan and David Chavis, 'Sense of Community: A Definition and Theory' (1986) 14 J. Community Psychology 6, 13 (explaining that shared values are key to cohesive communities).

[34] Karen Kovach notes that: "The international community is a community of the world's people, peoples, and states insofar as they take themselves to be part of a potentially universal agency. The international community is universal in the sense that every person and every social group is potentially a member and in the sense that it aspires to universality." 'The International Community as Moral Agent' (2003) 2 J. Military Ethics 99, 99.

[35] See Kenneth W. Abbott and Duncan Snidal, 'Why States Act through Formal International Organizations' (1998) 42 J. Conflict Resolution 3, 24 (explaining that international organizations "develop and express community norms and aspirations").

[36] Akira Iriye, *Global Community: The Role of International Organizations in the Making of the Contemporary World* (University of California Press 2002) 8 (discussing increasing globalization and the role of international organizations in creating a global community that transcends national societies).

"Global community" is not synonymous with "international community," although the terms are often used interchangeably. The former is a cosmopolitan concept that centers the individual as the unit of moral concern, whereas the latter centers the state. The global community thus derives its authority from the consent of people; the international community from that of states. International law, viewed as an instrument of the international community, is rooted in state consent. International criminal law is part of international law—and thus gives significant importance to state consent—but it also reflects global values pertaining to individuals.

The institution that most clearly demonstrates international criminal law's cosmopolitan identity is the ICC. The Rome Statute's preamble announces that "all peoples are united by common bonds," and that the Court is being established "for the sake of present and future generations" to adjudicate "the most serious crimes of concern to the international community as a whole."[37] This language leaves little doubt that the ICC was created to benefit all people, not merely nationals of states parties. It establishes that not only states are concerned about these crimes, but all people everywhere. The Court's jurisdictional regime further evidences its global nature. Although the Court was not given universal jurisdiction as some had hoped, its reach extends throughout the world. The Security Council can refer any situation to the Court through its Chapter VII mandate to maintain and restore peace and security; and a national of a non-state party can be brought before the ICC for a crime committed on the territory of a state party.[38]

Other international criminal law institutions also reflect global community objectives, at least in part. The *ad hoc* tribunals for the Former Yugoslavia, Rwanda, and Lebanon were established pursuant to the Security Council's Chapter VII mandate to restore and maintain international peace and security; they were not simply intended to address the local justice objectives of the affected states. Even the hybrid tribunals established with state consent, such as the Special Court for Sierra Leone and the Extraordinary Chambers in the Courts of Cambodia, have laid claim to an international status, and thus to serving humanity.[39] Likewise, the first modern international criminal courts—those at Nuremberg and Tokyo—purported to act on behalf of humanity even though the former was created by just four states, and the latter by a single state.

The global agendas of these institutions provide some evidence of a global community's existence—at least in the minds of those who created and support them. Doctrines of international criminal law provide further support. For

---

[37] Rome Statute (n. 21) preamble.

[38] Ibid. art. 12(2)(a).

[39] See, e.g., *Prosecutor v. Kallon* (Appeals Judgment) SCSL-2004-15-AR72(E) (March 13, 2004) para. 72. (holding that as an international body, the Special Court was not bound by a national amnesty); *Prosecutor v. KAING Guek Eav* (Judgment) 001/18-07-2007/ECCC/TC (July 26, 2010) para. 27–34 (looking to international law in determining how to apply the principle of legality).

instance, the universal jurisdiction doctrine permits any state in the world to adjudicate a case involving international crimes, even in the absence of any connection to the crime, perpetrator, or victims. Courts exercising this form of jurisdiction frequently assert that they do so on behalf of the global community.[40] Although the doctrine is controversial, it has widespread support across the globe.[41] The obligation to extradite or prosecute persons accused of certain crimes and the Responsibility to Protect doctrine's authorization of intervention to stop such crimes are additional examples.[42] Without a global community that strongly values the prosecution and prevention of certain crimes, such doctrines would make little sense. Why constrain states' sovereign right and obligation to act on behalf of their national constituencies unless there is another, broader community demanding respect for its goals?

Institutions with global agendas and globally oriented doctrines reflect the existence of a global community because they proclaim an intention to act in certain ways, on behalf of all people. Broad jurisdictional norms, such as the ICC's jurisdiction over non-party states and the universal jurisdiction doctrine are especially important in this regard. As Adeno Addis notes:

[J]urisdictional norms, perhaps more than other norms, play an important role in defining community and belonging .... To prescribe jurisdictional rules is to assert or to assume that for this or that purpose a particular territorial community is a community of interest.[43]

When the jurisdictional norms are global, they posit a global community of interest.[44] Indeed, in writing about this development, Markus Benzing notes that "[f]rom the perspective of the enforcement of community interests, international

---

[40] See, e.g., *Attorney-General of the Government of Israel v. Eichmann* (Israel Dist. Ct.) 36 ILR. 5, 26 (December 12, 1961) para. 12. ("The abhorrent crimes defined in this Law are not crimes under Israel law alone. These crimes, which struck at the whole of mankind and shocked the conscience of nations are grave offenses against the law of nations itself (*delicta juris gentium*)."); *Prosecutor v. Klaus Barbie* (French Court of Cassation Appeals) 78 ILR 124 (October 6, 1983) 126 (explaining that Barbie's appeal, which was based on a claim of faulty extradition, was dismissed in part on the grounds that crimes against humanity were "subject to an international criminal order to which the notion of frontiers, and extradition rules arising therefrom, were completely alien.").

[41] Amnesty International, 'Universal Jurisdiction: A Preliminary Survey of Legislation Around the World' (Amnesty International Publications 2011) 2 (finding that the laws of 147 out of 193 states surveyed provide for universal jurisdiction over one or more of the following crimes: war crimes, crimes against humanity, genocide, and torture).

[42] On the duty to extradite or prosecute, see M. Cherif Bassiouni and Edward M. Wise, *Aut dedere aut judicare: The Duty to Extradite or Prosecute in International Law* (Martinus Njihoff 1995). Regarding the Responsibility to Protect doctrine, see International Commission on Intervention and State Sovereignty, 'The Responsibility to Protect: Report of the International Commission on Intervention and State Sovereignty VII' (December 2001).

[43] Adeno Addis, 'Imagining the International Community: The Constitutive Dimension of Universal Jurisdiction' (2009) 31 Human Rights Q. 129, 145.

[44] Ibid.

criminal courts have ... become the most important guardians of community values."[45]

The increasing strength and reach of international human rights instruments and enforcement mechanisms in the past decades is further evidence of a global community oriented by global values. The debates about cultural relativism during the late twentieth century have largely been side-lined, and many people and states now accept the existence of universal rights and values. These developments signal a shift in thinking around the world toward a cosmopolitan vision of global justice. The statism that dominated international relations until the end of the Cold War, and even the communitarian approaches to justice that animated the cultural relativism debates, are increasingly being replaced by a vision of justice that places the individual at the center of moral analysis. As John Finnis wrote: "it now appears that the good of individuals can only be fully secured and realized in the context of international community...."[46]

The institutions, norms, and doctrines of international criminal law point to the existence of a global *justice* community. That is, a group—humanity—that holds shared goals and values concerning justice—in particular, criminal justice. This global justice community is one aspect of a broader global community of shared goals and values related to a whole host of issues from human rights to environmental norms. Many authors have written about the growing importance of the global community writ large.[47] In *Humanity's Law*, Ruti Teitel argues that a paradigm shift is taking place whereby we are "departing from the preexisting interstate regime and moving toward a regime [she terms] 'humanity law'—that is, the law of persons and peoples."[48] Giuliana Capaldo sees a "transition of the community of states toward a human world society (global community) based on global constitutional principles."[49] Rafael Domingo agrees that "[a]s global interdependence grows, a new pluralistic and global human community made up of all human beings and based on the dignity of each person emerges."[50] He sees the development of this community as a political imperative, asserting:

> These local, national, and supranational communities, being insufficient to provide global or international justice, therefore must be complemented by an international political community sufficient to provide global justice.[51]

---

[45] Markus Benzing, 'Community Interests in the Procedure of International Courts and Tribunals' (2006) 5 L. & Practice Intl. Courts & Tribunals 369, 373–4.

[46] John Finnis, *Natural Law and Natural Rights*, 2nd edn. (Oxford University Press 1980) 150.

[47] See, e.g., Gillian Brock, *Global Justice: A Cosmopolitan Account* (Oxford University Press 2009) 8.

[48] Ruti G. Teitel, *Humanity's Law* (Oxford University Press 2011) x.

[49] Giuliana Ziccardi Capaldo, 'Global Constitutionalism and Global Governance: Towards a UN-Driven Global Constitutional Governance Model', in M. Cherif Bassiouni (ed.), *Globalization and its Impact on the Future of Human Rights and International Criminal Justice* (Intersentia 2015) 629.

[50] Rafael Domingo, 'The New Global Human Community' (2012) 12 Chi. J. Intl. L. 563, 566.

[51] Ibid. 565.

Indeed, according to the editors of a volume entitled *The Political Philosophy of Cosmopolitanism*, "everyone has to be at least a weak cosmopolitan now if they are to maintain a defensible view, that is to say, it is hard to see how one can reject a view that all societies have some global responsibilities."[52] Many others have written along similar lines.[53]

Some scholars of international criminal law support this cosmopolitan vision of the regime. Kai Ambos's review of the scholarship endorsing a cosmopolitan normative theory of international criminal law cites German as well as Anglo-American scholars who take this view.[54] Ambos himself concludes that the normative justification for the regime rests in both Kantian and cosmopolitan theory. He writes:

A supranational *ius puniendi* can be inferred from a combination of the incipient stages of supranationality of a valued-based world order and the concept of a world society composed of world citizens whose law—the "world citizen law" (*Weltbürgerrecht*)—is derived from universal, indivisible and interculturally recognized human rights predicated upon a Kantian concept of human dignity.[55]

This cosmopolitan vision of international criminal law is not without its critics. Two scholars reacted to the creation of the ICC by writing that this "attempt to transcend political institutions ... and enthrone law and its institutions as the governing authority of the world" was a "fundamental mistake with potentially grave consequences."[56] Other scholars have critiqued international criminal law along similar lines.[57] Nonetheless, cosmopolitanism is becoming increasingly pervasive in the discourse of international criminal law.

---

[52] Gillian Brock and Harry Brighouse (eds.), *The Political Philosophy of Cosmopolitanism* (Cambridge University Press 2005) 3 (emphasis omitted).

[53] See, e.g., Richard Vernon, *Cosmopolitan Regard: Political Membership and Global Justice* (Cambridge University Press 2010) 2 (asserting that "both cosmopolitans and their critics now occupy what we may term a 'weak cosmopolitan plateau,' upon which struggles are waged not over whether we owe outsides anything, but how much, and what is it."); Thomas W. Pogge, 'Cosmopolitanism and Sovereignty' (1992) 103 Ethics 48, 48–9 (proposing global institutional reforms to promote cosmopolitan values); Carl Knight, 'In Defense of Cosmopolitanism' (2011) 58 Theoria: J. Social & Political Theory 19, 19 (asserting that "strong cosmopolitanism" is now the most common position taken by political philosophers writing on global justice).

[54] Kai Ambos, 'Punishment without a Sovereign?: The Ius Puniendi Issue of International Criminal Law: A First Contribution towards a Consistent Theory of International Criminal Law' (2013) 33 OJLS 293, 307–14.

[55] Ibid. 314 (some emphasis omitted). Claus Kress is another prominent proponent of this view. See Claus Kress, 'Preliminary Observations on the ICC Appeals Chamber's Judgment of 6 May 2019 in the Jordan Referral re Al-Bashir Appeal' (Torkel Opsahl Academic EPublisher 2019) 19 (arguing that the *ius puniendi* of the international community has come into existence through customary international law).

[56] John M. Czarnetzky and Ronald J. Rychlak, 'An Empire of Law: Legalism and the International Criminal Court' (2003) 79 Notre Dame L. Rev. 55, 62.

[57] See, e.g., Martti Koskenniemi, 'Between Impunity and Show Trials' in J.A. Frowein and R. Wolfram (eds.), *Max Planck Yearbook of United Nations Law*, 6th edn. (Kluwer Law International 2002); Christine Schwöbel (ed.), *Critical Approaches to International Criminal Law: An Introduction* (Routledge 2014).

In asserting that a global justice community exists and is a central community
of interest for international criminal law, this book does not mean to imply that the
regime's norms have achieved universal acceptance, or anything close to it. Nor
does it ignore the ways in which the regime's norms are created by, and reinforce,
Western ideas about justice. Indeed, I share the concerns of scholars writing in critical legal traditions—in particular, Third World Approaches to International Law
(TWAIL) scholars—that international law's structures reproduce and reinforce
patterns of domination, including those stemming from colonialism.[58] It is true
that "[e]xisting international legal structures have been used to marginalize and
subordinate groups, first outside and then within the liberal global community."[59]
Scholars like David Kennedy have correctly observed that the vehicles of global
governance, even those established to promote human rights, sometimes serve as
vehicles for injustice.[60] I am also keenly aware of my own status as a privileged
Northern scholar seeking to advance the cause of global justice. As Kennedy writes:

> We need to remember, as we speak about these things, that all of us in the profes-
> sional classes of the North confront the rest of humanity with our entitlements
> and lifestyle and also with our talk about the "international community" and
> "global governance." It is not enough any more to say we favor better law or good
> governance. We will need to ask for whom we govern, for what form of political,
> social and economic life do we propose a constitution.[61]

The version of global community this book presents seeks to take account of these
concerns by entrusting the responsibility of defining the substance of global values
not to scholars, jurists, or politicians with authority unilaterally to dictate those
values, but to a dialogic process of continual correction between global institutions
and the people of the global community.

While the book assumes that sufficient agreement about global justice values
exists to justify a regime aimed at implementing those values, it endorses only a
"thin universalism."[62] Although there exist moral values that apply to all people, no
one can lay claim to special knowledge about the nature of those values.[63] Rather,
building the global community is a discursive endeavor that requires the broadest

---

[58] Makua Mutua, 'What is TWAIL?' (2000) 94 ASIL Proc. 31, 31. Indeed, the ICC itself has been
criticized as an exercise in neo-colonialism. See, e.g., Asad G. Kiyani, 'International Crime and the
Politics of Criminal Theory: Voices and Conduct of Exclusion' (2015) 48 NYU J. Intl. L. & Politics 129,
134. Likewise, the Responsibility to Protect doctrine strikes some commentators as an opportunity to
perpetuate colonial legacies. See Sue Roberston, ' "Beseeching Dominance": Critical Thoughts on the
Responsibility to Protect Doctrine' (2005) 12 Australian Intl. L.J. 33, 43.
[59] Asher Alkoby, 'Three Images of "Global Community": Theorizing Law and Community in a
Multicultural World' (2010) 12 Intl. Community L. Rev. 35, 56.
[60] David Kennedy, 'The Mystery of Global Governance' (2008) 34 Ohio Northern Univ. L. Rev.
827, 853.
[61] Ibid.
[62] Alkoby (n. 59) 59.
[63] Ibid.

possible participation to ensure its legitimacy. Here, the book echoes Jürgen Habermas' discourse ethics, whereby universal moral values are identified through discursive process.[64]

The book's claim is that the process of building a global justice community is a nascent one. Communities exist in varying degrees,[65] and the global justice community is in an early stage of formation. As Antony Duff writes:

> We can … see the ICC as one of the ways in which the moral ideal of a human community might be given more determinate and effective institutional form: the existence of a community is often a matter more of aspiration than of achieved fact, and a recognition of human community could be a recognition of what we should aspire to create.[66]

For international criminal law's legitimacy to grow, the regime must continue the process of identifying globally shared goals and values; and the more voices that are heard in that process, the stronger the regime's legitimacy will be. Moreover, powerful actors have a particular responsibility in the discursive process to ensure and support the participation of the less powerful, including by asking whether they would accept the goals and values they espouse as global if the roles were reversed.[67] The dialogic process of uncovering shared goals and values is an unending one in which continual re-evaluation is both valuable and necessary.

The global values to which this book refers are not simply global *beliefs* about what is right. The theory thus diverges from that of David Beetham who argues that legitimacy depends on conformity to rules that are justified by reference to shared *beliefs* about "the rightful source of authority."[68] While this may be true with respect to sociological legitimacy where perceptions are key, normative legitimacy requires identifying universal global values that are deontological—values that are good in themselves, rather than good only insofar as they contribute to some further value. The discursive process I advocate is aimed at uncovering those deontological moral values.

The book assumes that building the global justice community is a valuable endeavor. Unlike communitarians[69] and some pluralists,[70] it posits that global moral

---

[64] Ibid. 60 (citing Jürgen Habermas, *Structural Transformation of the Public Sphere*, Thomas Burger (trans.) (MIT Press, 1989)).

[65] Georges Abi-Saab, 'Whither the International Community' (1998) 9 Eur. J. Intl. L. 248, 249.

[66] Antony Duff, 'Authority and Responsibility in International Criminal Law' in Samantha Besson and John Tasioulas (eds.), *The Philosophy of International Law* (Oxford University Press 2010) 601.

[67] Alkoby (n. 59) 66. For a related argument, see John Rawls, *A Theory of Justice* (Harvard University Press 1971) 136–7.

[68] David Beetham, *The Legitimation of Power*, 2nd edn. (Palgrave 1990) 16–17.

[69] For a discussion of the "cosmopolitan/communitarian divide," see Richard Shapcott, *Justice, Community and Dialogue in International Relations* (Cambridge University Press 2001) 33 (noting that according to communitarians "the contextual and historical nature of human social life" precludes the possibility of universal values).

[70] Alkoby (n. 59) 45. ("The pluralist approach then rests on the assumption that the state is the only legitimate container for common values and ethics. But rather than denying the importance of morality, it seeks to recognize its limits by putting forward the argument that morality cannot be realized at the global level.").

values exist, and that the development of an increasingly strong global justice community is an important goal, albeit a long-term one. It argues that global norms and institutions of criminal justice have the potential to contribute positively to global wellbeing.

One core global value that is already well recognized is that of human dignity. As Jürgen Habermas has argued, human dignity "is the moral 'source' from which all of the basic rights derive their meaning."[71] The argument in Chapter 3 that gravity should not serve as a high threshold to global adjudicative authority rests on the premise that human dignity is a fundamental global justice value and, as such, the regime's rules should not be structured in ways that undermine that value. Other parts of the book's argument, in particular those regarding comparative gravity for selection purposes, rely on my views about what global values are, or should be, emerging. Those prescriptive arguments are only valid to the extent they withstand the testing of the discursive process required to build global community. When decisions are made based upon the decision-makers' current understanding of global values, not everyone will agree. Critical feedback will enable future decision-makers to adjust accordingly.

International criminal law is thus as much about building community norms as about reflecting them. As Asher Alkoby writes with respect to international law more generally:

> To think of [international law] from a discursive perspective is to realize its dual function as both reflective of the elements of solidarity in *international society* (as positivists maintain) but also as a meaningful path to developing deeper communal bonds in the process of constructing a *global community*.[72]

Similarly, Adeno Addis argues that the norms surrounding genocide, including universal jurisdiction and the Responsibility to Protect doctrine, constitute an effort to construct a diverse, cosmopolitan community at the global level.[73] This claim can be extended to most—if not all—of international criminal law's doctrines and norms. From the definitions of crimes to the norms regarding the exercise of jurisdiction and defendants' rights, the international criminal law regime aspires to building a community of global justice norms that are accepted by all and apply to all. To do this work productively, international criminal law's institutions must engage in inclusive discourse.

---

[71] Jürgen Habermas, 'The Concept of Human Dignity and the Realistic Utopia of Human Rights' (2010) 41 Metaphilosophy 464, 466.

[72] Alkoby (n. 59) 75.

[73] Adeno Addis, 'Genocide and Belonging: Processes of Imagining Communities' (2017) 38 U. Pa. J. Intl. L. 1041, 1079.

IV. Global Goals for Global Institutions

Although the global community is a central community of interest for international criminal law, it is not the only one—the national communities most affected by crimes are also important. International criminal courts and tribunals are generally expected to serve both the international (or global) community and relevant national communities. This is evident in their constitutive documents and rules, as well as in the commentary about their work. The Rome Statute's preamble implies a global agenda for the Court when it states that the Court was created to help prevent grave international crimes that "threaten the peace, security and well-being of the world."[74] Yet the Statute also provides for a significant level of victim participation, indicating a desire to meet the needs of the communities most affected by the crimes.[75] The rules and policies of the ICC also reflect an intention to pursue global and national agendas simultaneously. For instance, the rules regarding the initiation of investigations require the Court to consider both the interests of victims and the broader "interests of justice."[76] The Prosecutor's policies commit her to considering both global justice goals, such as norm promotion, and national goals, in particular the needs of victims.[77]

However, the goals and values of national communities do not always align with those of the global community. When there is tension between goals, international criminal courts and tribunals must identify priorities.[78] Although few commentators have addressed how this task should be undertaken, the scholarship on the purposes of international criminal courts tends to fall into two broad camps. One vision sees international courts primarily as vehicles for national or "transitional" justice in societies emerging from conflict or dictatorial regimes.[79] According to this view, international courts should serve as back-ups for unavailable or inadequate national justice systems and should prioritize the justice needs of national

---

[74] Rome Statute (n. 21) preamble.
[75] Ibid. arts. 15(3), 19(3), 43(6), 54(3)(b), 68(3), 75(3), and 82(4).
[76] Ibid. art. 53.
[77] See the discussion in Chapter 4, section I.
[78] For discussion of this issue see, e.g., Alexander K.A. Greenawalt, 'Justice Without Politics? Prosecutorial Discretion and the International Criminal Court' (2007) 39 NYU J. Intl. L. & Politics 583, 658 (asserting that the ICC "must face the irreducible tension between the policy priorities of the international institution on the one hand, and those of the societies most directly affected by international crimes on the other"); Robert D. Sloane, 'The Expressive Capacity of International Punishment: The Limits of the National Law Analogy and the Potential of International Criminal Law' (2007) 43 Stanford J. Intl. L. 39, 41 (stating that "unlike national criminal law, ICL purports to serve multiple communities, including both literal ones—for example, ethnic or national communities—and the figurative 'international community,' which needless to say, is not monolithic; it consists of multiple, often competing, constituencies and interests").
[79] "Transitional justice" has been defined in various ways, but generally relates to efforts to redress large-scale harms stemming from armed conflict or repressive regimes. See Naomi Roht-Arriaza, 'The New Landscape of Transitional Justice' in Naomi Roht-Arriaza and Javier Mariezcurrena (eds.), *Transitional Justice in the Twenty-First Century* (Cambridge University Press 2006) 1–2.

populations. Proponents of this view see international courts as tools for the promotion of justice and rule of law in transitional or post-conflict societies.[80] As
such, they believe that international courts should give priority to the goals of the
national communities where the crimes occurred.[81] The second vision sees international criminal courts primarily as vehicles of global criminal justice. Global
criminal justice takes various forms in the literature, with the most prominent theories focusing on global retribution,[82] crime prevention,[83] or some combination.[84]
Theories of global crime prevention reference a range of utilitarian theories, including deterrence, rehabilitation, and norm expression.[85]

An observer's perspective on the primary purpose of international criminal
law tends to influence their views about how the regime ought to operate. For instance, advocates of the local justice vision assert that courts should not select situations and cases without conforming to the preferences of national populations.[86]
They also argue that victims should play important roles in international criminal
trials and sentencing proceedings.[87] Global justice advocates, on the other hand,
accord a less important role to such groups in the decision-making processes of
international criminal courts. Sergey Vasiliev, for instance, has urged the ICC to
disavow the goal of achieving " 'restorative justice' through victim participation."[88]

[80] UNSC 'The Rule of Law and Transitional Justice in Conflict and Post-Conflict Societies' (August 23, 2004) S/2004/616* para. 49 (asserting that "the most significant recent development in the inter-national community's long struggle to advance the cause of justice and rule of law was the establishment of the International Criminal Court").
[81] Jaya Ramji-Nogales, 'Designing Bespoke Transitional Justice: A Pluralist Process Approach' (2010) 32 Michigan J. Intl. L. 1, 24.
[82] See, e.g., Adil Ahmad Haque, 'Group Violence and Group Vengeance: Toward a Retributivist Theory of International Criminal Law' (2005) 9 Buffalo Crim. L. Rev. 273; Jens Ohlin, 'Proportional Sentences at the ICTY' in Bert Swart, Goran Sluiter, and Alexander Zahar (eds.), The Legacy of the International Criminal Tribunal for the Former Yugoslavia (Oxford University Press 2011).
[83] See, e.g., Payam Akhavan, 'Beyond Impunity: Can International Criminal Justice Prevent Future Atrocities?' (2001) 95 AJIL 7.
[84] See Mirjan R. Damaska, 'What is the Point of International Criminal Justice?' (2008) 83 Chi.-Kent. L. Rev. 329, 331 ("Beside standard objectives of national criminal law enforcement, such as retribution for wrongdoing, general deterrence, incapacitation, and rehabilitation, international criminal courts profess to pursue numerous additional aims in both the shorter and longer time horizon.").
[85] Stuart Ford, 'A Hierarchy of the Goals of International Criminal Courts' (2018) 27 Minn. J. Intl. L. 179, 221–2; Mark Drumbl, Atrocity, Punishment, and International Law (Cambridge University Press 2007) 169–75 (arguing that norm expression, not deterrence or retribution, is the most reasonable aim of punishment in international criminal law).
[86] See, e.g., Ramji-Nogales (n. 81) (arguing that the failure to incorporate local preferences in their decision-making has harmed the legitimacy of international criminal courts).
[87] See, e.g., Ralph Henham, 'Developing Contextualized Rationales for Sentencing in International Criminal Trials' (2007) 5 J. Intl. Crim. Justice 757, 758 (arguing "that international sentencing should be sensitive to the demands of victims and communities ravaged by war and social conflict"); Raquel Aldana-Pindell, 'In Vindication of Justiciable Victims' Rights to Truth and Justice for State-Sponsored Crimes' (2002) 35 Vanderbilt J. Transnational L. 1399, 1499 (asserting that "victim-focused prosecution norms, in societies in transition from authoritarian state-sponsored mass atrocities, comport and pro-vide the more effective means of promoting respect for human rights ....").
[88] Sergey Vasiliev, 'Victim Participation Revisited: What the ICC is Learning About Itself' in Carsten Stahn (ed.), The Law and Practice of the International Criminal Court (Oxford University Press 2015) 1187 (emphasis omitted).

Scholars who favor a national justice vision of the role of international criminal courts tend to promote pluralist approaches to the regime's legal rules and policies. A number of scholars argue, for instance, that the sentencing practices of international criminal courts should take into consideration the punishment norms of the societies most affected by the crimes at issue.[89] Advocates of global justice, on the other hand, believe that international courts should adopt and develop global norms.[90]

In addressing what I have elsewhere called the "global-local dilemma,"[91] categorical approaches should be avoided. Instead, to identify the primary community of interest for a particular institution requires an inquiry into the intentions of the people who established the institution, and when those intentions are unclear, as they often are, a determination of which community the institution is best suited to serve. Not all supra-national courts are legitimate participants in the global justice system. For instance, if two states formed a court to adjudicate crimes committed on their territories, perhaps to conserve resources or coordinate efforts, such a court, although supra-national, would not act on behalf of the global community. On the other hand, a national court exercising universal jurisdiction over crimes that the global community has asked all states to adjudicate in its name would be acting on behalf of that community and could decide to adopt and advance its goals. A court's ability to serve the global community depends on a number of factors, including, in particular, its access to information about global goals and to resources sufficient to enable it to conduct proceedings in line with those goals.

Applying these criteria to the international criminal courts created in recent decades suggests different conclusions for different institutions. Most importantly, the criteria, particularly that of suitability, suggest that the ICC should privilege global goals. Although the Rome Statute's drafters hoped the Court could address the needs of both national and global communities, many were particularly focused on global justice.[92] More importantly, the ICC's structures make it better suited to the pursuit of global than national community goals.

---

[89] Nancy Amoury Combs, 'Seeking Inconsistency: Advancing Pluralism in International Criminal Sentencing' (2016) 41 Yale J. Intl. L. 1, 36 (arguing that "if the tribunals are going to take even the first step towards obtaining respect for their judgments, they will need their sentencing laws to reflect— at least in broad outlines—community norms"); Stephanos Bibas and William W. Burke-White, 'International Idealism Meets Domestic Criminal Procedure Realism' (2010) 59 Duke L.J. 637, 692 (asserting that "it is more important for international sentences to track domestic ones in the territorial state (at least roughly) than to track the sentences of other international tribunals").

[90] See, e.g., Steven C. Roach, 'Value Pluralism, Liberalism, and the Cosmopolitan Intent of the International Criminal Court' (2005) 4 J. Human Rights 475, 487.

[91] Margaret M. deGuzman, 'The Global-Local Dilemma and the ICC's Legitimacy' in Harlan Grant Cohen et al. (eds.), *Legitimacy and International Courts* (Cambridge University Press 2018).

[92] For instance, one delegate at the conference where the Rome Statute was adopted stated: "A court of international criminal justice would contribute significantly to the maintenance of international peace and security. With clear provisions relating to its power and jurisdiction, such a court would constitute an effective global deterrent." Many similar statements were made throughout the drafting process. UN Diplomatic Conference of Plenipotentiaries on the Establishment of an International Criminal Court,

The Court lacks the resources to adjudicate more than a handful of cases in each situation, and thus is not able to provide meaningful justice to victims of large-scale crimes. Moreover, the Court's complementarity regime means that when national courts are prosecuting effectively, the ICC must stay its hand, limiting its ability to pursue a complete set of national goals in a given situation. Adjudicating a small number of cases will usually do little to promote national justice goals. The ICC also lacks knowledge of national norms and access to information about national preferences. Often, its judges do not speak the language spoken where the crimes were committed, let alone grasp the nuances of local history and culture.

To be sure, the ICC can, and should, promote national justice indirectly by seeking to stimulate, and perhaps assist local prosecutions. Indeed, encouraging national authorities to prosecute is a central purpose of the Court's complementarity regime. By investigating situations, or even threatening to do so, the ICC can motivate national prosecutions. And through "positive complementarity," the Court can provide information, evidence, and other assistance to national authorities to assist them in their pursuit of national justice goals.[93] But national goals should not be the central focus of the ICC's own prosecutions.

On the other hand, the ICC's structure and stature make it particularly suited to the promotion of global justice goals. Although the Court can prosecute only a small number of cases each year, its global audience means that through those prosecutions it can identify and express global norms regarding appropriate conduct. Indeed, the Court's access to global audiences makes it better positioned that any other criminal court for such expression, which also serves to prevent conduct that violates the norms.

Determining the primary community of interest for the *ad hoc* tribunals is more difficult than for the ICC. The intentions of their creators are even less clear. The process involved a relatively small number of people, mostly at the United Nations. The tribunals were established by resolution of the Security Council, indicating their primary purpose was to promote international peace and security, but they were established to address specific situations, suggesting a more local focus. Moreover, it is debatable whether their institutional structures were more suited to the promotion of global or national justice. Although they each adjudicated crimes in a single situation, and thus could potentially address national justice goals, like the ICC, they had the resources to complete only a small number of exemplary prosecutions, not to address the vast criminality that occurred in those conflicts. Nor

Summary Records of the Plenary Meetings and of the Meetings of the Committee of the Whole (June 15–July 17, 1998) UN Doc A/CONF.183/13 (Vol. II) 109, para. 58.

[93] William W. Burke-White, 'Proactive Complementarity: The International Criminal Court and National Courts in the Rome System of International Justice' (2008) 49 Harv. Intl. L.J. 53, 54–5.

did the tribunals have the resources to ascertain the wishes of local populations or the expertise to seek to promote their goals. The question is at least as complex for the hybrid tribunals. The Special Court for Sierra Leone (SCSL) and Extraordinary Chambers in the Courts of Cambodia (ECCC) were created in cooperation with national authorities who presumably hoped they would promote national justice agendas. Yet they also had limited resources to address mass criminality and had significant international participation. As Elena Baylis has written, the "internationals" at these institutions view themselves as participating in a global justice mission;[94] but national personnel likely have a different perspective.

Because most of these institutions have either completed their missions, or are winding down, I will not try to resolve the question of where their primary focus ought to lie. Nonetheless, my hope is that this book's emphasis on the importance of identifying institutional goals will encourage the creators of future *ad hoc* and hybrid tribunals to more clearly articulate their goals and priorities. Most of the remainder of the book's analysis will focus on global institutions, in particular the ICC.

V. The Central Global Justice Goal: Crime Prevention

If global courts are to pursue global justice goals based in global values, the challenge for such courts is to identify the relevant values and goals. Chapters 3 to 6 discuss some of the values and goals that ought to undergird the most important gravity-related decisions at international criminal courts. They examine decisions related to prescriptive and adjudicative authority, defendants' rights and defenses, and sentencing. In each of these contexts, I argue that the central global goal ought to be crime prevention.

Crime prevention should be the principal focus of global criminal justice institutions for several reasons. First, like the human rights regime, the international criminal law regime is premised on the moral value of respecting and protecting human dignity. Criminal courts, including international criminal courts, contribute to this endeavor by preventing crimes that harm human dignity. There is near universal agreement as to the importance of this goal. The preamble of the Rome Statute highlights crime prevention as a central reason for the Court's creation,[95] and its judges cite prevention as one of the most important goals of punishment.[96] The other most commonly cited goal of punishment, retribution, is not

[94] Elena Baylis, 'Tribunal-Hopping with the Post-Conflict Justice Junkies' (2008) 10 Oregon Rev. Intl. L. 361, 363–4.
[95] Rome Statute (n. 21) preamble.
[96] *Prosecutor v. Al Mahdi* (Trial Judgment) ICC-01/12-01/15-171 (September 27, 2016) para. 66; *Prosecutor v. Bemba Gombo* (Trial Sentence) ICC-01/05-01/08 (June 21, 2016) para. 10.

a globally shared value as Chapter 6 argues, and should not be a key driver of international criminal law.[97]

Additionally, among utilitarian goals, crime prevention is the goal to which global institutions are best able to contribute as a practical matter. In particular, global courts are well-suited to preventing crimes through deterrence and norm promotion. Although prevention can take other forms, including community restoration, economic development, and peace building, the structures of international courts, in particular their very limited resources, render them relatively ineffective at accomplishing these goals. International courts' comparative advantage is their ability to prevent crimes by deterring wrong-doers and promulgating global norms of conduct. The ICC's global constitution and profile make it a particularly apt tool for global norm expression, which may be achievable with exemplary prosecutions of a small number of cases.[98] As such, while the ICC should seek to prevent crimes in whatever ways it deems possible, it should give priority to deterrence and global norm expression.

By expressing global norms, international courts, such as the ICC, give voice to, and also constitute, the global justice community. In doing so, they promote the regime's normative legitimacy, and, by communicating their goals and priorities clearly and transparently, they may enhance its sociological legitimacy as well. Moreover, transparent norm expression will enable relevant audiences to evaluate the courts' work and provide feedback that can help to guide future decisions. This dialogic process of norm recognition and promulgation will enable something akin to a democratic process to take place at the global level. As already discussed, it will be important to take special care to give voice to marginalized communities in this process so that international courts do not simply reinforce patterns of domination.

Conclusion

This chapter has explained the book's use of legitimacy as a way to analyze the legal and moral norms that undergird international criminal law's authority, as well as perceptions about the justifications for that authority. It has also previewed the book's central argument that gravity ought to be reconceptualized as contingent on the values and goals of relevant communities, including the global community with respect to global courts. Finally, it has set forth a discursive theory of global

---

[97] See Chapter 6, section III.B.

[98] As James Alexander has argued, claims about the ICC preventing crimes through what he calls "general moral influence" require a long time horizon and are difficult to demonstrate. See James F. Alexander 'The International Criminal Court and the Prevention of Atrocities: Predicting the Court's Impact' (2009) 54 Villanova L. Rev. 1, 29.

community to support the book's prescriptions regarding gravity and the legitimacy of international criminal law. The chapter that follows provides a brief history of gravity's role in legitimizing international criminal law, demonstrating that the concept's prominence is a matter of historical circumstance rather than moral necessity.

2

A Brief History of Gravity

This chapter recounts the history of gravity's use in international criminal law, showing that the concept's centrality in the regime's discourse was not inevitable. Instead, it was dictated largely by historical circumstances. These include the decisions to establish supra-national courts in response to some of the most large-scale crimes the world has experienced, the International Law Commission's decision to focus on gravity in defining international criminality, and the need to reassure states that the International Criminal Court (ICC) would not infringe too much on their sovereignty.

The story begins with the emergence of natural law theory, which eventually came to undergird international criminal law, and with the development of universal jurisdiction over piracy, which provides the backdrop for the international jurisdiction of supra-national institutions. During this early phase, references to gravity did not relate to "atrocities" but instead to the importance of our common humanity. Next came the discussions of international accountability after World War I and the establishment of the International Military Tribunals after World War II. This is when the initial turn to gravity as "atrocity" happened, as a way of differentiating the circumstances that justified establishing those tribunals from those typical within nation states. Still, gravity was not as important a justification for international authority as it is now because the prevalence of power politics meant that the victors of those conflicts felt less need to justify their actions than would many victors today. Between World War II and the creation of the International Criminal Tribunal for the Former Yugoslavia (ICTY) in 1993, the most important developments in international criminal law occurred at the International Law Commission (ILC), an organ of the United Nations charged with "encourag[ing] the progressive development of international law and its codification."[1] The ILC's discussions of international criminality and jurisdiction reveal a conscious turn toward gravity as a justification, even as the members acknowledged the near-impossibility of defining that concept. By the time the ICTY and the International Criminal Tribunal for Rwanda (ICTR) were established, the ILC had established a precedent of reliance on gravity to justify international criminal authority, and that precedent is reflected in the Statutes of those tribunals.

---

[1] ILC, 'Statute of the International Law Commission' (November 21, 1947) UN Doc. A/RES/174(II) art. 17(1).

Shocking the Conscience of Humanity. Margaret M. deGuzman, Oxford University Press (2020). © Margaret M. deGuzman. DOI: 10.1093/oso/9780198786153.001.0001

The most important event in the history of gravity's role was the establishment of the ICC. The drafters of the Rome Statute relied heavily on gravity to justify both the ICC's authority generally and particular exercises of that authority. The creation of the ICC thus entrenched the international community's reliance on gravity to justify international criminal law's authority. Gravity is now a key legal requirement as well as a frequently invoked moral principle. However, the Rome Statute's drafters spent very little time discussing the concept's meaning. Indeed, they seem to have preferred to leave the concept vague, thus enabling actors with different visions of the ICC's role in the world to support the Court's establishment.

The Rome Statute may represent the zenith of gravity's justificatory role in international criminal law. Subsequent international and hybrid tribunals have relied less heavily on the concept, and the proposed regional criminal court for Africa seems to have moved in a significantly different direction. What follows explores these phases of international criminal law's development, showing how gravity's importance grew, and pointing to early indications of a possible future decline.

I. Natural Law Theory and Universal Jurisdiction

As Anthony D'Amato has written, "[t]he affinity of international law to natural law goes back a long way to the classic writers of international law, notably Suarez, Pufendorf and Grotius."[2] However, in more recent years, positivist theories have gained such prominence in international law that they have largely eclipsed natural law in many areas.[3] Fernando Tesón has noted that despite a "venerable lineage," the argument that international law includes natural law norms is profoundly unpopular.[4] Nonetheless, natural law remains influential in human rights law,[5] humanitarian law,[6] and their offspring, international criminal law.[7]

Human rights law is based on the premise that all people have natural rights and that rulers have duties to uphold those rights. Humanitarian law is likewise rooted in the idea that wars should be conducted in ways that respect certain natural

---

[2] Anthony D'Amato, 'Is International Law a Part of Natural Law?' (1989) 9 Vera Lex 8, 8.

[3] H.L.A. Hart is one of the many positivist theorists whose theories came to dominate those of naturalists. See generally H.L.A. Hart, 'Positivism and the Separation of Law and Morals' (1958) 71 Harv. L. Rev. 593.

[4] Fernando R. Tesón, 'Natural Law As Part of International Law: The Case of the Armenian Genocide' (2013) 50 San Diego L. Rev. 813, 813–14.

[5] See, e.g., John Finnis, *Natural Law and Natural Rights*, 2nd edn. (Oxford University Press 1980).

[6] An important example of the natural law influence on international humanitarian law is the Martens Clause of the 1899 Hague Convention, which states that until the positive laws of war develop further "populations and belligerents remain under the protection and empire of the principles of international law, as they result from the usages established between civilized nations, from the laws of humanity and the requirements of the public conscience." 'Laws and Customs of War on Land (Hague, II)' (1899) 1 Bevans 247.

[7] See, e.g., Tesón (n. 4) 824–8 (making the case that the prohibition on state-conducted mass murder is a natural law norm).

rights.[8] International criminal law draws on these bodies of law and, as such, is also an outgrowth of the natural law tradition. Hugo Grotius, a natural law thinker who is considered the father of modern international law, declared: *"crimen grave non potest non esse punibile"* (a serious crime cannot be unpunishable).[9] Grotius believed that any ruler was authorized to punish injuries that "excessively violate the law of nature or of nations."[10] Indeed, he asserted that such crimes require states to either prosecute or extradite their perpetrators.[11]

Natural law ideas about the right, or even obligation to punish certain serious crimes gave rise to the doctrine of universal jurisdiction. The first widely recognized universal jurisdiction crime was piracy.[12] Pirates were labeled *hostes humani generis*, the enemies of all mankind. Their crimes were considered grave, if at all, only in the sense that they harmed humanity by discouraging travel by sea. But the justification for universal jurisdiction over piracy was less its particular gravity than the fact that it took place outside the territory of any state.[13] Eugene Kontorovich has shown that invoking gravity to justify universal jurisdiction over piracy is a recent revisionist move to help justify universal jurisdiction over the so-called "core crimes": war crimes, crimes against humanity, genocide, and aggression.[14] Such arguments overlook the fact that piracy, which is essentially maritime robbery, was never considered an "atrocity" crime in the sense often attributed to the core crimes. As such, the pervasive analogies between piracy and the core international crimes by those seeking to justify gravity-based jurisdiction over the latter must be regarded with caution.[15]

In sum, current appeals to gravity to justify international criminal law's authority have historical roots in the natural law tradition and in universal jurisdiction over

---

[8] M. Cherif Bassiouni, *Crimes Against Humanity: Historical Evolution and Contemporary Application*, 2nd edn. (Cambridge University Press 2011) 96–111 (describing the evolution of humanitarian law based on "humanistic principles"). But see Eyal Benvenisti and Doreen Lustig, 'Taming Democracy: Codifying the Laws of War to Restore the European Order, 1856–1874' (2017) Cambridge Faculty of Law Research Paper 28/2017, 1, available at https://papers.ssrn.com/sol3/papers.cfm?abstract_id=2985781 (last accessed on September 19, 2019) (arguing that the desire to protect civilians was less central to the development of humanitarian law than is generally believed).

[9] Hugo Grotius, *Hugonis Grotii De Jure Belli Et Pacis Libri Tres: Accompanied by an Abridged Translation*, William Whewell (trans.) (J.W. Parker 1853), Book 2, Chapter XX, s. II(3), 244.

[10] Ibid., Book 2, Chapter XX, s. XL(1), 308.

[11] Ibid., Book 2, Chapter XXI, s. IV(1), 347.

[12] Eugene Kontorovich, 'The Piracy Analogy: Modern Universal Jurisdiction's Hollow Foundation' (2004) 45 Harv. Intl. L.J. 183, 190. Some states also asserted universal jurisdiction over slave trading, but this was more controversial. See Roger Clark, 'Steven Spielberg's Amistad and Other Things I Have Thought About in the Past Forty Years: International (Criminal) Law, Conflict of Laws, Insurance and Slavery' (1998) 30 Rutgers L.J. 371, 390 n. 55.

[13] David Luban, 'Fairness to Rightness: Jurisdiction, Legality, and the Legitimacy of International Criminal Law' in Samantha Besson and John Tasioulas (eds.), *The Philosophy of International Law* (Oxford University Press 2010) 570–71.

[14] Kontorovich (n. 12).

[15] See, e.g., Kenneth C. Randall, 'Universal Jurisdiction Under International Law' (1988) 66 Texas L. Rev. 785, 798 (asserting that "[t]he concept of universal jurisdiction over piracy has had enduring value, however, by supporting the extension of universal jurisdiction to certain modern offenses somewhat resembling piracy.").

piracy, but those roots reflect a rather different understanding of the concept from the one that prevails today.

II. International Trials as a Response to World War

The idea that especially grave crimes warrant international adjudication emerged largely in response to the World Wars.[16] Writing in 1950, diplomat and international lawyer Ricardo Alfaro observed:

> After the termination of the First World War, the conviction crystallized in the minds of thinking people that the horrors of war must be spared to men, that war is a crime against humankind and that such a crime must be prevented and punished. Great was the clamour against the atrocities perpetrated in violation of the laws and customs of war, as embodied in the unwritten law of humanity and civilization as well as in the positive provisions of The Hague and Geneva conventions and other international agreements. [17]

Such invocations of the "atrocity" of the crimes of World War I motivated the victorious Allies to consider, at the Paris Peace Conference, creating an international military tribunal to try the Germans for both "acts which provoked the World War" and "violations of the law and customs of war and the laws of humanity."[18] The Treaty of Versailles included a provision to try Kaiser Wilhelm II for "a supreme offence against international morality and the sanctity of treaties";[19] and the Allies considered trying the Ottoman Turks for "crimes against humanity and civilization" for their massacres of Armenians.[20] However, neither trial ultimately occurred. The reasons were complex, but seem to have included concerns based in the principle of legality.[21]

---

[16] Some earlier instances of supra-national adjudication exist. For an interesting discussion of the early history, see Ziv Bohrer, 'International Criminal Law's Millennium of Forgotten History' (2016) 34 L. & History Rev. 393.

[17] ILC, 'Report of Ricardo J. Alfaro, Special Rapporteur, on the Question of International Criminal Jurisdiction' (March 3, 1950) UN Doc. A/CN.4/15 para. 6.

[18] Commission on the Responsibility of the Authors of the War and on Enforcement of Penalties, 'Report Presented to the Preliminary Peace Conference' (1920) 14 AJIL 95, 118.

[19] Treaty of Versailles (adopted on June 28, 1919, entered into force on January 10, 1920) 2 Bevans 43, 136 art. 227. For an in-depth discussion of the effort to try the Kaiser, see William A. Schabas, *The Trial of the Kaiser* (Oxford University Press 2018).

[20] Egon Schwelb, 'Crimes against Humanity' (1946) 23 Brit. Y.B. Intl. L. 178, 181 (quoting Armenian Memorandum presented by the Greek delegation to the Commission of Fifteen on March 14, 1919).

[21] Steven D. Roper and Lillian A. Barria, *Designing Criminal Tribunals: Sovereignty and International Concerns in the Protection of Human Rights* (Ashgate 2006) 5–6 (noting that the "US representatives objected to the tribunal on the grounds that such a court had no precedent in international law"); Carnegie Endowment for International Peace, 'Violations of the Laws and Customs of War: Reports of Majority and Dissenting Reports of American and Japanese Members of the Commission of Responsibilities For the Conference of Paris', Pamphlet No. 32, (1919) 76.

Nonetheless, the discussions of possible prosecutions after World War I sowed the seeds for the eventual creation of an international criminal court. In fact, in 1920, there were discussions at the League of Nations about establishing a "High Court of Justice ... competent to try crimes constituting a breach of international public order or against the universal law of nations."[22] The effort was short-lived, however, because states repeated earlier objections that no international crimes or jurisdiction existed.[23] Still, the committee working on the issue foreshadowed the establishment of an international criminal court, noting: "If crimes of this kind should in future be brought within the scope of international penal law, a criminal department might be set up in the Court of International Justice."[24]

The seeds sown after World War I yielded fruit after World War II. Once again, the world had witnessed unimaginable atrocities, and this time the victorious Allies decided to try some of the vanquished perpetrators. The establishment of the International Military Tribunal at Nuremberg (IMT) and International Military Tribunal for the Far East (IMTFE) is often cited as inaugurating modern international criminal law.[25] Although state sovereignty remained a powerful concept in international law and relations, the scale of the Nazi crimes seems to have catalyzed a shift in world opinion around issues of human rights. The idea that states had absolute rights within their borders was no longer palatable. Already in 1950, Joseph Keenan and Brendan Brown wrote:

> It is the authors' contention that the Tokyo and Nuernberg war crimes trials were a manifestation of an intellectual and moral revolution which will have a profound and far-reaching influence upon the future of world society .... They maintain that the international moral order must be regarded as the cause, not the effect, of positive law; that such law does not derive its essence from physical power, and that any attempt to isolate such law from morals is a symptom of juridical schizophrenia caused by the separation of the brain of the lawyer from that of the human being.[26]

This reuniting of law and morality harkened back to the natural law tradition[27] and gave rise to the human rights movement, including the adoption of documents

---

[22] ILC, 'Historical Survey of the Question of International Criminal Jurisdiction' (1949) UN Doc. A/CN.4/7/Rev.1 10.
[23] Manley O. Hudson, 'The Proposed International Criminal Court' (1938) 32 AJIL 549, 550.
[24] ILC, 'Historical Survey' (n. 22) 12.
[25] See, e.g., Roper and Barria (n. 21) 6 (claiming that "the horrific abuses of the Holocaust finally forced states to end impunity for individual actions under the laws of war."); but see Bohrer (n. 16) (arguing that this common narrative overlooks important prior history).
[26] Joseph B. Keenan and Brendan F. Brown, *Crimes Against International Law* (Public Affairs Press 1950) v–vi.
[27] See, e.g., Robert J. Beck, *International Rules: Approaches from International Law and International Relations*, Anthony Clark Arend and Robert D. Vander (eds.) (Oxford University Press 1996) 34.

such as the Universal Declaration of Human Rights and the International Covenant on Civil and Political Rights.

The concept of gravity played an important role in justifying the creation of the IMT and IMTFE. Concerns about sovereignty and the principle of legality were overcome with references to the extreme gravity of the crimes at issue. Political statements before the war ended already reflected the importance of gravity to the eventual international trials. In 1943, Roosevelt, Churchill, and Stalin issued a statement "Regarding Atrocities" in which they announced that the Nazis would be tried for their "abominable deeds" either in the places where the crimes occurred or, in "the case of major criminals, whose offenses have no particular geographic location," by joint decision of the Allies.[28] The US President asserted that the Nazi's "wholesale systematic murder of the Jews of Europe" was "one of the blackest crimes of all history," and it was "therefore fitting that we should again proclaim our determination that none who participate in these acts of savagery shall go unpunished."[29] The Soviet Union issued a declaration asserting "that the Hitlerite Government and its accomplices would not escape responsibility and deserved punishment for all the *unprecedented atrocities* perpetrated against the peoples of the USSR and against all the freedom-loving countries."[30]

In opening the Nuremberg trials, the US Chief Prosecutor, Robert Jackson, famously stated: "The wrongs which we seek to condemn and punish have been so calculated, so malignant, and so devastating, that civilization cannot tolerate their being ignored, because it cannot survive their being repeated."[31] Jackson's appeal to the gravity of the crimes was aimed in part to counter charges of retroactive and victors' justice—for crimes this bad, Jackson implied that such flaws were excusable.

Despite the prevalence of such gravity rhetoric, the concept did not play the central role in justifying international authority after World War II that it does today. First, international law and relations were perhaps more rooted in power than they are now. As victors, the Allies claimed the authority to adjudicate the crimes in lieu of the defeated governments. As such, the IMT and IMTFE are sometimes considered "an assertion of sovereignty."[32] Second, while the decision to establish the tribunals was justified in terms of gravity, unlike many of the crimes in the Rome Statute, the crimes in the tribunals' Statutes were not defined by their gravity. The tribunals had jurisdiction over war crimes, crimes against

---

[28] US Department of State, 'Report of Robert H. Jackson, United States Representative to the International Conference on Military Trials' (1945) 11–12.

[29] Ibid. 12–13.

[30] Ibid. 16 (emphasis added).

[31] IMT, 'Trial of the Major War Criminals Before the International Military Tribunal Proceedings' (Nuremberg, November 14–30, 1945) Vol. II, 98–9 (opening statement of Justice Robert H. Jackson, November 21, 1945).

[32] Roper and Barria (n. 21) 6.

humanity, and crimes against peace without regard to the scale or nature of harm they caused.[33] War crimes had never required harm that was especially serious in terms of scale or scope, but instead were designed to minimize suffering in war generally. Likewise, crimes against humanity as defined in the Nuremberg Charter aimed to capture crimes committed by a government against its own people rather than crimes of particular gravity. Crimes against peace were perhaps most obviously associated with gravity, but those were poorly defined in the Charter.[34] Thus, while the post-World War II tribunals are widely viewed as "[r]epresent[ing] a first effort by the international community to create a judicial mechanism for addressing *atrocities* committed during war,"[35] the justifications for such a mechanism were not strongly rooted in gravity. Indeed, the most immediate legacy of the tribunals' work was not the creation of other international courts, but rather the development of human rights and humanitarian law regimes, that seek to prevent all violations, not merely particularly serious ones. In sum, although gravity was used to help justify the establishment of the IMT and IMTFE, it was not relied upon as heavily as it is today.

Another important legacy of the post-war tribunals was the further codification of the law of armed conflict, in particular, the adoption of the four Geneva Conventions in 1949. Each Convention criminalizes "grave breaches" of the laws of war and requires states parties to either prosecute or extradite persons on their territories who are suspected of these offenses.[36] Gravity clearly plays a role in defining these offenses, but again, not in the "atrocity" sense in which it is most frequently employed today. Grave breaches are "grave" relative to other breaches of the Conventions that do not necessarily merit criminal sanction. With regard to non-grave breaches of the Conventions and Protocols, states are free—at least as a matter of treaty law—to pursue non-criminal means of prevention.[37]

The crimes of World War II also catalyzed Rafael Lemkin's campaign to create the crime of genocide. The negotiations surrounding the Genocide Convention

[33] Charter of the International Military Tribunal, 'Agreement for the Prosecution and Punishment of the Major War Criminals of the European Axis' (August 8, 1945) 82 UNTS 280 art. 6; Charter for the International Military Tribunal for the Far East (April 26, 1946) 1589 TIAS 20 art. 5.

[34] The Charter defines crimes against peace as the "planning, preparation, initiation or waging of a war of aggression, or a war in violation of international treaties, agreements or assurances ...." IMT Charter (n. 33) art. 6(a). By not defining "war of aggression," this definition fails clearly to explain the prohibited conduct.

[35] Roper and Barria (n. 21) 9 (emphasis added).

[36] Geneva Convention for the Amelioration of the Condition of the Wounded and Sick in Armed Forces in the Field (adopted on August 12, 1949, entered into force on October 21, 1950) 75 UNTS 31 art. 49; Geneva Convention for the Amelioration of the Condition of the Wounded, Sick and Shipwrecked Members of Armed Forces at Sea (adopted on August 12, 1949, entered into force on October 21, 1950) 75 UNTS 85 art. 50; Geneva Convention Relative to the Treatment of Prisoners of War (adopted on August 12, 1949, entered into force on October 21, 1950) 75 UNTS 135 art. 129; Geneva Convention Relative to the Protection of Civilian Persons in Time of War (adopted on August 12, 1949, entered into force on October 21, 1950) 75 UNTS 287 art. 146.

[37] Geneva Convention Joint Committee, 'Final Record of the Diplomatic Conference of Geneva of 1949' vol. II-B, 115.

are an important part of the story of gravity's rise to prominence in international criminal law. Reacting to the Holocaust, which had decimated his family, Lemkin sought to define a crime that would be subject to international jurisdiction because it would concern all of humanity. Lemkin had a particular vision of *why* genocide concerns humanity: for him, the harm of genocide lay not in the number of people harmed or the severity of their suffering, but in the impoverishment of humanity's diversity when a defined group of people is partly or completely eliminated.[38]

The negotiating history of the Genocide Convention reveals resistance from states concerned about protecting their sovereignty.[39] Ultimately, however, most states agreed that when a person commits specific acts with intent to destroy a national, ethnic, racial, or religious group in whole or in part they have committed an international crime. Moreover, although the Genocide Convention does not provide for universal jurisdiction, it does require prosecution by the state where the crime was committed and grants jurisdiction to "such international penal tribunal as may have jurisdiction with respect to those Contracting Parties which shall have accepted its jurisdiction."[40] The Convention thus anticipates the creation of an international court without itself establishing one.

The adoption of the Genocide Convention helped to promote gravity's role as a central concept in international criminal law. Genocide is often called the "crime of crimes" and its mention evokes images of the Holocaust and the massive slaughter of Tutsis in Rwanda. Yet, as a legal matter, genocide does not require large-scale harm. Rather, the gravity of the crime lies in the intent to destroy a group, not in whether the intent is realized, or whether the group is a large one.

III. Work of the International Law Commission

An important chapter in the history of gravity's role in international criminal law is the ILC's work in the years between the establishment of the IMT and of the ICTY.[41] For several decades after World War II, Cold War politics inhibited the legal development of the international criminal law regime, but the conceptual

---

[38] Raphael Lemkin, 'Genocide as a Crime Under International Law' (1947) 41 AJIL 145, 147 (discussing the difference between "mass murder" and "genocide" definitions and noting that, "mass murder does not convey the specific losses to civilization in the form of the cultural contributions which can be made only by groups of people united through national, racial or cultural characteristics").

[39] William Schabas, *Genocide in International Law: The Crime of Crimes* (Cambridge University Press 2009) 65 (citing a comment by Venezuela to the effect that an international criminal court to prosecute genocide would violate state sovereignty).

[40] Convention on the Prevention and Punishment of the Crime of Genocide (December 9, 1948) 78 UNTS 277 art. 6.

[41] The ILC was established by the General Assembly with the purpose of promoting the "progressive development of international law and its codification." UNGA Res. 174(II) (November 21, 1947) UN Doc. A/RES/174(II) art. 1.

efforts of the ILC during this period laid a strong foundation for the regime's rapid evolution once the Cold War ended.[42] One of those conceptual contributions was the decision to emphasize gravity as an important justification for international authority.

In 1947, the United Nations General Assembly assigned the ILC two related tasks: (1) to formulate the principles established by the Nuremberg tribunal and judgment; and (2) to draft a Code of Offenses against the Peace and Security of Mankind (Draft Code).[43] A year later, in connection with the drafting of the Genocide Convention, the General Assembly asked the ILC to study the desirability of creating an international criminal court to adjudicate genocide and "other crimes over which jurisdiction will be conferred upon that organ by international conventions."[44]

A significant impetus for these efforts was the urgent need to avoid future wars. The idea of formulating the Nuremberg Principles and developing a Draft Code originated in correspondence between Nuremberg Justice Francis Biddle and US President Truman. Justice Biddle wrote a report recommending codification of offenses against the peace and security of mankind in order to both reaffirm the principle against aggression as the supreme crime and "afford an opportunity to strengthen the sanctions against lesser violations of international law."[45] Truman's response focused more narrowly on the crime of aggression. He wrote that a "code of international criminal law to deal with all who wage aggressive war ... deserves to be studied and weighed by the best legal minds the world over" and expressed the hope that the United Nations would pursue this endeavor.[46] But Ricardo Alfaro, when he was appointed Special Rapporteur on the Question of International Jurisdiction, viewed the task somewhat more broadly. In his 1950 report to the ILC, Alfaro wrote:

> The essential question before the Commission is whether it is desirable and feasible to institute an international criminal jurisdiction for the prevention and punishment of international crimes. My answer to that question is unhesitatingly in the affirmative. The community of States is entitled to prevent *crimes against the peace and security of mankind and crimes against the dictates of the human conscience*, including therein the hideous crime of genocide.[47]

---

[42] The ILC was not writing on a blank slate. Various other efforts to develop the notion of an international criminal jurisdiction had taken place in both official and unofficial fora. For an overview, see ILC, 'Report of Ricardo J. Alfaro' (n. 17).

[43] UNGA Res. 177(II) (November 12, 1947) UN Doc. A/RES/177(II).

[44] UNGA Res. 260B(III) (December 9, 1948) UN Doc. A/RES/260(III).

[45] Correspondence between Justice Biddle and President Truman, cited in ILC, 'Report by Jean Spiropoulos, Special Rapporteur, Draft Code of Offences Against the Peace and Security of Mankind' (April 26, 1950) UN Doc. A/CN.4/25 para. 9.

[46] Ibid. para. 10.

[47] ILC, 'Report of Ricardo J. Alfaro' (n. 17) para. 136.

Alfaro's distinction between "crimes against the peace and security of mankind" and "crimes against the dictates of the human conscience" is interesting. Although he did not explain the difference, he implied that a category of offenses exists that offends the human conscience without also threatening peace and security. Whether such crimes offend the conscience because they are especially grave in an "atrocity" sense or for some other reason is unclear. His report did suggest that "crimes against humanity" extend beyond "atrocities," when it defined such crimes as "atrocities *and other inhumane acts* committed against a civilian population ...."[48]

The ILC's first Draft Statute for an international criminal court avoided the question of how to distinguish international crimes from others by simply giving the proposed court jurisdiction over "crimes under international law, as may be provided in conventions or special agreements among States parties to the present Statute."[49] But the Report of the Committee on International Criminal Jurisdiction suggests that gravity was part of the discussions. It stated that a proposal to include crimes such as drug trafficking and damage to submarine cables was defeated because such crimes "are of minor importance compared to international crimes proper."[50] The question of what constitute "international crimes proper" was not addressed.[51]

In its early efforts to define "offences against the peace and security of mankind" for purposes of the Draft Code, the ILC focused not on gravity, but on the political nature of such crimes. Its 1950 Report asserted that the Code "should be limited to offences which contain a political element and which endanger or disturb the maintenance of international peace and security."[52] While the Report did not define the term "political element," Special Rapporteur Jean Spiropoulis asserted that "political element" refers to "offences which, on account of their specific character, normally would affect international relations in a way dangerous for the *maintenance of peace*."[53] In other words, for Spiropoulis, "political" essentially amounted to a threat to peace and security.

This early focus on peace and security is a legacy of the Nuremberg Charter. The Charter gave the IMT jurisdiction over war crimes and crimes against peace, each of which clearly threatens peace and security, as well as crimes against humanity. Although more recent definitions of crimes against humanity do not entail

[48] Ibid. para. 37 (Alfaro's definition also includes "persecutions on political, racial or religious grounds in execution of, or in connexion with, any crime within the jurisdiction of the Tribunal.").
[49] Draft Statute for an International Criminal Court, Annex to Rep. of the Committee on International Criminal Jurisdiction (August 31, 1951) UN Doc. A/2136 art. 1.
[50] ILC, 'Report of the Committee on International Criminal Jurisdiction' (August 31, 1951) UN Doc. A/2136 para. 33.
[51] Ibid.
[52] ILC, 'Report of the ILC Covering the Work of its Second Session' (June 5–July 29, 1950) UN Doc A/CN.4/34 para. 149.
[53] ILC, 'Report by J. Spiropoulos, Special Rapporteur, on Draft Code of Offences Against the Peace and Security of Mankind' (April 26, 1950) UN Doc. A/CN.4/25 para. 35.

a threat to peace and security, the IMT definition required a nexus with war crimes or crimes against peace.[54] As such, all of the Nuremberg Charter crimes involved a threat to peace and security.

By 1951, some ILC delegates took the position that crimes against humanity need not be associated with crimes against peace or war crimes, calling into question the peace and security rationale, but other delegates disagreed.[55] Control Council Law Number 10, the law used to prosecute the "lesser" war criminals after World War II, had omitted the so-called "war nexus,"[56] but some delegates nonetheless felt the nexus was essential. The draft text the ILC submitted to governments that year for their consideration thus expanded the definition of crimes against humanity somewhat by, for instance, including crimes committed in connection with state-sponsored terrorism, but it maintained the focus on crimes that threaten peace.[57]

The Commission expressed the view that a "violation of the laws and customs of war" does not affect the peace and security of mankind, but included such violations in the Draft Code because they were listed in the Nuremberg Charter.[58] The Commission also rejected the idea of limiting war crimes in the Draft Code to "acts of a certain gravity," asserting that "*every* violation of the laws or customs of war [should] be considered as a crime under the code."[59] At this stage, therefore, gravity clearly was not a requirement of international criminality.

By 1954, the nexus for crimes against humanity had been replaced with a different "political element"—the involvement of state actors. The 1954 Draft Code defined crimes against humanity as: "Inhuman acts ... committed against any civilian population on social, political, racial, religious or cultural grounds by the authorities of a State or by private individuals acting at the instigation or with the toleration of such authorities."[60] Whereas the earlier version allowed "private individuals" to be perpetrators, the Commission now felt that: "In order not to characterize any inhuman act committed by a private individual as an

---

[54] IMT Charter (n. 33) Annex to the Agreement for the Prosecution and Punishment of the Major War Criminals of the European Axis art. 6(c).

[55] See ILC, 'Second Report by J. Spiropoulos, Special Rapporteur, on Draft Code of Offences Against the Peace and Security of Mankind' (April 12, 1951) UN Doc. A/CN.4/44 paras. 116–24.

[56] Control Council Law No. 10, Punishment of Persons Guilty of War Crimes, Crimes Against Peace and Against Humanity art. 2 (December 20, 1945), reprinted in Telford Taylor, *Final Report to the Secretary of the Army on The Nuremberg War Crimes Trials Under Control Council Law No. 10* (US Government Printing Office 1949) 250.

[57] ILC, 'Report on the Work of Its Third Session, Draft Code of Offenses Against the Peace and Security of Mankind' (May 16–July 27, 1951) UN Doc. A/CN.4/48 and Corr.1 and 2 para. 59, art. 2. Interestingly, the draft text does not use the term "crimes against humanity," perhaps because the definition does not reflect that in the Nuremberg Charter.

[58] ILC, 'Second Report by J. Spiropoulos, Special Rapporteur, on Draft Code of Offences Against the Peace and Security of Mankind' (n. 55) 59, para. 10(b).

[59] Ibid. 59 para. 10(c).

[60] ILC, 'Report of the ILC Covering the Work of its Sixth Session' (June 3–July 28, 1954) UN Doc A/CN.4/88 para. 50, art. 2(11).

international crime, it was found necessary to provide that such an act constitutes an international crime only if committed by the private individual at the
instigation or with the toleration of the authorities of a State."[61] To the extent the
Commission required gravity at this point, therefore, it took the form of a state
action requirement.

Meanwhile, the UN Committee on International Criminal Jurisdiction was
debating the feasibility of establishing an international criminal court.[62] The
Committee's 1953 Report reveals that some members were opposed to the idea,
arguing that:

> An international criminal court presuppose[s] an international community with
> the power necessary to operate the court, and such power did not exist. A sur-
> render of some present State sovereignty would be the condition of the establish-
> ment of the court, and such surrender was highly unlikely.[63]

The objection was also raised that international criminal law was not sufficiently
defined in conventions for a court to have jurisdiction over it. Other members
countered that international law was beginning to recognize the rights of individuals and that states' unanimous affirmation of the Nuremberg Principles testified
to the existence of common norms for a court to apply.[64]

The Committee's 1954 Draft Statute, like an earlier 1951 version, did not specify which crimes would be within the court's jurisdiction but this revision allowed
for the international court to adjudicate crimes under national law "where appropriate."[65] At this early stage in the deliberations, therefore, it was far from clear that
gravity would play an important role in justifying the authority of an international
criminal court, or in defining international crimes.

It was in the early 1980s, when the ILC resumed work on the Draft Code after a
long hiatus, that the Commission began to rely more directly on gravity as a justification for international prescriptive and adjudicative authority. By this time, the
human rights regime was firmly established, and the idea that violations of human
rights concern those outside a state's borders was less controversial. As such, the
peace and security rationale had lost some of its force. The new Special Rapporteur,
Doudou Thiam, can be credited with shifting the Commission's work toward
gravity. In his first report, Thiam addressed the question of what makes a crime

---

[61] Ibid. Comment.
[62] UNGA 'Report of the 1953 Committee on International Criminal Jurisdiction' (August 20,
1953) UN Doc. A/2645 para. 1 (explaining that the committee was established "for the purpose of
preparing one or more preliminary draft conventions and proposals relating to the establishment and
the statute of an international criminal court").
[63] Ibid. para. 17.
[64] Ibid. para. 18.
[65] Ibid. Annex art. 2.

international, noting that "it is clear that the distinction between crimes under internal law and crimes under international law is relative and at times arbitrary."[66] He disagreed with the 1954 Draft Code's focus on a political element, arguing instead that gravity should be the decisive factor:

> It is nevertheless an offence against the peace and security of mankind if its seriousness and scope are such as to impair fundamental interest of the international community. It may be that the authors of the Charter of the Nürnberg Tribunal were struck not so much by the political content of the crimes with which they were concerned as by their gravity, their atrociousness, their scale and their effects on the international community.[67]

It is notable that Thiam mentioned atrociousness and scale separately from gravity, implying a distinction that is often not drawn today. In Thiam's view, international criminality did not require atrociousness or large-scale harm. He considered crimes "international by their nature," when they "assail sacred values or principles of civilization—for example, human rights or peaceful coexistence of nations—which are protected as such."[68] Assaults on human rights thus concerned the international community sufficiently to give rise to international criminality, even in the absence of large-scale harm.

Thiam gave specific attention to the meaning of gravity. He asserted that gravity involves an objective criterion—"the fundamental interest of the international community"—and a subjective criterion—"the evaluation of the offence by the international community itself."[69] According to Thiam: "It is the subjective element—the evaluation of the offence by the international community and the way in which the offence is perceived by that community—which determines whether the offence is to be transposed from the internal to the international level and made a crime under international law."[70] He did not explain how the presence of either the objective or subjective components of gravity might be ascertained.

The ILC accepted Thiam's suggestion that the offenses in the Draft Code should be identified according to their seriousness rather than by any political aspect. Indeed, the Commission asserted that such offenses are not only more serious than national crimes but also relative to other international crimes. The ILC's 1983 Report states:

---

[66] ILC, 'First Report by Mr. Doudou Thiam, Special Rapporteur, on the Draft Code of Crimes against the Peace and Security of Mankind' (March 18, 1983) UN Doc. A/CN.4/364 para. 35.

[67] Ibid. para. 37.

[68] Ibid. para. 35.

[69] Ibid. para. 40.

[70] Ibid.

> From the standpoint of *seriousness*, there is … a kind of hierarchy of these international crimes. Offences against the peace and security of mankind are at the top of the hierarchy. They are in a sense *the most serious of the most serious offences*.[71]

The Commission thus decided unanimously to include in the Code only "those crimes which are at the top of the scale because of their especial seriousness."[72] Such crimes are "characterized by the particular horror which they evoke in the universal conscience."[73]

After identifying gravity as the key factor legitimizing international criminal authority, the ILC spent many years grappling with the meaning of the concept. In his second report, Thiam noted the complexity of this endeavor, explaining that gravity is "highly subjective" and "is bound up with the state on the international conscience at a given moment."[74] This subjectivity made it difficult to define international crimes. For example, Thiam opined that the distinction between crimes against humanity and other human rights violations is a matter of degrees of seriousness, but he gave no indication of how a line between the two might be drawn.[75]

The Commission's 1984 Report reflected the members' struggle to explain gravity as a criterion for identifying offenses against the peace and security of mankind.[76] The Report noted that the Commission had discussed several possible distinguishing criteria including:

> the inspiration of the criminal act (for example an act based on racial, religious or political conviction); the status of the victim of the criminal act (for example, a State or a private individual); the nature of the law or interest infringed (the interest of security appearing more important than a purely material interest); or lastly, the motive, etc.[77]

However, none of these criteria were considered sufficient because:

> The seriousness of an act was judged sometimes according to the motive, sometimes according to the end pursued, sometimes according to the particular nature of the offence (the horror and reprobation it arouses), sometimes according to the

---

[71] ILC, 'Report on the Work of Its Thirty-Fifth Session' (May 3–July 22, 1983) UN Doc. A/38/10 para. 47.

[72] Ibid. para. 48.

[73] Ibid. para. 59.

[74] ILC, 'Second Report by Mr. Doudou Thiam, Special Rapporteur, on the Draft Code of Crimes Against the Peace and Security of Mankind' (February 1, 1984) UN Doc. A/CN.4/377 and Corr.1 para. 8.

[75] Ibid. para. 40.

[76] ILC, 'Report on the Work of Its Thirty-Sixth Session' (May 7–July 27, 1984) UN Doc. A/39/10 para. 47 (noting that "[s]ome breaches might constitute only a minor infringement, reprehensible no doubt, but not falling within that category of offences.").

[77] Ibid. para. 34.

physical extent of the disaster caused. Furthermore, these elements seemed difficult to separate and were often combined in the same act.[78]

Despite its inability to define seriousness with any precision, the Commission excluded several crimes from the Draft Code on the basis of insufficient seriousness,
including forging passports. In justifying this move, the ILC employed very general language about gravity, stating:

> The code ought to retain its particularly serious character as an instrument
> dealing solely with offences distinguished by their especially horrible, cruel,
> savage and barbarous nature. These are essentially offences which threaten the
> very foundations of modern civilization and the values it embodies. It is these
> particular characteristics which set apart offences against the peace and security
> of mankind and justify their separate codification.[79]

Crimes that the Commission favored adding to the Draft Code, again without providing specifics regarding their seriousness, included "colonialism, apartheid and
possibly serious damage to environment and economic aggression."[80]

In its 1987 Report, the ILC again sought to explain what seriousness means for
purposes of identifying crimes against the peace and security of mankind:

> These are crimes which affect the very foundations of human society. Seriousness
> can be deduced either from the nature of the act in question (cruelty, monstrous-
> ness, barbarity, etc.) or from the extent of its effects (massiveness, the victims
> being peoples, populations or ethnic groups), or from the motive of the perpet-
> rator (for example, genocide), or from several of these elements. Whichever factor
> makes it possible to determine the seriousness of the act, it is this seriousness
> which constitutes the essential element of a crime against the peace and security
> of mankind—a crime characterized by its degree of horror and barbarity—and
> which undermines the foundations of human society.[81]

Like the earlier statements, this adds little in the way of specific criteria to distinguish the crimes that should be subject to international jurisdiction. However, the
emphasis on gravity eventually led to changes in the elements of the crimes included in the Draft Code. The 1991 Draft Code replaced crimes against humanity
with "systematic or mass violations of human rights."[82] The Commentary noted

---

[78] Ibid.

[79] Ibid. para. 63.

[80] Ibid. para. 65(c)(ii).

[81] ILC, 'Report on the Work of Its Thirty-Ninth Session' (May 4–July 17, 1987) UN Doc. A/CN.4/404
para. 66.

[82] ILC, 'Report on the Work of Its Forty-Third Session' (April 29–July 19, 1991) UN Doc. A/46/10
para. 176.

that since the acts in question must be extremely serious, only systematic or mass violations of human rights should qualify.[83] It stated that "systematic" relates to a "constant practice or methodical plan to carry out such violations," while "[t]he mass scale element relates to the number of people affected."[84] Likewise, the Draft Code included only "exceptionally serious" war crimes. This change was made in an effort to be "faithful to the criterion that the draft Code should cover only the most serious among the most serious crimes."[85]

Around the same time, the ILC resumed consideration of the related question of establishing an international criminal court.[86] In this context, the role of gravity became more controversial. Although the Commission had broadly accepted gravity as the key criterion for international prescriptive authority, views regarding the justification for international adjudicative authority were more varied. While some members of the Commission felt the jurisdiction of an international criminal court should be restricted to a small category of extremely grave crimes, others wanted to expand its reach to crimes with transnational components—crimes that came to be known as "treaty crimes" in the Rome Statute negotiations.[87] Indeed, the initial impetus for the request to reopen discussion of an international criminal court was a plea by Trinidad and Tobago for international assistance in addressing its serious drug trafficking problem.[88] Still, others took a middle position that linked the question of subject matter jurisdiction of the ICC to its adjudicative jurisdiction. They suggested that the Court's jurisdiction should be compulsory for exceptionally serious crimes and optional for other crimes of international character, such as the seizure of aircraft.[89] Another suggestion was that the Court could have exclusive jurisdiction over some crimes and concurrent jurisdiction over others.[90] Gravity's role in determining the scope of the Court's authority was thus contested in the early ILC debates.

When the ILC proposed a Draft ICC Statute in 1994, gravity was at the heart of the proposal. The Draft included both "crimes of an international character" and treaty crimes such as those concerning trafficking, but it accorded the Court jurisdiction over the latter only in cases that "constitute exceptionally serious crimes

---

[83] Ibid.
[84] Ibid.
[85] Ibid.
[86] ILC, 'Report on the Work of Its Forty-Fifth Session' (May 3–July 23, 1993) UN Doc. A/48/10 para. 29.
[87] ILC Report 1991 (n. 82) paras. 119–21.
[88] UNGA Res. 44/39 (1989). See also Paul D. Marquardt, 'Law Without Borders: The Constitutionality of an International Criminal Court' (1995) 33 Columbia J. Transnational L. 73, 90–1 (describing the request to the UN by a Latin American coalition constituted by the Trinidadian government that an international court be established to combat drug trafficking).
[89] ILC, 'Report on the Work of Its Forty-Fourth Session' (May 4–July 24, 1992) UN Doc. A/47/10 para. 37.
[90] Ibid. para. 41 (stating that some held the view that exclusive jurisdiction could be applied to crimes of extreme gravity, but not to lesser crimes such as international drug trafficking or seizing of aircraft).

of international concern."[91] It also limited war crimes to "serious violations," although it dropped the Draft Code's qualifier of "exceptional" seriousness.[92] The term "crimes against humanity" was reintroduced in place of "systematic and mass violation of human rights," but the Commission noted that "the hallmarks of such crimes lie in their widespread and systematic nature."[93]

The 1994 Draft Statute also reflected a discretionary version of what later became the mandatory gravity threshold for admissibility in the Rome Statute. The Court would be permitted to find inadmissible any case that "is not of such gravity to justify further action by the Court."[94] In this regard, the ILC Report noted:

> There were also suggestions that the court should have discretion to decline to exercise its jurisdiction if the case was not of sufficient gravity or could be adequately handled by a national court. This suggestion was explained in terms of ensuring that the court would deal solely with the most serious crimes, it would not encroach on the functions of national courts, and it would adapt its caseload to the resources available.[95]

Some members of the Commission felt the admissibility provision was unnecessary because the relevant considerations could be taken into account in determining jurisdiction, but others asserted "that the circumstances of particular cases could vary widely and could anyway be substantially clarified after the court assumed jurisdiction so that a power such as that contained in Article 35 was necessary if the purposes indicated in the preamble were to be fulfilled."[96] There does not seem to have been much discussion of how the court would determine which crimes are insufficiently grave to merit its attention.

In 1995, the ILC members tried again to come up with gravity criteria but to no avail.[97] The Report states:

> There were various suggestions concerning other relevant criteria that might be considered by the Commission in determining the list of crimes, including: acts committed by individuals which posed a serious and immediate threat to the peace and security of mankind, drawing upon the general definition contained in article 1; the highest threshold of gravity and the public interest; the gravity of the

---

[91] ILC, 'Report on the Work of Its Forty-Sixth Session' (May 2–July 22, 1994) UN Doc A/49/10 37 para 10(a).

[92] Ibid. 39 para. 10.

[93] Ibid. 40 para. 14.

[94] Rome Statute of the International Criminal Court (adopted on July 17, 1998, entered into force on July 1, 2002) art. 17(d).

[95] ILC Report 1994 (n. 91) para. 50.

[96] Ibid. para. 52.

[97] ILC, 'Report on the Work of Its Forty-Seventh Session' (May 2–July 21, 1995) UN Doc. A/50/10 para. 57.

act itself, its consequences or both and the designation of the act as a crime by the international community as a whole, notwithstanding an element of ambiguity in the motion of consensus reflected in the second criterion; and the effect of the crime on the international community as a whole.[98]

By the time it adopted its final Draft Code in 1996, the ILC seems to have largely given up on elaborating detailed criteria for international criminality. When re-nowned international jurist Allain Pellet deplored the absence of a general concep-tual definition in the Draft Code, Thiam responded simply that the criterion for inclusion in the Code was "extreme gravity."[99] The ILC's 1996 Report states:

> The Commission decided not to propose a general definition of crimes against the peace and security of mankind. It took the view that it should be left to practice to define the exact contours of the concept of crimes against peace, war crimes, and crimes against humanity.[100]

In other words, the Commission essentially punted to the prosecutors and judges who would interpret the crimes the task of explaining their gravity component.

The 1996 Draft Code reflects a consensus that aggression, genocide, crimes against humanity, and war crimes are sufficiently serious for international jurisdic-tion, but other crimes, such as drug trafficking and harm to the environment, re-mained controversial.[101] Moreover, the core crimes had acquired some new gravity elements. Although the qualifier "serious" had been deleted from the title of the war crimes provision, the provision restricted war crimes to acts "committed in a systematic manner or on a large scale."[102] Crimes against humanity had the same limitation and also had to be "instigated or directed by a Government or by any organization or group."[103] The commentary noted: "The instigation or direction of a Government or any organization or group, which may or may not be affili-ated with a Government, gives the act its great dimension and makes it a crime against humanity imputable to private persons or agents of a State."[104] The "polit-ical element" had thus made its way back into the definition alongside—or as part of—the gravity requirement.

By the end of the ILC's work on the Draft Code and Draft Statute, gravity had thus taken center stage in discussions about international prescriptive and adju-dicative authority. However, little progress had been made in identifying what the

---

[98] Ibid.
[99] ILC, 'Report on the Work of Its Forty-Eighth Session' (May 6–July 26, 1996) UN Doc. A/51/10 para. 50.
[100] Ibid. 17.
[101] Ibid. paras. 112–13, 119.
[102] Ibid. para. 50 art. 20.
[103] Ibid. para. 50 art. 18.
[104] Ibid.

concept entailed. In some contexts, scale and systematicity were emphasized, yet many delegates also favored including crimes that did not meet these criteria. For crimes against humanity, the involvement of political actors seemed to contribute to their gravity, but this was not important for many of the other crimes. Some of the discussions had emphasized ideas like atrociousness and barbarity, yet the definitions of crimes did not clearly reflect these notions. This combination of emphasis on gravity, alongside ambiguity about its meaning, would later characterize the ICC negotiations as well.

IV. International Criminal Tribunals for the Former Yugoslavia and Rwanda

While the work of the ILC helped to develop the conceptual framework of international criminal law, the most important post-Nuremberg chapter in the evolution of the regime began with the establishment of the ICTY in 1993 and the ICTR one year later. The Cold War had ended, enabling the major powers on the Security Council to establish the tribunals as a measure to promote international peace and security under Chapter VII of the UN Charter. The impressive development of the human rights regime in the post-war years, as well as the push to hold dictators accountable in some countries, promoted the idea that accountability for human rights violations advances international peace and security.

Nonetheless, state sovereignty remained a core principle of international law, and the establishment of a supra-national court required a justification sufficient to overcome concerns about sovereignty. Although people and governments around the world increasingly recognized that sovereignty had to be limited to protect individual rights, discussions about when such limitations justified supra-national criminal adjudication were only just beginning. As with the post-war tribunals, the concept of gravity was used to explain why it was legitimate for the international community to establish a tribunal to adjudicate individual criminal responsibility.[105]

Although the question of which crimes are grave enough to merit supra-national adjudication remained unanswered, there was little resistance to creating the ICTY and ICTR for two reasons. First, the scale and barbarity of the crimes at issue was beyond dispute. In the Former Yugoslavia, more than 100,000 people had been killed and another two million people were forcibly removed from their homes due

---

[105] See Statute of the ICTY (adopted on May 25, 1993) UN Doc. S/RES/827 preamble (expressing "grave alarm at continuing reports of widespread and flagrant violations of international humanitarian law" and establishing the ICTY); Statute of the ICTR (adopted on November 8, 1994) UN Doc. S/RES/955 preamble (expressing "grave concern at the reports indicating that genocide and other systematic, widespread and flagrant violations of international humanitarian law have been committed in Rwanda" and establishing the ICTR).

to their ethnicity.[106] In Rwanda, between 800,000 and one million members of the Tutsi ethnic group were slaughtered in 100 days in an effort to destroy the group itself.[107] Second, no states were strongly asserting their sovereignty in opposition to the Security Council's decisions. The Former Yugoslavia was a failed state, and the new Rwandan government initially supported establishment of the ICTR and, even after it changed its mind, put up little resistance.[108] Indeed, the tribunals were given primary jurisdiction over crimes in their Statutes, meaning that they, rather than national courts, had the first right to pursue cases; and this move was widely accepted.

Although gravity was important in justifying the establishment of the tribunals, it is less central to the elaboration of their subject matter jurisdictions. The drafters of the ICTY Statute, apparently wishing to preclude objections based on the principle of legality, relied largely on the IMT Charter and Geneva and Genocide Conventions in defining the crimes. The definitions therefore omitted some of the gravity requirements that the ILC had adopted in its 1991 Draft Code. War crimes had to be "serious" but not "exceptionally serious" and crimes against humanity were not limited to "systematic or mass violations of human rights." The ICTR Statute expanded the importance of gravity somewhat by adding the requirement that crimes against humanity must be part of a widespread or systematic attack. It also required that the widespread or systematic attack be committed "on national, political, ethnic, racial or religious grounds," introducing a discrimination element not present in the Nuremberg Charter.[109]

The ICTY Statute maintained the IMT Charter's war nexus for crimes against humanity, implying that this was at least part of the basis for the international community's concern over such crimes; but the ICTR Statute omitted this requirement. The ICTY held in its first case that criminal liability for war crimes is not restricted to international armed conflict, as most authorities had previously believed; it can also arise in internal armed conflict.[110] The judges referenced natural law and gravity, asserting that "principles and rules of humanitarian law reflect elementary considerations of humanity widely recognized as the mandatory minimum for conduct in armed conflicts of any kind" and that "no one can doubt the gravity of the acts at issue, nor the interest of the international community in their

---

[106] See ICTY, 'The Conflicts', available at http://www.icty.org/en/about/what-former-yugoslavia/conflicts (last accessed on July 28, 2017).

[107] See 'The Genocide' (United Nations Mechanism for International Criminal Tribunals: Legacy Website of the International Criminal Tribunal for Rwanda), available at http://unictr.unmict.org/en/genocide (last accessed on July 28, 2017).

[108] The Rwandan government disagreed with the decision to omit the death penalty from the punishments the ICTR could impose. See Jens David Ohlin, 'Applying the Death Penalty to Crimes of Genocide' (2005) 99 AJIL 747, 748.

[109] ICTR Statute (n. 105) art. 3.

[110] *Prosecutor v. Tadić* (Decision on the Defence Motion for Interlocutory Appeal on Jurisdiction) IT-94-1-AR72 (October 2, 1995) para. 78.

prohibition."[111] The ICTR had no need for such a ruling since its Statute included violations of common Article 3 of the Geneva Conventions, which applies to non-international armed conflicts.[112]

The tribunals have relied on gravity to justify their jurisdiction, but judges have not substantially explained what the term means. For instance, when a defendant argued that the ICTY should not have primacy over national courts, the ICTY Appeals Chamber stated that, without such jurisdiction, international crimes might be treated as "ordinary crimes."[113] Tribunals use this distinction between "ordinary crimes" and "crimes which are so horrific as to warrant universal jurisdiction" to justify various decisions, without a clear explanation of what makes crimes adequately "horrific."[114]

The ICTY and ICTR have also used vague language to explain the meaning of "serious" in the context of their jurisdiction over war crimes. They have held that this limitation does not restrict the tribunals' jurisdiction to people in positions of authority;[115] rather, the crime must "constitute a breach of a rule protecting important values, and the breach must involve grave consequences for the victim."[116] The substance of these values and consequences is left unexplained. Instead, the tribunals use such ambiguous descriptive phrases as: "shocking to the conscience of mankind,"[117] "fundamental human values deliberately negated,"[118] and "crimes [that] threaten not only the foundations of the society in which they are perpetrated but also those of the international community as a whole."[119] In sum, gravity emerged as important in justifying both the creation of the *ad hoc* tribunals and their subject matter jurisdiction, but its role was unclear and its content ambiguous.

V. Negotiating the Rome Statute

Gravity assumed a much more central role in the negotiations surrounding the ICC than it had for prior international tribunals. Previous institutions were established to respond to situations that the international community had already judged to be extremely grave, whereas the ICC was to have the power to respond to future

---

[111] Ibid. paras. 128–30.

[112] ICTR Statute (n. 105) art. 4.

[113] *Tadić* (Decision on Interlocutory Appeal) (n. 110) para. 58.

[114] See, e.g., *Prosecutor v. Tadić* (Decision on the Prosecutor's Motion Requesting Protective Measures for Victims and Witnesses) IT-94-1-AR72 (August 10, 1995) paras. 26–28.

[115] See *Prosecutor v. Johan Tarćulovski* (Judgment) IT-04-82-A (May 19, 2010) para. 52 (rejecting appeal on the grounds that the court lacks jurisdiction because "the subordinate role of an accused is legally irrelevant in determining his individual criminal responsibility").

[116] *Tadić* (Decision on Interlocutory Appeal) (n. 110) para. 94.

[117] See, e.g., *Prosecutor v. Tadić* (Opinion and Judgment) IT-94-1-T (May 7, 1997) para. 709.

[118] *Prosecutor v. Elizaphan & Gérard Ntakirutimana* (Judgment and Sentence) ICTR-96-10 & ICTR-96-17-T (February 21, 2003) para. 88.

[119] Ibid.

situations. Any gravity-based limitation to the ICC's jurisdiction therefore had to be written into the Court's Statute. Gravity's ability to limit the ICC's prescriptive and adjudicative authority was thus an important issue in the treaty negotiations.

Beginning in its preamble, the Rome Statute leaves little doubt that gravity is an important justification for the ICC's authority. The preamble notes "that during this century millions of children, women and men have been victims of unimaginable atrocities that deeply shock the conscience of humanity"; it recognizes "that such grave crimes threaten the peace, security and well-being of the world"; it affirms "that the most serious crimes of concern to the international community as a whole must not go unpunished"; and it asserts the drafters' determination therefore to establish an international criminal court "with jurisdiction over the most serious crimes of concern to the international community as a whole."[120] This strong commitment to gravity as a justification for the ICC's authority masks underlying divisions about the role of the Court in the global legal order.

The central ideological divide at the Rome Conference was between states that preferred broad accountability for human rights violations, and those more concerned about protecting state sovereignty. States in the former category eventually formed a group and adopted the label "like-minded" states. States in the latter category tended to endorse positions that would limit the jurisdiction of the Court. This was not a neat divide; many states took some positions that demonstrated a commitment to creating a strong court and other positions more protective of sovereignty. Nonetheless, the relationship between accountability and sovereignty was a central theme in the negotiations.

Gravity quickly emerged as the concept that would mediate between these competing values. This was not surprising since the process was based on the foundation the ILC had laid in its Draft Code and Draft Statute, both of which highlighted the importance of gravity. The idea that the Rome Statute should be limited to the most serious crimes led states to exclude "treaty crimes" from the Court's jurisdiction,[121] although a few states insisted that the Rome Conference's Final Act recommend future consideration of the inclusion of terrorism and drug crimes.[122] Efforts to expand the Court's jurisdiction in this way have gained little traction. Limiting the crimes to those considered most grave enabled states to agree to a broader form of jurisdiction than some of them initially preferred. Instead of states parties having to accept the Court's jurisdiction on an *ad hoc* basis, the Court was given inherent jurisdiction over core crimes committed by a national or on the territory of a state party.

---

[120] Rome Statute (n. 94) preamble.
[121] UNGA, 'Report of the Ad Hoc Committee on the Establishment of an International Criminal Court' (September 6, 1995) UN Doc. A/50/22 para. 81.
[122] See Final Act of the UN Diplomatic Conference of Plenipotentiaries on the Establishment of an International Criminal Court (July 17, 1998) UN Doc. A/CONF.183/10 7-8.

The concept of gravity was also important in obtaining consensus on the definitions of crimes within the Court's jurisdiction. For war crimes, a number of states concerned about sovereignty, including the United States, favored a mandatory gravity threshold.[123] In fact, some states had proposed that war crimes be excluded from the Court's mandatory jurisdiction entirely and instead made subject to *ad hoc* acceptances, but the effort failed.[124] Many states preferred to include broad jurisdiction over war crimes, a position endorsed by the International Committee of the Red Cross. The compromise ultimately adopted is awkwardly phrased as an optional limit to the Court's jurisdiction—an oxymoron. Article 8 of the Rome Statute states: "The Court shall have jurisdiction in respect of war crimes in particular when committed as part of a plan or policy or as part of a large-scale commission of such crimes."[125] This provision demonstrates the importance of including gravity limits to gain agreement from states concerned about sovereignty, but it also shows that those limits could be largely rhetorical.

With regard to crimes against humanity, there were heated debates about three gravity-related issues: (1) whether to require a widespread *and* systematic "attack against a civilian population" or to make the qualifiers alternatives; (2) whether there should be a nexus to armed conflict and, if so, whether it should be limited to international armed conflict; and (3) whether there should be a discrimination requirement. States advocating broader jurisdiction prevailed on the last two issues. With regard to the first issue, another compromise emerged: the attack can be widespread *or* systematic, but must be limited to "a course of conduct involving the multiple commission of acts referred to in paragraph 1 against any civilian population, pursuant to or in furtherance of a State or organizational policy to commit such attack."[126] This "policy element," which remains controversial, ensures that the gravity of crimes against humanity is not rooted entirely in the widespread nature of the harm.

The negotiations surrounding the crime of aggression, which were concluded at a Review Conference in 2010, also highlighted the importance of gravity in mediating between accountability and sovereignty. Because aggression is essentially a crime of state, a charge that a state's leader has committed the crime of aggression amounts to a call for regime change—a direct attack on state sovereignty. Participants in the negotiations were reasonably united in believing that the concept of gravity, which is highlighted in the definition and in the "understandings" appended to the definition, would help to ensure that accountability for aggression was privileged over state sovereignty only in appropriate cases. The definition of the crime of aggression requires "an act of aggression which, by its character, gravity

---

[123] See Roy S. K. Lee (ed.), *The International Criminal Court: The Making of the Rome Statute* (Martinus Nijhoff 1999) 106.

[124] Author's notes from negotiations regarding jurisdiction, June 22, 1998 (on file with author).

[125] Rome Statute (n. 94) art. 8(1).

[126] Ibid. art. 7(2)(a).

and scale, constitutes a manifest violation of the Charter of the United Nations."[127] It is notable that "character" and "scale" are listed separately from gravity, since the former are often considered elements of gravity. Moreover, one of the "under-standings" stipulates that each of these three must be independently sufficient to meet the "manifest violation" standard. This insistence on separating the idea of gravity from character and scale will surely prove challenging for those charged with interpreting the concept in the context of aggression.

These gravity-based limits on the ICC's subject matter jurisdiction are supple-mented by the requirement that the Court deem inadmissible cases "not of suf-ficient gravity to justify further action by the Court."[128] This gravity threshold survived many rounds of negotiations largely unchanged after its first inclusion in the ILC's 1994 Draft Statute. The only difference between the 1994 version and the Rome Statute is that the threshold is now mandatory, rather than discretionary.

As discussed earlier, the original idea behind the gravity threshold seems to have been to ensure that the Court would not encroach on the province of national courts and would make the best use of its limited resources.[129] Part of the motiv-ation seems to have been that "treaty crimes" might not always be sufficiently ser-ious to warrant international adjudication.[130] Yet even after the treaty crimes were omitted from the Statute, the gravity threshold remained. Indeed, it was so uncon-troversial that it was rarely discussed in several years of negotiations. Although at one of the Preparatory Committee meetings some delegations expressed a pref-erence that the provision be deleted or placed elsewhere in the Statute,[131] no one seems to have felt strongly about it. A lone delegation pleaded that "there was a need to explain more clearly the vague reference . . . to sufficient gravity in regard to the justification of the Court's further action," but the concern fell on deaf ears.[132]

The broad support for the gravity threshold, along with the failure to elaborate the concept, suggests that gravity's ambiguity was useful in generating support for the creation of the ICC. It enabled states with rather different visions of the Court's role in the world to vote to adopt the Statute. The like-minded states that wanted broad accountability for human rights, could tell their constituents that the Court had broad-based authority, while states concerned about preserving sovereignty

---

[127] Ibid. art. 8.

[128] Ibid. art. 17(d).

[129] See nn. 94–96 and accompanying text.

[130] In supporting inclusion of the threshold, the US member of the Commission noted that it would help alleviate concerns about the inclusion of such crimes as drug trafficking and terrorism in the Draft Statute. ILC, 'Summary Record of the 2332nd Meeting' (May 5, 1994) UN Doc. A/CN.4/SR.2332 para. 59.

[131] UN Diplomatic Conference of Plenipotentiaries on the Establishment of an International Criminal Court, Rep. of the Preparatory Committee on the Establishment of an International Criminal Court, UN Doc. A/CONF.183/2/Add.1 (April 14, 1998) art. 15(1)(d) n. 44.

[132] UN Diplomatic Conference of Plenipotentiaries on the Establishment of an International Criminal Court, Committee of the Whole, Summary Record of the 11th Meeting, UN Doc. A/CONF.183/C.1/SR.11 (November 20, 1998) para. 29.

could adopt a more robust interpretation of gravity to portray the Court's jurisdiction as limited.

VI. "Hybrid" International Criminal Tribunals

Gravity's role in legitimizing international criminal law's authority is complicated by the existence of a number of "hybrid" tribunals, several of which were created after the adoption of the Rome Statute. These tribunals combine elements of national and international criminal law in different ways. For instance, the Special Court for Sierra Leone (SCSL) applies international and national law, the government of Sierra Leone appoints a minority of the judges, and the UN Secretary General appoints the majority of the judges and the prosecutor.[133] The Extraordinary Chambers in the Courts of Cambodia (ECCC) also apply national and international laws; however, unlike at the SCSL, national judges and prosecutors retain significant control over the proceedings.[134] The Special Tribunal for Lebanon employs international and Lebanese personnel, but it applies only Lebanese law.[135] Some of these so-called "hybrid" or "mixed" tribunals were established by agreement with the state concerned, while others were set up under the auspices of a UN governing authority.[136] The Special Tribunal for Lebanon was created by the Security Council acting under Chapter VII. The extent to which each of these courts is "international" is therefore debatable.[137]

Because the structures of the hybrid courts account for the sovereignty of the concerned states in various ways, gravity's role might be presumed to be less central to legitimizing their authority. Indeed, the jurisdiction of these courts is not always limited to the most serious international crimes.[138] Although two hybrid

---

[133] Agreement Between the United Nations and the Government of Sierra Leone on the Establishment of a Special Court for Sierra Leone (January 16, 2002) 2178 UNTS 138, arts. 1–3.

[134] Law on the Establishment of the Extraordinary Chambers in the Courts of Cambodia for the Prosecution of Crimes Committed During the Period of Democratic Kampuchea, with inclusion of amendments (October 27, 2004) NS/RKM/1004/006.

[135] Agreement between the United Nations and the Lebanese Republic on the Establishment of a Special Tribunal for Lebanon (annexed to S.C. Res. 1757, May 30, 2007) UN Doc. S/RES/1757 art. 2.

[136] For example, the Special Court for Sierra Leone was established by agreement between the United Nations and the Government of Sierra Leone (SCSL Statute (n. 133)), and the Special Panels for Serious Crimes in East Timor were established by the United Nations transitional authority. United Nations Transitional Administration in East Timor Regulation No. 2001/15 on the Establishment of Panels with Exclusive Jurisdiction Over Serious Criminal Offenses (June 6, 2000) UNTAET/REG/2000/15.

[137] Compare Herbert D. Bowman, 'Not Worth the Wait: Hun Sen, The UN, and the Khmer Rouge Tribunal' (2006) 24 UCLA Pacific Basin L.J. 51, 68 (arguing that the ECCC is not international, but rather a domestic court with international personnel), with Anees Ahmed and Robert Petit, 'A Review of the Jurisprudence of the Khmer Rouge Tribunal' (2010) 8 North Western J. Intl. Human Rights 165, 166 (describing the ECCC as an international court).

[138] For example, the SCSL, ECCC, and Special Tribunal for Lebanon have jurisdiction of the domestic crimes of murder and rape. See SCSL Statute (n. 133) art. 2; ECCC Statute (n. 134) art. 5; STL Statute (n. 135) art. 2(a).

court Statutes—those of the SCSL and ECCC—restrict prosecutions to those most responsible for the crimes at issue,[139] that limitation seems to be more tied to resource constraints than to concerns about legitimate authority. Moreover, the hybrid courts have not adopted some of the gravity-based limitations in the Rome Statute. For instance, some of them have omitted the policy requirement for crimes against humanity,[140] and none of them has a gravity threshold for admissibility.

Conclusion

The history of the development of international criminal law shows a gradual evolution in the role of gravity as a justification for international prescriptive and adjudicative authority. Natural law theory and the recognition of universal jurisdiction over piracy provided the foundation for the idea of international jurisdiction over certain crimes, but those crimes were not limited to atrocities. Reactions to the World Wars, in particular WWII, generated new demands for accountability, and shifted the rhetoric to focus more on atrocities.

The ILC in the 1980s and 1990s further promoted gravity's importance as a legitimizing factor for international criminal law, although the Commission struggled, largely unsuccessfully, to identify the content of the concept. The establishment of the ICTY and ICTR likewise popularized the idea of international adjudication for particularly heinous crimes, and the law of those tribunals was somewhat more dependent on gravity than was that of the IMT and IMTFE.

With the Rome Statute, the concept of gravity reached center stage as a determinant of the legitimacy of the international criminal law regime. The Court's subject matter jurisdiction and its authority to exercise that jurisdiction are directly linked to the concept of gravity. When the Rome Statute was negotiated, gravity was deployed to mediate between calls for international authority and concerns about limiting national authority. While gravity has been less central to the work of the hybrid tribunals, this makes sense since they derive some of their legitimacy from their affiliation with national legal systems.

This historical evolution of gravity as a legitimizing force in international criminal law shows that gravity's centrality in the regime today is more a function of its usefulness as a consensus builder than of any agreement about the moral values that it reflects. Indeed, the international community has yet to identify clearly the interests that legitimize its authority to prescribe and adjudicate particular crimes.

[139] See SCSL Statute (n. 133) art. 1(1) ("The Special Court shall ... have the power to prosecute persons who bear the greatest responsibility for serious violations of international humanitarian law."); ECCC Statute (n. 134) Chapter 1 art. 1 ("The purpose of this law is to bring to trial ... those who were most responsible for the crimes and serious violations of Cambodian penal law.").
[140] See SCSL Statute (n. 133) art. 2; United Nations Transitional Administration in East Timor, Reg. 2000/15 (June 6, 2000) s. 5.1.

As Chapter 3 shows, most theories of international prescriptive authority—that is, efforts to explain the nature of international criminality—rely on a gravity threshold below which the international community's authority must not extend. Yet these normative theories are not reflected in current legal norms of international criminality, which are quite broad and still expanding. The chapter presents a new theory of international criminality that links the international interest in prescribing conduct to the right to humanity dignity, and assigns gravity roles as a minimal threshold and as an aid in identifying prescriptive priorities.

3
Global Prescriptive Authority

One of the most important roles that the international criminal law regime ascribes to gravity is that of defining the scope of global prescriptive authority—the authority of the global community to prescribe rules of conduct and consequences for violating those rules. This authority is exercised when state actors draft treaties and court Statutes, and when courts interpret those Statutes and treaties.[1] Prescriptive authority in criminal law generally resides with states, which are supposed to seek to promote the values and goals of national communities. States uphold the national community's norms of conduct by seeking to prevent conduct that violates those norms, and, for retributivists, by ensuring deserved punishment. As I explained in Chapter 1, international criminal law presupposes and reflects the existence of a global community with its own values and goals in the domain of criminal law. If such a community did not exist, international criminal law could only legitimately seek to bind consenting states. Thus, if states agreed to coordinate their criminal law efforts by adopting prescriptive rules, those rules could apply only to consenting states. But international criminal law does not purport to constrain conduct only on the territories of, or by, or against, the nationals of consenting states. When regime actors prescribe rules of international criminal law by defining crimes in Statutes or treaties and elucidating the definitions in case law, they claim to act on behalf of the entire global community. This global orientation existed even at Nuremberg, where Justice Jackson insisted that the crimes included in the International Military Tribunal (IMT) Statute applied equally to all people, even though the IMT judged only German defendants.[2]

The global community's central goal in prescribing rules of conduct mirrors that of national communities: to prevent conduct that violates community values—in this case, global values.[3] As such, for the global community's prescriptive efforts to be legitimate they must reflect global values. But what are those values? Various theories have been advanced, virtually all of which rely on the concept of gravity, but almost none of them give principled content to the concept. This reliance on a largely undefined notion of gravity obscures important questions about global

---

[1] For a discussion of prescriptive authority in international law, see Myres S. McDougal and W. Michael Reisman, 'The Prescribing Function in World Constitutive Process: How International Law is Made' (1980) 6 Yale Studies in World Public Order 249.

[2] Robert H. Jackson, *Report of Robert H. Jackson, United States Representative to the International Conference on Military Trials* (U.S. Department of State 1949) vii–viii.

[3] As I elaborate in Chapter 6, I do not include retribution as a goal because, in my view, it is not a globally shared value.

Shocking the Conscience of Humanity. Margaret M. deGuzman, Oxford University Press (2020). © Margaret M. deGuzman.
DOI: 10.1093/oso/9780198786153.001.0001

values, discourages discussion of those values, and hinders the progressive development of the global justice community. This undermines the regime's moral legitimacy. Additionally, vague ideas about gravity are embedded in the definitions of the core international crimes—war crimes, crimes against humanity, genocide, and aggressions. This causes instability in the legal norms, thereby undermining the regime's legal legitimacy.

After critiquing current theories of international criminality regarding the core crimes, this chapter proposes a new theory that grounds the global community's authority to prescribe in its interest in upholding human dignity. It argues that all humans, as part of the global community, have an interest in preventing harms to human dignity wherever, and to whomever, they occur. As such, the global community has legitimate authority to prescribe rules of conduct regarding all harms to human dignity—at least when there is broad global agreement that the harms merit criminal sanction. The only role that gravity should play in *limiting* global prescriptive authority therefore, is to provide a low threshold: one that excludes conduct that threatens or harms human dignity so minimally that it may not warrant criminal sanction at all. All conduct above this minimal gravity threshold ought to be considered a legitimate subject of global prescription.

In addition to providing a minimal threshold for legitimate global prescription, gravity can be used in a way that helps to legitimize the global community's choices about which crimes to prescribe above the threshold. Although the global community can legitimately prescribe all harms to human dignity, its limited resources require it to identify priorities. Current vague invocations of gravity fail adequately to support the global community's choices in this regard, particularly its focus on the core crimes. If gravity is reconceptualized in relation to global goals, however, it can serve to legitimize global prescriptive choices. This approach would facilitate the efficient pursuit of the global community's most important global goals, and thus promote the regime's normative legitimacy. For instance, rather than citing undefined gravity to justify global prescription over war crimes, regime supporters could assert that preventing harms to human dignity in armed conflict is a greater global priority than doing so in peacetime because armed conflicts disproportionately harm the world's most vulnerable populations. Or they could argue that crimes in armed conflicts, even non-international conflicts, threaten additional, ongoing harms in ways that similar crimes in peacetime do not. Similar goal-based arguments can be made for each of the core crimes.

This theory differs from most theories of international criminality in several respects. First, it adopts only a minimal threshold compared to the undefined, but implicitly substantial, gravity thresholds in many theories. Second, where most theories look to global interests to justify international criminality, this one sees those interests as merely supporting prescriptive priorities. Thus, rather than finding it *illegitimate* for the global community to proscribe conduct that harms human dignity but fails to align with a very important global interest, this theory deems such a prescription to be less strongly legitimate than one that reflects a more important interest. In other words, it deems global prescription to be more strongly legitimate for crimes in which the global community has a stronger interest. This approach favors flexible legal norms that can evolve with changing global priorities, but also requires transparent communication about the global interests that justify prescriptive actions.

Finally, the theory differs from other theories of international criminality in that it delinks the question of when global prescription is legitimate from that of when global *adjudication* is legitimate, which is the subject of Chapter 4. As explained below, most commentators conflate these questions, arguing that once a prohibition is sufficiently grave to be an "international crime" the global community has legitimate authority to adjudicate. This is too simplistic. Once the global community chooses to proscribe certain conduct, a separate decision must be made as to whether it is legitimate to exercise *adjudicative* authority over that conduct under particular circumstances, which is the subject of Chapter 4. As that chapter explains, the legitimacy of global adjudication depends not only on the global community's values and goals, but also on those of the most affected national communities. When these are in tension, global adjudication is legitimate only when global values outweigh national values. In contrast, global prescription does not require the same kind of analysis. Global prescription is legitimate for any crime that harms human dignity; and a global focus on particular crimes is legitimate as long as it promotes appropriate global values.

This chapter begins by critiquing the most common theories of international criminality, in particular, their reliance on poorly explained claims about gravity. It then demonstrates how gravity's ambiguous role in justifying global prescriptive authority destabilizes the legal norms governing international crimes. Finally, it proposes a new theory of legitimate global prescriptive authority.

I. Which Crimes Concern the Global Community?

In seeking to justify global prescriptive authority, most scholarship points to global interests underlying the category "international crimes," or a particular crime in that category. Sometimes the relevant global interest is simply said to rest in the gravity of the crimes, with little explanation of what that entails. Other times, one or more specific global interests is identified, such as the need to prevent crimes committed by states, or against particular groups; but these theories usually also include an undefined gravity threshold below which global authority is said not to be legitimate.

Many legal sources are also unclear about gravity's role in legitimizing global authority. For instance, the Rome Statute asserts that the crimes it defines are "the most serious crimes of concern to the international community as a whole."[4]

---

[4] Rome Statute of the International Criminal Court (adopted on July 17, 1998, entered into force on July 1, 2001) Preamble.

This statement can be read to mean that the crimes in the Statute concern the international community *because of their seriousness*, as most people assume, or instead, that they concern the international community for some other reason, but only the most serious instances of the crimes are within the ICC's jurisdiction. The Statute also states that "during this century millions of children, women and men have been victims of unimaginable atrocities that deeply shock the conscience of humanity" and that "such grave crimes threaten the peace, security and well-being of the world."[5] Apart from the reference to a large number of victims, there is no indication of what constitutes an "unimaginable atrocity" or of what it takes to "deeply shock the conscience of humanity." The implicit assumption is that the crimes in the Statute *are* the "atrocities ... that deeply shock the conscience of humanity," but these include instances of crimes that look very similar to domestic crimes, such as the illegal killing of a single person in armed conflict. Such uncertainty about gravity's role is pervasive in international criminal law.

This section reviews the main theories of international criminality in the commentary and jurisprudence, including that international crimes: (1) threaten international peace and security; (2) shock humanity's conscience; (3) result from state action or inaction; and (4) victimize groups. It highlights the confusion and ambiguity surrounding gravity's role and meaning in each theory. Such confusion includes a lack of clarity about whether the cited interest is what makes the crime sufficiently grave to be international, or whether an additional, undefined gravity threshold must be reached.

A. Threats to International Peace and Security

Before the human rights movement began to erode the notion of absolute state sovereignty, the most common justification for international criminality, at least with respect to the so-called "core crimes," was that they threatened international peace and security. This was taken literally to mean that the crimes caused or threatened to cause war. Thus, the IMT and International Military Tribunal for the Far East (IMTFE) had jurisdiction over "crimes against peace," which is now called "aggression," as well as war crimes committed in *international* armed conflict and crimes against humanity connected to such conflict. The IMT judgment famously called aggression, "the supreme international crime differing only from other war crimes in that it contains within itself the accumulated evil of the whole."[6] War crimes and crimes against humanity connected to war also literally threaten international peace and security in that they may aggravate tensions between states and prolong international conflicts.

---

[5] Ibid.
[6] Judgment of the Nuremberg International Military Tribunal 1946 (1947) 41 AJIL 172, 186.

As the human rights movement gained traction, the idea that international crimes threaten peace and security has expanded to include threats of a more figurative nature. When the concept is invoked today, it often means that crimes either threaten armed conflict *or* cause a more general sense of unease around the world. Thus, the Rome Statute preamble references threats to peace and security but also to the "well-being of the world."[7] This can be read quite expansively: arguably any threat of harm to human dignity threatens the well-being of the world.

The expansion of this rationale beyond literal threats to international peace began soon after World War II. Control Council Law No. 10, which the Allies used to prosecute lesser war criminals after the Nuremberg trial, did not require crimes against humanity to be associated with war,[8] and the drafters of the Genocide Convention rejected any link to armed conflict.[9] In fact, even the IMT judges seemed uncomfortable with the war nexus as a limitation on their jurisdiction. Although they declined to assert jurisdiction over crimes committed before 1939 on the grounds that they were insufficiently connected to the war, they emphasized the "revolting and horrible" nature of many of those crimes,[10] foreshadowing the shift to a more figurative harm to humanity as the basis for global authority.

Although the drafters of the International Criminal Tribunal for the Former Yugoslavia (ICTY) Statute included the war nexus for crimes against humanity to avoid challenges of retroactive application of law, the Tribunal's judges held that the nexus was no longer part of customary international law.[11] Having rejected the war nexus as a source of authority, the judges turned to gravity, reading into the Statute a requirement that the crimes be part of a widespread or systematic attack on a civilian population.[12]

The ICTY judges also revolutionized the law concerning war crimes by holding that such crimes can be committed in non-international armed conflict.[13] In doing so, the judges invoked gravity without explaining what makes crimes committed in internal armed conflicts sufficiently serious to concern the international community.[14] The decision seems to have been catalyzed by the increasingly

[7] Rome Statute (n. 4) preamble.

[8] Control Council Law No. 10, Punishment of Persons Guilty of War Crimes, Crimes Against Peace and Against Humanity (December 20, 1945) art. II(1)(c) in Telford Taylor, *Final Report to the Secretary of the Army on The Nuremberg War Crimes Trials Under Control Council Law No. 10* (US Government Printing Office 1949) 250.

[9] William A. Schabas, *Genocide in International Law: The Crime of Crimes*, 2nd edn. (Cambridge University Press 2009) 52–3 (noting the Cuban representative's insistence that genocide should not be limited to armed conflict).

[10] Nuremberg Judgment (n. 6) 249.

[11] *Prosecutor v. Tadić* (Decision on the Defence Motion for Interlocutory Appeal on Jurisdiction) IT-94-1 (October 2, 1995) paras. 140–1.

[12] *Prosecutor v. Tadić*, (Appeal Judgment) IT-94-1-A (July 15, 1999) para. 248.

[13] *Tadić* (Decision on the Defence Motion for Interlocutory Appeal on Jurisdiction) (n. 11) para. 78.

[14] Ibid. para. 129.

popular view that there should be no impunity for "atrocities." According to scholar and international judge, Theodore Meron: "This advance can be explained by the pressure, in the face of atrocities, for a rapid adjustment of law, process and institutions."[15]

Despite the ICTY jurisprudence, the issue of whether war crimes can be committed in non-international armed conflict was again controversial at the Rome Conference. A significant minority of states, including India and China, preferred a definition in line with the literal peace and security rationale limiting war crimes to international armed conflict.[16] Although this view did not ultimately prevail, a discretionary gravity threshold was included in the Statute to reassure such states that their sovereignty would be adequately protected: The International Criminal Court (ICC) has jurisdiction over war crimes "in particular when committed as part of a plan or policy or as part of a large-scale commission of such crimes."[17] This provision originated with the US delegation, which proposed a mandatory gravity threshold: the Court's jurisdiction over war crimes would extend only to those that are part of a policy or committed on a large scale.[18] The compromise reached does not rely entirely on either gravity or international peace and security, but gestures to both. The reference to policy or scale is a nod to gravity; but the peace and security rationale survives as well in that the Statute includes a more limited set of war crimes in non-international than in international armed conflict. For instance, the Statute criminalizes the use of certain weapons only in international armed conflict.[19] In sum, the Rome Statute's provisions contain a mix of gravity and peace and security rationales, without defining either.

The scholarship on international criminality reflects similar uncertainties. Larry May, one of the few philosophers to address the normative grounding of international crimes, advances a complex theory of international criminal liability that blends several rationales. He starts with a literal peace and security rationale for war crimes, asserting that there is little controversy over the justification for such crimes because they often cross borders.[20] In his view, crimes against humanity and genocide are harder to justify because they raise more significant sovereignty concerns.[21] Yet the assertion that war crimes "often cross borders" is debatable,

---

[15] Theodor Meron, *The Humanization of International Law* (Martinus Nijhoff 2006) 94.

[16] Twenty-sixth meeting on Wednesday, July 8, 1998, A/CONF.183/C.1/SR.26 paras. 84–7, in UN Diplomatic Conference of Plenipotentiaries on the Establishment of an International Criminal Court, Summary Records of the Plenary Meetings and of the Meetings of the Committee of the Whole (June 15–July 17, 1998) UN Doc. A/CONF.183/13 (Vol. II) 279.

[17] Rome Statute (n. 4) art. 8(1).

[18] Bartram Brown, 'The Statute of the ICC: Past, Present, and Future', in Sarah B. Sewall and Carl Kaysen (eds.), *The United States and the International Criminal Court* (Roman & Littlefield Publishers 2000) 69.

[19] Compare Rome Statute (n. 4) art. 8(2)(b) with arts. 8(2)(c) and (e).

[20] Larry May, *Crimes Against Humanity: A Normative Account* (Cambridge University Press 2004) 8.

[21] Ibid.

particularly for crimes committed in non-international armed conflict. The direct effects of such crimes are often contained within borders, particularly when the conflict is small scale or short-lived. Such crimes do not literally threaten the world's peace, and yet they are core international crimes.

Others argue that war crimes committed within state borders threaten peace and security because they have the potential to cause instability outside those borders.[22] However, this approach fails to distinguish war crimes from other kinds of harms. Certain human rights abuses in "peacetime"[23] may have greater potential to cause international instability than small-scale abuses in armed conflict. As Myres McDougal and Michael Reisman argued in justifying Security Council action against the racist Rhodesian regime:

[I]n the contemporary world, international peace and security and the protection of human rights are inescapably interdependent and ... the impact of the flagrant deprivation of the most basic human rights of the great mass of the people of a community cannot possibly stop short within the territorial boundaries in which the physical manifestations of such deprivations first occur.[24]

This statement reflects the figurative threat to peace and security rationale; and, like most commentators, McDougal and Reisman include a substantial gravity threshold: the harms must affect "the great mass of the people of a community" to threaten international peace and security.

Even for the crime of aggression—the crime that most obviously concerns peace and security—gravity has come to play an important, if ambiguous, role. After many years of debating the definition of aggression—an effort that stalled the creation of the ICC[25]—states adopted a definition at the Kampala review conference in 2010 that reads:

For the purpose of this Statute, "crime of aggression" means the planning, preparation, initiation or execution, by a person in a position effectively to exercise control over or to direct the political or military action of a State, of an act of

---

[22] See Ravi Mahalingam, 'The Compatibility of the Principle of Nonintervention with the Right of Humanitarian Intervention' (1996) 1 UCLA J. Intl. L. & Foreign Affairs 221, 252–3 (noting that "[w]hereas the Charter expressed a strong distinction between international conflict and matters of an essentially domestic nature, the U.N. of the 1990's has internationalized many internal conflicts on the rationale that they create potential international threats to peace and security").

[23] The distinction between "peacetime" and "war time" is not without its critics. For an interesting discussion, see Mary L. Dudziak, *War Time: An Idea, Its History, Its Consequences* (Oxford University Press 2012).

[24] Myres S. McDougal and W. Michael Reisman, 'Rhodesia and the United Nations: The Lawfulness of International Concern' (1968) 62 AJIL 1, 18.

[25] Leila N. Sadat, 'The Establishment of the International Criminal Court: From the Hague to Rome and Back Again' (1999) 8 J. Intl. L. & Practice 97, 110–11 (noting that the draft code of offenses was put off for decades due to a lack of agreement over the definition of the crime of aggression).

aggression which, by its character, gravity and scale, constitutes a manifest violation of the Charter of the United Nations.[26]

The undefined concept of gravity is thus central to a finding of aggression at the ICC. Indeed, because "scale" and "character" are usually considered components of gravity,[27] the definition seems to require gravity in three different ways.

In sum, although the relevance of the literal threat to peace and security justification has diminished over time, efforts to justify international criminality, including in the ICC Statute, continue to reflect that rationale, albeit with modifications rooted in gravity. In none of its formulations, however, does this rationale provide a principled basis for global prescription.

B. Shocking Humanity's Conscience: The Atrocity Rationale

Although the peace and security rationale was important in the early days of the international criminal law regime, most efforts to justify international criminality today rely more explicitly on gravity. The claim is formulated in various ways, including that the crimes "shock the conscience of humanity."[28] As Frédéric Mégret has stated:

> The emphasis today is on the sheer gravity of international crimes, their cosmopolitan nature, and the extent to which they may "shock the conscience of mankind," rather than the relatively anecdotal question of whether their commission involved some straddling of borders.[29]

Terje Einarsen has similarly asserted that: "A philosophical starting point for identifying universal crimes is that some crimes are of such magnitude or gravity

[26] 'The Crime of Aggression', ICC Doc. RC/Res.6 (June 11, 2010).

[27] See, e.g., ICC-OTP, 'Policy Paper on Case Selection and Prioritisation' (September 15, 2016) para. 32 (listing "scale" and "nature" of crimes as factors in the gravity assessment for purposes of case selection).

[28] See, e.g., *Attorney Gen. of Israel v. Eichmann*, 36 I.L.R. 18, 26 (Isr. Dist. Ct. Jm. 1961) ("The abhorrent crimes ... which struck at the whole of mankind and shocked the conscience of nations, are grave offences against the law of nations itself ... "); Diane F. Orentlicher, 'Whose Justice? Reconciling Universal Jurisdiction with Democratic Principles' (2003) 92 Georgetown L.J. 1057, 1116 (citing a post-World War II case, *United States v. Otto Ohlendorf*, stating that "[h]umanity can assert itself by law"); *Prosecutor v. Al-Bashir* (Judgment in the Jordan Referral re Al-Bashir Appeal) ICC-02/05-01/09 OA2 (May 6, 2019) para. 123 ("The obligation to cooperate with the Court reinforces the obligation *erga omnes* to prevent, investigate, and punish crimes that shock the conscience of humanity."); *Prosecutor v. Bikindi* (Trial Judgment) ICTR-01-72-T (December 2, 2008) para. 448 ("Genocide is, by definition, a crime of the most serious gravity which affects the foundations of society and shocks the conscience of humanity.").

[29] Frédéric Mégret, 'A Special Tribunal for Lebanon: The Council and the Emancipation of International Criminal Justice' (2007) 21 Leiden J. Intl. L. 485, 506-7.

that they shock the consciousness of human beings wherever they live and regardless of their connection to the victims or to the place where the crimes were committed."[30] In his view, the definitions of all international crimes should include gravity requirements.[31]

Bruce Broomhall likewise believes that the "conscience of humanity" rationale is the primary justification for war crimes, as well as for crimes against humanity since the elimination of the war nexus.[32] According to Broomhall, the abandonment of the war nexus "affirm[ed] that individual responsibility under international law may justifiably rest not on the stability of the international order alone, but on the power of such acts to shock the conscience of humanity."[33]

Sometimes, the peace and security and conscience-shocking rationales are provided as alternatives. For instance, Egon Schwelb has written that a crime against humanity is an offense that concerns the international community *either* because "it has repercussions reaching across international frontiers" *or* because "it passes in magnitude or savagery any limits of what is tolerable by modern civilisations."[34] Cherif Bassiouni, in contrast, claimed that a crime is a universal norm if it *both* shocks the conscience of humanity *and* threatens the peace and security of mankind, and that "[t]he argument [for universality] is less compelling, though still strong enough, if only one of these elements is present."[35]

The idea that the world shares a collective conscience has a long historical pedigree rooted in natural law. The Martens Clause of the 1899 Hague Convention on the Laws and Customs of War on Land states:

Until a more complete code of the laws of war is issued, the High Contracting Parties think it right to declare that in cases not included in the Regulations adopted by them, populations and belligerents remain under the protection and empire of the principles of international law, as they result from the usages established between civilized nations, from the laws of humanity and *the requirements of the public conscience.*[36]

---

[30] Terje Einarsen, *The Concept of Universal Crimes in International Law* (Torkel Opsahl Academic EPublisher 2012) 23.

[31] Ibid. 254.

[32] Bruce Broomhall, *International Justice and the International Criminal Court: Between Sovereignty and the Rule of Law* (Oxford University Press 2004) 45–9.

[33] Ibid. 49.

[34] Egon Schwelb, 'Crimes Against Humanity' (1946) 23 Brit. Y.B. Intl. L. 178, 195.

[35] M. Cherif Bassiouni, 'International Crimes: The Ratione Materiae of International Criminal Law' in M. Cherif Bassiouni (ed.), *International Criminal Law: Sources, Subjects and Content* (3rd edn., Leiden 2008) 176.

[36] Hague Convention (II) with Respect to the Laws and Customs of War on Land and Its Annex: Regulations Concerning the Laws and Customs of War (signed on July 29, 1899, entered into force on September 4, 1900) 187 C.T.S. 429 preamble (emphasis added).

This century-old proclamation affirms that the world shares a collective conscience and also that global moral norms are enshrined in "laws of humanity." Both of these ideas were central to the creation of the category "crimes against humanity."[37] The Allies referenced this rationale to justify the inclusion of these crimes in the Statute of the IMT and IMTFE Statutes. Subsequently, the *ad hoc* tribunals also justified their work in part by invoking the conscience-shocking rationale and the related notion that international crimes are "Universally Condemned Offences."[38]

When courts and scholars justify prescriptive authority by asserting that crimes shock humanity's conscience, they rarely specify what it takes to cause such shock. In discussing the relative competencies of national and international courts, scholar Alain Pellet stated:

> [I]t must be kept in mind that only crimes which "deeply shock the conscience of humanity" can justify an internationalization of their prosecution, which involves a far-reaching blow to the competence of domestic courts on an issue which otherwise would come under "matters which are essentially within the domestic jurisdiction of States."[39]

Given the importance that Pellet placed on distinguishing international from domestic crimes, one might expect him to elaborate on the notion of crimes that "deeply shock the conscience of humanity," but no explanation is provided. Similarly, judge and scholar Antonio Cassese, asserted that international courts are the best forum for adjudicating international crimes because such crimes "infringe values that are transnational and of concern for the whole world community."[40] Cassese too, failed to explain the content of these "values" or how they "concern" the world community.

An important manifestation of the conscience-shocking rationale is the movement to label international crimes "atrocities." Indeed, the idea that international crimes are "atrocities" has become the most popular argument for international

---

[37] See Commission on the Responsibility of the Authors of the War and on Enforcement of Penalties, 'Report Presented to the Preliminary Peace Conference' (1920) 14 AJIL 95, 117 (proposing criminal prosecutions of persons "guilty of offenses against the laws and customs of war and the laws of humanity").

[38] See, e.g., *Prosecutor v. Nikolic* (Decision on Interlocutory Appeal Concerning Legality of Arrest) IT-94-2-AR73 (June 5, 2003) paras. 24–5; *Prosecutor v. Kambanda* (Trial Judgment and Sentence) ICTR 97-23-S (September 4, 1998) para. 61. See also William A. Schabas, *The UN International Criminal Tribunals: The Former Yugoslavia, Rwanda and Sierra Leone* (Cambridge University Press 2006) 151 (noting that the *ad hoc* tribunal judges have capitalized "Universally Condemned Offenses" "suggesting that they may be attempting to coin a new term subsuming genocide, crimes against humanity and war crimes").

[39] Alain Pellet, 'Internationalized Courts; Better than Nothing . . .' in Cesare P.R. Romano et al. (eds.), *Internationalized Criminal Courts: Sierra Leone, East Timor, Kosovo, and Cambodia* (Oxford University Press 2004) 438.

[40] Antonio Cassese, 'The Rationale for International Criminal Justice' in Antonio Cassese et al. (eds.), *The Oxford Companion to International Criminal Justice* (Oxford University Press 2009) 127.

prescriptive authority in the past decade or so. David Scheffer, who represented the US at the Rome Conferences, has been a key proponent of this move. In a 2006 article he wrote:

> There also is a critical need for a new term—"atrocity crimes"—and a new field of international law—atrocity law—to … enable public and academic discourse to describe genocide, crimes against humanity (including ethnic cleansing), and war crimes with a single term that is easily understood by the public and accurately reflects the magnitude and character of the crimes adjudicated before international and hybrid criminal tribunals and of the law being applied by such tribunals, by governments and international organizations. The purpose would be to simplify and yet render more accurate both public dialogue and legal terminology describing genocide and other atrocity crimes.[41]

Like others who endorse the conscience-shocking rationale, Scheffer has devoted little attention to specifying the requisite "magnitude" or "character" of atrocity crimes. Yet Scheffer's labeling effort has been highly successful; the term "atrocity crimes" has become almost synonymous with international crimes.[42] For instance, Gregory Gordan has written a book on "Atrocity Speech Law" wherein he defined "atrocity" as including the core crimes in the Rome Statute.[43]

This turn to what can now be called the "atrocity rationale" is problematic both because the term is usually undefined, and because any definition will be under or over-inclusive of the crimes that are generally considered to be legitimate subjects of global prescription. For instance, a U.S. human rights commission conducting a hearing on how to pursue accountability for "mass atrocities" defined them "as large-scale, deliberate attacks against civilians, and include[d] genocide, crimes against humanity and war crimes."[44] The Commission went on to assert that the results of such crimes are the "suffering and deaths of hundreds of thousands of

---

[41] David Scheffer, 'Genocide and Atrocity Crimes' (2006) 1 Genocide Stud. & Prevention 229, 248. See also David Scheffer, 'Atrocity Crimes Framing the Responsibility to Protect' (2008) 40 Case W. Res. J. Intl. L. 111, 111 (discussing the R2P doctrine's application to "genocide, war crimes, ethnic cleansing, and crimes against humanity" which are "categories of significant crimes that should be designated as *atrocity crimes* both for the purposes of accuracy … and for simplicity").

[42] Gareth Evans, *The Responsibility to Protect: Ending Mass Atrocity Crimes Once and For All* (Brookings Institution Press 2008) 11 ("[T]he expressions 'mass atrocities' or 'mass atrocity crimes' are used more or less interchangeably to refer to what is now embraced by the description 'genocide, war crimes, ethnic cleansing, and crimes against humanity.'"); Thorsten Benner et al., 'Effective and Responsible Protection from Atrocity Crimes: Toward Global Action' (Global Public Policy Institute 2015) 7 ("Our research has focused on the crimes covered by the 2005 World Summit definition of Responsibility to Protect: genocide, crimes against humanity, war crimes, and ethnic cleansing (which we collectively refer to as atrocity crimes).").

[43] Gregory S. Gordon, *Atrocity Speech Law: Foundation, Fragmentation, Fruition* (Oxford University Press 2017) 379.

[44] Tom Lantos Human Rights Commission, 'Hearing on Pursuing Accountability for Atrocities', held at US Congress, Washington DC, on June 13, 2019, available at https://humanrightscommission.house.gov/events/hearings/pursuing-accountability-atrocities (last accessed on August 9, 2019).

people" and the displacement of millions.[45] Yet most courts and commentators would not limit atrocities, or crimes deserving global adjudication, to those committed on such a large scale. Nor would they exclude from the purview of such crimes, those committed on a large scale against non-civilians.

The label "atrocity" is particularly awkward with regard to war crimes. First, war crimes need not be committed on any significant scale. An individual soldier's misuse of a flag of truce or destruction of property not justified by military necessity can be a war crime. Indeed, not all war crimes even qualify as *malum in se*—inherently morally wrong. The Rome Statute recognizes this in providing for a defense of superior orders when the defendant did not know the order was unlawful and it was not "manifestly unlawful."[46] According to the Statute, genocide and crimes against humanity are always manifestly unlawful; but conduct that constitutes war crimes may appear to be lawful. It is hard to characterize as an atrocity a crime that appeared lawful to its perpetrators.

Many commentators who endorse the atrocity rationale focus on the scale of the crimes as an important determinant of international concern. Broomhall has written that only some "atrocities [are] of a magnitude capable of being labeled crimes against humanity, genocide, or violations of the laws and customs applicable in non-international armed conflict."[47] Dinah PoKempner, general counsel of Human Rights Watch, likewise wrote that: "By their nature, international crimes involve large-scale harm, careful planning and coordination, and a knowledge of their scope or potential scope by participants."[48] Yet such commentators rarely specify the quantities of harm required to qualify for international criminality. Scheffer for instance defined atrocity crimes as requiring "a relatively large number of victims" without further specificity regarding either the number or to what it is relative.[49] Even authors who attempt to elucidate the issue rarely succeed. For instance, Professors Andrew Altman and Christopher Wellman have advocated limiting global adjudication to crimes that are widespread or systematic. In defining "widespread" they wrote:

> "Widespread" is a purely quantitative notion referring mainly to the number of violations: it takes account of the number of people victimized, weighted by the relative importance of the rights violated. In some cases, the total population size

---

[45]   Ibid.

[46]   Rome Statute (n. 4) art. 8(2).

[47]   Broomhall (n. 32) 50. Broomhall leaves the role of scale unclear, however, as he also argues that even small-scale war crimes should be considered international crimes. Ibid. 51.

[48]   Dinah PoKempner, 'The Tribunal and Cambodia's Transition to a Culture of Accountability' in Jaya Ramji and Beth Van Schaack (eds.), *Bringing the Khmer Rouge to Justice: Prosecuting Mass Violence Before the Cambodian Courts* (E. Mellen Press 2005) 340. International criminal law jurisprudence frequently references scale in the context of adjudicating crimes against humanity. See, e.g., *Prosecutor v. Akayesu* (Judgment) ICTR-96-4-T (September 2, 1998) para. 580 (defining "widespread" and "systematic" in the context of international crimes).

[49]   Scheffer, 'Genocide and Atrocity Crimes' (n. 41) 238.

will be relevant, but above a certain threshold number of victims, it probably does not matter what proportion of the total population the victims represent. For example, the Serbian massacre of 7,000 Muslim males at Srebrenica counted as widespread, no matter what fraction it was of the total Bosnian population.[50]

This passage suggests that the scale required can be a matter of absolute victim numbers or population percentages, and that 7,000 deaths certainly qualify as widespread; but these general conclusions obviously leave a host of open questions.

In sum, one of the most common justifications for international crimes is that they are so serious that they shock the conscience of humanity and qualify as "atrocities." But commentators rarely elucidate the characteristics necessary to merit such labels. Although they often reference the scale of harm, they rarely do so in a way that meaningfully limits the category. It thus remains unclear what is required to shock humanity's conscience.

C. State Action

Another popular rationale for international criminality is that the crimes are perpetrated by, or with the acquiescence of, states, or that relevant states have failed to prevent or punish them. Commentators who take this "state action" approach often extend the criteria to organizations with state-like characteristics, in particular, control over territory. The state action rationale is sometimes linked to gravity and it is sometimes treated as a distinct argument. In its early efforts to define international crimes, the ILC considered the two rationales to be separate.[51] Some scholars have likewise distinguished the two rationales. For instance, William Schabas has suggested that state action and gravity operate as "competing justifications" for the exercise of international jurisdiction.[52] Larry May also differentiated the rationales in his elaborate theory of international criminality. May argued that to be truly international, crimes must fulfill both what he called the "harm principle" and the "security principle."[53] The security principle requires that the state was complicit, unwilling, or unable to prosecute the crimes—an argument akin to the state action rationale.[54] The "harm principle" requires that the crime harms humanity either by harming an individual "because of that person's group membership or other non-individualized characteristic" (the rationale discussed

---

[50] Andrew Altman and Christopher Heath Wellman, 'A Defense of International Criminal Law' (2004) 115 Ethics 35, 48.
[51] See Chapter 2, section III.
[52] William A. Schabas, *An Introduction to the International Criminal Court* (Cambridge University Press 2007) 82–3.
[53] May, *Crimes Against Humanity* (n. 20) 63–95.
[54] Ibid. 68.

in the section D) or because "the harm occurs due to the involvement of a group such as the State" (another reference to the state action rationale).[55] According to May, such group-based harms affect the international community because they are likely to be widespread or systematic (a gravity reference), they "assault the common humanity of the victims," and they "risk crossing borders" (the peace and security rationale).[56] In his view, the normative basis for international criminality is strongest when a crime both harms humanity and is perpetrated by a group.[57] May's theory thus combines several of the rationales for international crimes found in the literature, with a strong emphasis on state action.

Notably, May has also highlighted gravity as an independent requirement of international criminality. He has argued that humanity must not merely be offended but rather assaulted, and that "[a]ssaults on humanity are a class of offenses that are especially egregious and deserving of sanction."[58] Although May has not elaborated on what makes such assaults "egregious," he has noted that harming individuals is not sufficient, implying that some kind of scale is required.[59]

Antony Duff has also relied on both an undefined requirement of seriousness, and the involvement of state officials to explain the legitimate ambit of international criminal justice. In Duff's view, criminal offenders are primarily answerable to the political communities against which they have offended; but there are two roles for international criminal courts: they can address crimes with international impacts, particularly those committed by states; and they can act on behalf of national communities whose courts fail to act, for instance, because the offender is an official of the state.[60] But, at least in the latter cases, the crimes involved must be "serious enough to warrant the costs involved."[61]

Other scholars treat the gravity of international crimes not as a separate requirement, but as deriving, at least in part, from the involvement of a state.[62] Kirsten Fisher adopted this view in her book, *Moral Accountability and International Criminal Law*, which is subtitled *Holding Agents of Atrocity Accountable to the World*. The book states: "The travesty of political organization is what makes international crimes so atrocious as to require the explicit condemnation of the

---

[55] Ibid. 83.
[56] Ibid.
[57] Ibid.
[58] Ibid. 86.
[59] Ibid.
[60] Antony Duff, 'Authority and Responsibility in International Criminal Law' in Samantha Besson and John Tasioulas (eds.), *The Philosophy of International Law* (Oxford University Press 2010) 598.
[61] Ibid. 599.
[62] Kirsten Fisher, *Moral Accountability and International Criminal Law: Holding Agents of Atrocity Accountable to the World* (Routledge 2013). See also Mark J. Osiel, 'Why Prosecute? Critics of Punishment for Mass Atrocity' (2000) 22 Human Rights Q. 118, 118 (asserting that "[t]he harm wrought by state sponsors of mass atrocity is so colossal that even skeptics of the criminal law's coherence and defensibility find themselves longing for their doubts to be allayed, at least for perpetrators such as these").

international community."[63] According to Fisher, the normative legitimacy of international crimes requires that they meet what she calls the "associative threshold," whereby a state or other organization has perpetrated serious harms or failed to protect people from such harms. Although she also posited that a "seriousness threshold" must be met, in her view the threshold does not require a certain quantity of harm, but rather describes the quality of harm—the crime must violate the right to physical security.[64]

Still other commentators have implied that state action is part of what makes international crimes grave by linking the state action rationale with the peace and security and conscience-shocking rationales. For instance, Bassiouni asserted that a "state-action or state-favoring policy" is implicit in the peace and security rationale and sometimes also in the conscience-shocking rationale.[65] Since Bassiouni also wrote that international crimes are hierarchically superior to national crimes,[66] it appears that for him the additional gravity derives significantly, if not entirely, from the state action requirement. Professor Jan Klabbers agrees that "what makes [international crimes] special is precisely the link between individuals and their states."[67] He has rejected the idea that the gravity of international crimes derives from their perpetrators being more evil than other criminals, noting that those who committed the My Lai massacre shared their lunch with survivors.[68] Schabas likewise has endorsed the organizational policy requirement, expanding it to organizations with state-like characteristics.[69] George Fletcher has framed the requirement as one of "collective perpetration" and asserted that: "[w]hatever the pretense of liberal international lawyers, the crimes of concern to the international community are collective crimes."[70]

The state action rationale is frequently advanced to justify international authority over crimes against humanity. Philosophers David Luban and Richard Vernon have each elaborated a "political" view of crimes against humanity. In elaborating his theory of crimes against humanity, Luban began by noting that the term "humanity" is subject to two interpretations: it can refer either to "the quality of being human" or to humans as a group.[71] Unlike many commentators,

---

[63] Fisher (n. 62) 23.

[64] Ibid.

[65] Bassiouni, 'The *Ratione Materiae* of International Criminal Law' (n. 35) 176.

[66] Ibid. 136–7.

[67] Jan Klabbers, 'The Spectre of International Criminal Justice: Third States and the ICC' in Andreas Zimmermann (ed.), *International Criminal Law and the Current Development of Public International Law* (Dunker & Humblot 2003) 49, 60.

[68] Ibid.

[69] See William A. Schabas, 'State Policy as an Element of International Crimes' (2007) 98 J. Crim. L. & Criminology 953, 972 (arguing that the concept of "state policy" should be broadly construed to include state-like actors such as the FARC or Republika Srpska, but not Hell's Angels or the mafia).

[70] George P. Fletcher, 'The Storrs Lectures: Liberals and Romantics at War: The Problem of Collective Guilt' (2002) 111 Yale L.J. 1499, 1514. But see Robert D. Sloane, 'The Expressive Capacity of International Punishment: The Limits of the National Law Analogy and the Potential of International Criminal Law' (2007) 43 Stanford J. Intl. L. 39, 56–7 (disagreeing with the categorical nature of Fletcher's claim).

[71] David Luban, 'A Theory of Crimes Against Humanity' (2004) 29 Yale J. Intl. L. 85, 86–7.

Luban has emphasized the former, arguing that it is not the scale of the crimes that makes them special but the particular human quality they violate: our nature as political beings.[72] Crimes against humanity are committed by state actors abusing their power and thus represent "politics gone cancerous."[73] Vernon has made a similar argument, hinging the distinctiveness of crimes against humanity on the state's violation of its sovereign obligation to protect people.[74] Both authors have also argued that crimes against humanity must be targeted at groups rather than individuals—the rationale I address in the next section.

Former ICC judge Hans-Peter Kaul adopted the state policy vision of crimes against humanity in a dissenting opinion in the Kenya situation. Kaul's review of the law and scholarship on crimes against humanity led him to conclude:

> Crimes of this nature and magnitude were made possible only by virtue of an existing State policy followed in a planned and concerted fashion by various segments of public power targeting parts of the civilian population who were deprived totally and radically of their basic fundamental rights. It was not (only) the fact that crimes had been committed on a large scale but the fact that they were committed in furtherance of a particular (in-humane) policy. Consequently, it was felt that the threat emanating from such State policy is so fundamentally different in nature and scale that it concerned the entire international community. In other words, the presence of a policy element elevated those crimes to the international level.[75]

Like Kaul, many of the authors who have adopted the state action rationale for crimes against humanity seem to be motivated at least in part by a desire to avoid a definition that relies too heavily on the scale of the crimes. According to Vernon, his model of crimes against humanity "may help to deal with the troubling question of the scale of atrocity."[76] He has noted that on the one hand "the greatness of evil owes something to its extent," while on the other, "moral sense rebels at the thought that numbers count in this way …."[77] Vernon claims to solve this problem by suggesting that it is the power of the state to harm that matters, as opposed to the number of victims actually harmed.[78] Adil Haque has also taken this position,

---

[72] Ibid. 90–1.

[73] Ibid.

[74] Richard Vernon, 'What is Crime Against Humanity?' (2003) 10 J. Political Philosophy 231; Richard Vernon, 'Crimes Against Humanity: A Defense of the "Subsidiarity" View' (2013) 26 Canadian J.L. & Jurisprudence 229.

[75] *Situation in the Republic of Kenya* (Decision Pursuant to Article 15 of the Rome Statute on the Authorization of an Investigation into the Situation in the Republic of Kenya, Dissenting Opinion of Judge Hans-Peter Kaul) ICC-01/09-19 (March 31, 2010) para. 60.

[76] Richard Vernon, *Cosmopolitan Regard: Political Membership and Global Justice* (Cambridge University Press 2010) 162.

[77] Ibid.

[78] Ibid. 162–3.

stating: "International law makes group perpetration and group victimization—not numbers of victims—the central features of crimes against humanity."[79] Luban takes the point further, asserting that crimes against humanity include even individual incidents of government abuses. To Luban, the idea that "small-scale, government-inflicted atrocities remain the business of national sovereigns" is a "profoundly cynical conclusion."[80] Bassiouni similarly asserted that the state action and group targeting requirements avoid the problems of uncertainty and subjectivity inherent in a definition of crimes against humanity that relies on their scale.[81] Nonetheless, unlike Luban and Vernon, Bassiouni maintained that some notion of scale is required in addition to state action and group targeting.[82] Likewise, international lawyer Geoffrey Robertson argued that: "The individuals responsible for any *widespread* pattern of barbarity, imposed or supported by the State (through its politicians or police or military) or by armed organizations fighting to attain some (or more) power, should be indictable" for crimes against humanity.[83]

For some authors, the requirement of state action is less a description of the particular gravity of international crimes than a practical consideration: states are unlikely to prosecute crimes their agents commit, making international jurisdiction necessary.[84] Win-chiat Lee has taken this argument to its logical extreme. According to Lee, "international crimes proper" include only those that a state perpetrates against its own citizens and crimes a state is unable or unwilling to prevent or punish.[85] When crimes cross borders, the state on whose territory the crimes are committed has an incentive to prosecute, making international jurisdiction less essential. According to Lee, therefore, genocide and crimes against humanity committed by the agents of one state against the citizens of another are not international crimes in the strict sense.[86] Such acts are crimes against the other state, rather than crimes against the international community. Although he used the term "serious crimes," Lee's account of international crimes does not rely on a quantitative notion of gravity, implying instead that even small-scale crimes by state actors are international.[87] He asserted that "neither the egregiousness of the crimes nor

---

[79] Ahmad Haque, 'Group Violence and Group Vengeance: Toward A Retributivist Theory of International Criminal Law' (2005) 9 Buffalo Crim. L. Rev. 273, 298.

[80] Luban, 'A Theory of Crimes Against Humanity' (n. 71) 107.

[81] M. Cherif Bassiouni, *Crimes Against Humanity in International Criminal Law* (Kluwer Law International 1999) 246.

[82] Ibid. 243.

[83] Geoffery Robertson, *Crimes Against Humanity: The Struggle for Global Justice* (New Press 2006) 429.

[84] See, e.g., Schabas, 'State Policy as an Element of International Crimes' (n. 69) 974 (stating that "[o]ver the decades, a principal rationale for prosecuting crimes against humanity as such has been the fact that such atrocities generally escape prosecution in the State that normally exercises jurisdiction, under the territorial or active personality principles, because of the State's own involvement or acquiescence").

[85] Win-chiat Lee, 'International Law and Universal Jurisdiction' in Larry May and Zachary Hoskins (eds.), *International Criminal Law and Philosophy* (Cambridge University Press 2010) 21.

[86] Ibid. 33.

[87] Ibid. 37.

the universality of the values protected" is sufficient to distinguish international and national crimes. For Lee, the distinction only makes sense if it rests on the state's abdication of its duty to adjudicate crimes.[88]

Similarly, Altman and Wellman have advanced a theory of international criminality that depends on "whether the state is adequately performing the requisite political functions."[89] But these authors included a gravity requirement, restricting the appropriate reach of international criminal law to situations involving crimes that are "widespread or systematic."[90] Moreover, unlike many authors, Altman and Wellman included a notion of scale even in the "systematic" alternative. For them, "systematic" does not necessarily require the involvement of a government or government-like organization in perpetrating the crimes—a popular interpretation of the term. Rather, it is "a partly quantitative notion, referring to acts that are part of some plan whose execution would result in *many* rights violations," but also a qualitative idea because "there is some aim or objective that cannot be specified solely in numerical terms."[91] Since their understanding of "systematic" is partly quantitative, it appears that their theory of international crimes is especially focused on the element of scale, even if it also includes some other notion of aims or objectives.

Notably, although Altman and Wellman claimed that their theory does not rest on a distinction between international and domestic crimes, their emphasis on scale effectively creates such a distinction. Indeed, they seemed to admit as much when they wrote:

> In order to be normatively plausible, any standard dictating when international criminal jurisdiction is triggered must point to the kinds of considerations that we have discussed in cashing out "widespread or systematic," that is, those regarding the scope and severity of violations of basic rights.[92]

Although they asserted that international crimes are not "supercrimes" and that even "generic" murders and rapes are eligible for international prosecution when the state is not operating properly,[93] their theory seems to rest international criminality significantly on an evaluation of the quantity of harm caused.

Some scholars have rejected the idea that international crimes generally require state action. For instance, Broomhall has criticized Bassiouni's insistence on state

---

[88]   Ibid. 31–2.
[89]   Altman and Wellman (n. 50) 63. Alejandro Chehtman likewise rejects the idea that international crimes must "harm humanity," but nonetheless retains the requirement that they be sufficiently serious, large-scale, or part of a plan or policy. See Alejandro Chehtman, *The Philosophical Foundations of Extraterritorial Punishment* (Oxford University Press 2010) 109.
[90]   Altman and Wellman (n. 50) 35.
[91]   Ibid. 48 (emphasis added).
[92]   Ibid. 50, n. 24.
[93]   Ibid. 65.

action, asserting that state action is an element of aggression and sometimes of crimes against humanity, but is not always an aspect of war crimes or genocide.[94] Unlike Bassiouni, Broomhall does not believe that the peace and security or conscience shocking rationales require state action. On the contrary, Broomhall has asserted that requiring state action would undermine the international community's ability to prevent crimes that threaten the peace or shock the conscience. In rejecting the state action requirement, Broomhall wrote:

> The fundamental international interest in peace and security and the ability of international law to respond appropriately to affronts to the public conscience are important enough that the possibility of flexible future development should not be closed off in the name of conceptually neat but restrictive doctrinal arrangement.[95]

Otto Triffterer was similarly critical of the claim that "genocide, war crimes and crimes against humanity can only be committed when the political framework in a State would permit such behavior."[96] According to Triffterer, this approach is misguided because the mission of international criminal law is "to protect the highest values of the international community as a whole against grave violations."[97]

In sum, the involvement of a state or state-like organization or the failure of the state to prevent or punish is frequently cited as critical to the normative legitimacy of international criminality. Commentators sometimes treat this rationale as an explanation for, or component of, the gravity of international crimes and sometimes view the two justifications as separate. Frequently, the relationship between state action and gravity is left unclear, and gravity's role in justifying international prescriptive authority remains undefined.

D. Group Victimization

A final justification for international criminality in the literature is that the crimes target groups. As noted earlier, May considers this to be one of the potential normative justifications for international crimes. In his view, either group victimization or group perpetration (in the form of state or organizational action) must be present for the international community to have an interest in the crimes that warrants international prosecution.[98] Luban and Vernon place more importance on

---

[94] Broomhall (n. 32) 51.
[95] Ibid.
[96] Otto Triffterer, 'The Preventive and Repressive Function of the International Criminal Court' in Mauro Politi and Guiseppe Nesi (eds.), *The Rome Statute of the International Criminal Court* (Routledge 2001) 147.
[97] Ibid.
[98] May, *Crimes Against Humanity* (n. 20) 89.

group victimization than May does, making it a requirement, at least for crimes against humanity. Luban has asserted that crimes against humanity are committed by states or organizations and "inflicted on victims because of their membership in a population or group rather than their individual characteristics."[99] Group-on-group violence generates the "political infernos" that he believes crimes against humanity are designed to address.[100]

Vernon has taken a slightly different view of the group victimization requirement. According to him, groups are the natural locus of protection for individuals and the state supplants that status by purporting to provide the required protection.[101] When states attack groups instead of protecting them, they "invite charges of travesty."[102] Allison Marston Danner, has taken a similar position, arguing that crimes against humanity are more serious then war crimes because the former involve "both group perpetration and group victimization."[103]

While group victimization is inherent in the definition of genocide, which requires intent to destroy a group, some commentators reject that requirement for other international crimes.[104] For Altman and Wellman, for example, what matters most is whether the relevant government is willing and able to prosecute the crimes. Thus, in a failed state, large-scale murders and rapes that are not committed by or against a group can be international crimes.[105] However, as discussed earlier, Altman and Wellman qualify this claim with a scale-based gravity threshold: only when a *significant number* of perpetrators who played important roles in the crimes are left unprosecuted is international criminal jurisdiction triggered.[106] Neither Altman and Wellman's threshold, nor theories that require group-based harm, specify the kind of gravity that is required for international criminality. Their supporters often use quantitative terms like "significant number" but without stipulating a required quantity of harm.

In sum, although various theories have been advanced to justify global prescriptive authority, none of them provides a principled basis for such authority. They virtually all rely on an unexplained gravity requirement and, consequently, they fail adequately to explain the global community's interest in proscription. The next section explores the implications of this reliance on undefined gravity for the

---

[99] Luban, 'A Theory of Crimes Against Humanity' (n. 71) 103.

[100] Ibid. 109.

[101] Vernon, 'Crimes Against Humanity' View' (n. 74) 236.

[102] Ibid.

[103] Allison Marston Danner, 'Constructing a Hierarchy of Crimes in International Criminal Law Sentencing' (2001) 87 Va. L. Rev. 415, 474–5.

[104] See, e.g., Bassiouni, *Crimes Against Humanity in International Criminal Law* (n. 81) 247 (asserting that crimes against humanity do not require group targeting); Alexander R. J. Murray, 'Does International Criminal Law Still Require a "Crime of Crimes"? A Comparative Review of Genocide and Crimes Against Humanity' (2011) 3 Goettingen J. Intl. L. 589, 591 ("Crimes against humanity present a broader range of offences and there is no requirement for a specific group to be targeted.").

[105] Altman and Wellman (n. 50) 49.

[106] Ibid. 49 (emphasis added).

doctrine of international crimes, before elaborating, in the final section, a human dignity theory of international criminality that reconceptualizes gravity.

II. Normative Uncertainty Produces Unstable Legal Norms

This brief survey of theories of international crimes reveals extensive uncertainty concerning the moral justification for labeling crimes "international." While most commentators agree that international crimes concern the international community in some way, there is significant disagreement about the nature of that concern and gravity's role in it. In other words, the moral basis for international criminal law's prescriptive authority—its moral legitimacy—remains unclear. This lack of clarity about the moral basis for international prescriptive authority fosters instability in the legal norms governing international crimes; and this instability undermines the regime's legal legitimacy.

The reasons for the international community's failure to reach consensus about, or even to interrogate deeply, the normative basis for international criminality can be traced to the historical evolution of the regime. International criminal law has not generally been crafted through a purposive process of identifying the values the global community wishes to uphold and establishing priorities among them. Instead, the regime's early institutions, in particular the post-WWII and *ad hoc* tribunals, were created in reaction to particular situations that many people felt demanded international action. Since those institutions were created to adjudicate crimes that had already been committed, there was no time—or need—to craft theoretically optimal international crimes. Indeed, the institutions had to rely, and be seen to rely, on pre-existing law to comply with the principle of legality and to maximize their sociological legitimacy. They therefore turned to international humanitarian law, a pre-existing legal regime, that was not one originally intended for international prosecution. Because crimes against humanity were linked with war crimes in the Nuremberg Charter, little effort was made to develop an independent normative underpinning for them either. Until the Rome Conference, the only international crime that had been defined through a deliberative process of international negotiation was genocide, and the politics surrounding those negotiations left important normative questions unresolved, including the role of gravity.

In Rome, there was too much historical baggage for a true engagement with normative principles in crafting the definitions of crimes. The idea of revisiting the definition of genocide, for instance, was quickly rejected: the Genocide Convention was widely ratified, and the notion of reopening those difficult negotiations struck few participants as a good idea.[107] Normative coherence with regard to war crimes

---

[107] UN Conference on the Establishment of an ICC (n. 16) 146.

and crimes against humanity was inhibited by the political compromises necessary to reach agreement.[108] In sum, the normative uncertainty regarding international criminality, including gravity's role, stems in significant part from the somewhat haphazard way the regime evolved.

This normative uncertainty has contributed to instability in the legal norms governing international crimes. The legal norms are unstable in the sense that prosecutors, courts, and advocates often disagree about their content. Although most law is subject to normative contestation, the degree of uncertainty in international criminal law's criminality norms is particularly high. For instance, the definitions of crimes against humanity at the various international courts and tribunals contain important differences, reflecting divergent perspectives on their normative justification. The ICTY definition has a war nexus,[109] the ICTR's definition includes a discrimination element,[110] and the ICC version requires a state or organizational policy not required by either of the other two.[111] Although many commentators assumed the ICC definition would prove authoritative,[112] other courts have rejected the ICC's state plan or policy element since the Rome Statute was adopted.[113] The definitions reflect different normative rationales: peace and security is particularly important at the ICTY, group victimization at the ICTR, and group perpetration at the ICC.

Even within institutions, opinions are divided about the values that animate crimes against humanity. For instance, at the ICC, judges disagree about whether the organizational policy element requires a high degree of institutional organization—a "state-like" organization—or a looser requirement of group perpetration.[114] The ICC judges have also reached different conclusions about the degree of formalization that the policy element requires.[115] Likewise, judgments

---

[108] For discussion, see n. 142 and accompanying text.

[109] Statute of the ICTY (May 25, 1993) UN Doc. S/RES/827 art. 5.

[110] Statute of the ICTR (November 8, 1994) UN Doc. S/RES/955 art. 3.

[111] Rome Statute (n. 4) art. 7(2)(a).

[112] Darryl Robinson, 'Defining "Crimes Against Humanity" at the Rome Conference' (1999) 93 AJIL 43, 56–7 (stating that "Article 7 of the ICC statute sets forth a modernized and clarified definition of crimes against humanity that should provide a sound basis for international criminal prosecution in the future").

[113] See, e.g., *Prosecutor v. Fofana* (Trial Judgment) SCSL-04-14-T (August 2, 2007) paras. 112–13; *Prosecutor v. Kunarac* (Appeals Judgment) IT-96-23 & IT-96-23/1-A (June 12, 2002) para. 98; *Prosecutor v. Semanza* (Appeals Judgment) ICTR-97-20-A (May 20, 2005) para. 269.

[114] Compare *Situation in the Republic of Kenya* (Decision Pursuant to Article 15 of the Rome Statute on the Authorization of an Investigation into the Situation in the Republic of Kenya) ICC-01/09-19 (March 31, 2010) para. 92 (holding that the policy of an organization not linked to a state can fulfill the policy requirement), with *Situation in the Republic of Kenya* (Decision Pursuant to Article 15 of the Rome Statute on the Authorization of an Investigation into the Situation in the Republic of Kenya, Dissenting Opinion of Judge Hans-Peter Kaul) (n. 75) para. 51 (interpreting the policy requirement to include only states and organizations with "quasi-State" abilities).

[115] Compare *Prosecutor v. Gbagbo* (Judgment on the Appeal of the Prosecutor Against the Decision of Pre-Trial Chamber I of June 3, 2013 entitled 'Decision Adjourning the Hearing on the Confirmation of Charges Pursuant to Article 61(7)(c)(i) of the Rome Statute') ICC-02/11-01/11 OA 5 (December 16, 2013) para. 215 (asserting that "an attack which is planned, directed, or organized—as opposed to spontaneous or isolated acts of violence—will satisfy the policy criterion, and that there is no requirement

of the ICTY reflect different perspectives about whether crimes against humanity encompass crimes harming a limited number of victims.[116] And courts have struggled to identify the requirements of the constitutive acts of crimes against humanity, including the definitions of "persecution"[117] and "other inhumane acts,"[118] both of which are required to match the gravity of the other constitutive acts of crimes against humanity under the Rome Statute.[119]

The scholarship on crimes against humanity reflects similar debates about the elements of those crimes. Scholars disagree about whether crimes against humanity should require a state or organizational policy and, if so, what the attributes of such a policy should be.[120] Opinions also diverge about whether crimes against humanity should include many terrorist acts[121] or government failures to alleviate suffering after natural disasters.[122] Similar debates occur in the political sphere. For instance, when the Lebanon Tribunal was established to prosecute those responsible for killing Prime Minister Rafik Hariri and a few others, the UN Secretary General believed that the crimes could be charged as crimes against humanity

---

that the policy be formally adopted"), overturning *Prosecutor v. Gbagbo* (Decision Adjourning the Hearing on the Confirmation of Charges Pursuant to Article 61(7)(c)(i) of the Rome Statute) ICC-02/11-01/11 (June 3, 2013) para. 44 (requiring evidence of formalization).

[116] Compare *Prosecutor v. Krstić* (Trial Judgment) IT-98-33-T (August 2, 2001) para. 501 (stating that "while extermination generally involves a large number of victims, it may be constituted even where the number of victims is limited"), with Prosecutor v. Limaj (Trial Judgment) IT-03-66-T (November 30, 2005) para. 187 (asserting that the "population" element of crimes against humanity cannot be satisfied by "a limited and randomly selected number of individuals").

[117] See, e.g., *Prosecutor v. Blagojević & Jokić* (Trial Judgment) IT-02-60-T (January 17, 2005) paras. 588–602 (discussing whether various crimes, including destruction of personal property, forcible transfer of population, and terrorizing the civilian population, are grave enough to constitute persecution as a crime against humanity).

[118] See, e.g., *Prosecutor v. Vasiljevic* (Trial Judgment) IT-98-32-T (November 29, 2002) paras. 234–7.

[119] Rome Statute (n. 4) art. 7.

[120] Compare, e.g., M. Cherif Bassiouni, *Crimes Against Humanity: Historical Evolution and Contemporary Application* (Cambridge University Press 2011) xxxii (supporting a policy element); Schabas, 'State Policy as an Element of International Crimes' (n. 69) 953 (same), with Charles Chernor Jalloh, '(Re)defining Crimes Against Humanity' in Larry May and Elizabeth Edenberg (eds.), *Just Post Bellum and Transitional Justice* (Cambridge University Press 2013) 118 (arguing against a policy element); Guénaël Mettraux, 'The Definition of Crimes Against Humanity and the Question of a "Policy" Element' in Leila Nadya Sadat (ed.), *Forging a Convention for Crimes Against Humanity* (Cambridge University Press 2011) 151–2 (same). See also Robert Cryer et al., *An Introduction to International Criminal Law and Procedure* (Cambridge University Press 2007) 198 (suggesting a minimalist interpretation of the ICC's policy element).

[121] Compare Johan D. Van der Vyver, 'Prosecuting Terrorism in International Tribunals' (2010) 24 Emory Intl. L. Rev. 527, 539 ("Being an instance of 'inhumane acts ... causing great suffering, or serious bodily injury to body or mental or physical health,' terrorism clearly qualifies for purposes of ICC jurisdiction as a crime against humanity."), with William A. Schabas, 'The International Criminal Court: The Secret of Its Success' (2001) 12 Crim. L.F. 415, 427 ("It would be a terrible distortion for the International Criminal Court to become focused on so-called 'terrorist' activity rather its truly intended target, namely gross violations of human rights committed by a government on its own civilian population.").

[122] Stuart Ford, 'Is the Failure to Respond Appropriately to a Natural Disaster a Crime Against Humanity?' (2010) 38 Denver J. Intl. L. & Policy 227, 235.

despite the small number of victims, but some members of the Security Council disagreed.[123]

Even genocide, despite being defined in a widely accepted convention, remains the subject of significant normative debate. Scholars, judges, and advocates continue to disagree about what makes genocide a particularly serious crime—a crime of concern to the international community. The legal definition implies that genocide's gravity stems entirely from the mental element—the intent to destroy a group—but many commentators argue that more is required. Schabas, who has written extensively about genocide, asserts that, like other crimes against humanity, genocide can only be committed as part of a state or organizational policy.[124] Schabas finds support for his position in some of the jurisprudence.[125] Moreover, the ICC Statute's Elements for genocide require that "[t]he conduct took place in the context of a manifest pattern of similar conduct directed against that group or was conduct that could itself effect such destruction."[126] On the other hand, the ICTY famously held that a lone madman operating in isolation could be guilty of genocide.[127] Some scholars agree that the intent to destroy a group is all that is necessary to make genocide a crime of concern to the global community.[128] Other scholarship and jurisprudence seems to imply that what makes genocide concern the world is the quantity of harm it inflicts.[129]

Another unresolved legal issue concerning the gravity of genocide is what "part" of a group the perpetrator must intend to destroy.[130] The case law generally requires the intent to destroy a "substantial" part of the group. "Substantial" has been interpreted to mean either a large number of people in absolute terms or a significant proportion of the group, even if that means only a small number of people are harmed.[131] Such pronouncements do little to clarify the issue. How many deaths in a group are "significant"? If only two members of an ethnic group remain on

---

[123] UNSC, 'Report of the Secretary-General on the Establishment of a Special Tribunal for Lebanon' (November 15, 2006) UN Doc. S/2006/893 paras. 24–5.

[124] Schabas, *Genocide in International Law: The Crime of Crimes* (n. 9) 491; but see Jordan J. Paust, 'The International Criminal Court Does Not Have Complete Jurisdiction Over Customary Crimes Against Humanity and War Crimes' (2010) 43 John Marshall L. Rev. 681, 696–7 (arguing that genocide has no plan or policy requirement).

[125] Schabas, *Genocide in International Law: The Crime of Crimes* (n. 9) 438-2 (discussing cases).

[126] ICC, *Elements of Crimes* (International Criminal Court 2011) art. 6(a)(4).

[127] *Prosecutor v. Jelisic* (Trial Judgment) IT-95-10-T (December 14, 1999) para. 100.

[128] See, e.g., Triffterer, (n. 96) 149; Laurelyn Whitt and Alan W. Clarke, 'Bringing It Home: North American Genocides' (2017) 20 J. Gender Race & Justice 263, 268–9 (asserting that "[a]s an inchoate crime, genocide does not require completion for prosecution or conviction. The specific intent to destroy a protected group in whole or in part, together with the prohibited acts aimed at the group, suffice 'whether or not those acts actually result in the group's destruction' ").

[129] See, e.g., Israel W. Charny, 'Toward a Generic Definition of Genocide' in George J. Andreopoulos (ed.), *Genocide: Conceptual and Historical Dimensions* (University of Pennsylvania Press 1994) 76 (asserting that "[g]enocide in the generic sense is the mass killing of substantial numbers of human beings...").

[130] See David Alonzo-Maizlish, 'In Whole or In Part: Group Rights, The Intent Element of Genocide, and the "Quantitative Criterion" ' (2002) 77 NYU L. Rev. 1369, 1385.

[131] See Scheffer, 'Genocide and Atrocity Crimes' (n. 41) 240 (discussing cases).

earth, is killing one of them genocide? One commentator worries that the substantiality criteria could become an "insurmountable obstacle"[132] to prosecutions for genocide, but the opposite conclusion—that it will be relatively easy to prove—is equally plausible. The meaning of "in part" will remain unclear unless consensus emerges on what quantity of harm, if any, is required for the crime of genocide to concern the world.

A similar problem arises with regard to the crime of incitement to genocide. Since incitement requires no actual harm, the question becomes how much harm must be threatened and how serious must the threat be. Professor Susan Benesch has argued for a "reasonably possible consequences" test,[133] while others have taken different approaches, including looking to imminence.[134]

The definition of aggression also remains uncertain, in particular with regard to the role of gravity. Aggression is essentially a crime of state—it is committed by leaders of one state against the sovereignty of another. However, not all acts of aggression are criminal. Under the Rome Statute, it is the gravity of an act, along with its "character" and "scale" that determines whether it is a "manifest" violation of the UN Charter and thus a crime.[135] While an "understanding" appended to the definition declares that gravity, character, and scale must each be "significant enough" for aggression to be a crime,[136] this fails to clarify the matter since most definitions of gravity encompass notions of both character and scale. As such, the moral and legal legitimacy of aggression depends in part on what is meant by gravity. As for the other crimes, however, this issue has been left unresolved. It thus remains unclear when an act of aggression rises to the level of an international crime.

Although war crimes have the longest historical pedigree, the basis for their status as crimes subject to international adjudication remains unclear. The law of war crimes was developed for use in national courts, particularly the courts of the states most affected by the crimes. Indeed, jurisdiction over such crimes in national courts was not based in international law but required implementing legislation.[137] The basis for prosecuting war crimes before the post-WWII tribunals was less their seriousness or the concern of the world than the well-established right of the parties to a conflict to adjudicate crimes committed therein. Thus, in 1951, the ILC concluded that war crimes were not crimes against the peace and security of mankind, although it included them in its Draft Code nonetheless on the grounds that

---

[132] Alonzo-Maizlish, 'In Whole or In Part' (n. 130) 1396.

[133] Susan Benesch, 'Vile Crime or Inalienable Right: Defining Incitement to Genocide' (2008) 48 Va. J. Intl. L. 485, 494.

[134] See, e.g., Joshua Wallenstein, 'Punishing Words: An Analysis of the Necessity of the Element of Causation in Prosecutions for Incitement to Genocide' (2001) 54 Stanford L. Rev. 351, 374.

[135] The Crime of Aggression, RC/Res.6 (adopted on June 11, 2010) Annex I, para. 2, art. 8*bis*(1).

[136] Ibid. Annex III, para. 7.

[137] Georges Abi-Saab, 'The Concept of "War Crimes"' in Sienho Yee and Wang Tieya (eds.), *International Law in the Post-Cold War World* (Routledge 2001) 100.

they were in the Nuremberg Charter.[138] Later, the ILC added a requirement of "exceptional seriousness," and then just "seriousness," in an effort to ensure that war crimes concerned the entire world.[139] Eventually, the threshold was elaborated to include only war crimes "committed in a systematic manner or on a large scale," and included in the Rome Statute with the Preface "in particular."[140] The Rome Statute's optional gravity threshold is thus the legal manifestation of normative uncertainty about when war crimes constitute "serious crimes of concern to the international community as a whole."

Another area of legal uncertainty pertains to the relationship among the core crimes. Some judges and scholars claim that there is a hierarchy among these crimes, generally placing war crimes at the bottom and sometimes elevating genocide above crimes against humanity.[141] This hierarchy is sometimes based on the claim that crimes involving discriminatory targeting are more serious than non-discriminatory crimes.[142] Others reject the hierarchy.[143] For instance, the International Commission of Inquiry on Darfur, in controversially concluding that genocide did not occur there, stated: " '[G]enocide is not necessarily the most serious international crime. Depending upon the circumstances, such international offences as crimes against humanity or large scale war crimes may be no less serious and heinous than genocide.' "[144] Some commentators, including former ICTY Judge Patricia Wald, have even suggested that the distinction between genocide and crimes against humanity should be rethought in light of the extreme gravity of both crimes.[145]

These are just some of the ways in which the law governing international crimes remains in flux. While law is generally subject to gradual evolution, the definitions of international crimes are particularly unstable. Although the regime's youth is part of the explanation for this uncertainty, it is also due to the absence of clear

---

[138] ILC, 'Report on the Work of Its Third Session, Draft Code of Offenses Against the Peace and Security of Mankind' (May 16–July 27, 1951) UN Doc. A/CN.4/48 and Corr. 1 and 2 135 para. 59.

[139] ILC, 'Report on the Work of Its Forty-Third Session, Draft Code of Crimes Against the Peace and Security of Mankind' (April 29–July 19, 1991) UN Doc. A/46/10 97 para. 176, art. 22; ILC 'Report of the Commission to the General Assembly on the Work of Its Forty-Sixth Session, Draft Statute for an International Criminal Court' (May 2–July 22, 1994) UN Doc, A/CN.4/Ser.A/1994/Add.1 38 para. 91, art. 20.

[140] These developments are discussed in detail in Chapter 2, section III.

[141] This issue is discussed in detail in Chapter 6, section I.

[142] See, e.g., Allison Marston Danner, 'Constructing a Hierarchy of Crimes' (n. 103) 474–5 (arguing that "[c]rimes against humanity . . . should be considered more serious than war crimes because of their characteristics of group perpetration and group victimization").

[143] See, e.g., *Prosecutor v. Tadić* (Appeals Sentencing Judgment) IT-94-1-A and IT-94-1-A*bis* (January 26, 2000) para. 69 ("After full consideration, the Appeals Chamber takes the view that there is in law no distinction between the seriousness of a crime against humanity and that of a war crime.").

[144] International Commission of Inquiry on Darfur, 'Report of the International Commission of Inquiry on Darfur to the United Nations Secretary-General, Pursuant to the Security Council Resolution 1564 of 18 September 2004' (January 25, 2005) para. 522 (emphasis omitted).

[145] Patricia M. Wald, 'Genocide and Crimes Against Humanity' (2007) 6 Wash. U. Global Studies L. Rev. 621, 633.

guiding moral principles regarding the nature of international criminality. The next section seeks to identify a more stable moral footing for international prescriptive authority.

III. Reforming Gravity: A Human Dignity Theory of International Criminality

This chapter has shown that gravity is central to virtually all efforts to justify international prescriptive authority. Gravity is almost universally cited to distinguish "international crimes" from "national" or "ordinary" crimes, but little substance is given to the concept. As explained earlier, this reliance on an uncertain gravity threshold has led to instability in the regime's legal norms that threatens its legitimacy. To alleviate this problem, gravity should be reconceptualized as a function of global values and goals. The central value that undergirds the global community's prescriptive authority is that of human dignity; and the associated goal should be to protect human dignity to the greatest possible extent.

Human dignity is the concept at the heart of the human rights regime.[146] It derives from a natural law frame that merges law and morality;[147] and has been the subject of lengthy discussions among philosophers, political scientists, and legal scholars.[148] The concept can be traced at least to the Stoics, and some authors claim that it goes back to the first or second century BC.[149] More recently, it has been incorporated in the constitutions of many countries.[150]

Although the meaning of human dignity is contested, for present purposes it encompasses both a recognition of the equal moral worth of all humans, and an acknowledgement of the rights all humans therefore enjoy.[151] This view of human dignity features prominently in the main legal instruments of the human rights regime. The Universal Declaration of Human Rights asserts that "all human beings are born free and equal in dignity and rights";[152] and the preamble to the

---

[146] See, e.g., Paolo G. Carozza, 'Human Dignity and Judicial Interpretation of Human Rights: A Reply' (2008) 19 Eur. J. Intl. L. 931, 932 (asserting that "the idea of human dignity serves as the single most widely recognized and invoked basis for grounding the idea of human rights generally").

[147] See J. Benton Heath, 'Mapping Extensive Uses of Human Dignity in International Criminal Law' in Siljia Vöneky (ed.), *Ethics and Law: The Ethicalization of Law* (Springer Press 2013) 256 (asserting that "dignity is the paradigmatic hybrid of a legal and moral concept").

[148] See, e.g., Jürgen Habermas, 'The Concept of Human Dignity and the Realistic Utopia of Human Rights' (2010) 41 Metaphilosophy 464, 465; Rhoda E. Howard and Jack Donnelly, 'Human Dignity, Human Rights, and Political Regimes' (1986) 80 American Political Science Rev. 801, 802; Oscar Schachter, 'Human Dignity as a Normative Concept' (1983) 77 AJIL 848, 849.

[149] Adeno Addis, 'The Role of Human Dignity in a World of Plural Values and Ethical Commitments' (2013) 31 Netherlands Q. of Human Rights 403, 408.

[150] Ibid. 411.

[151] Paolo G. Carozza, 'Human Dignity' in Dinah Shelton (ed.) *The Oxford Handbook of International Human Rights Law* (Oxford University Press 2013) 345.

[152] Universal Declaration of Human Rights (adopted on December 10, 1948) UNGA Res 217 A(III) art. 1.

International Covenant on Civil and Political Rights (ICCPR) declares that "recognition of the inherent dignity and of the equal and inalienable rights of all members of the human family is the foundation of freedom, justice and peace in the world."[153] The ICCPR further recognizes that human rights "derive from the inherent dignity of the human person."[154] Other international human rights instruments contain similar provisions.[155] Indeed, the UN General Assembly has stated that all human rights instruments should "derive from the inherent dignity and worth of the human person."[156]

Although the understanding of human dignity advocated herein is substantively universalist, it is procedurally pluralist because it recognizes the importance of plural process for ascertaining the content of the rights human dignity entails. Here I echo an argument that Adeno Addis made in an article entitled "The Role of Human Dignity in a World of Plural Values and Ethical Commitments." Addis argued for a notion of human dignity linked to political process, stating:

> To tie human dignity to a political process is to leave it to humans themselves in their daily construction of their lives and their relationships to determine the contours of what constitutes a dignity worthy of humans.[157]

The goal is to uncover "overlapping consensus" among societies with "different ways of dignifying humans."[158] This is the approach advocated in Chapter 1 for identifying the values of the global community more broadly. Although global values are universal in nature, discovering them requires a dialogic process that takes account of as many divergent views as possible. This approach is essential for uncovering the content of human dignity for purposes of determining legitimate global prescriptive authority. Paolo Carozza describes this process as building "the global *ius commune* of human rights."[159] He notes:

> The universal value of human dignity remains in a complex and concrete relationship with the particular positive law of any given, specific legal context, such that it remains informal, flexible and pluralistic in its relationship to local law and culture.[160]

---

[153] ICCPR (adopted on December 16, 1966, entered into force on March 23, 1976) 999 UNTS 171 preamble.

[154] Ibid.

[155] See, e.g., UNGA International Covenant on Economic, Social and Cultural Rights (adopted on December 16, 1966, entered into force on January 3, 1976) 993 UNTS 3 preamble; UNGA Convention Against Torture and Other Cruel, Inhuman or Degrading Treatment or Punishment (adopted on December 10, 1984, entered into force on June 26, 1987) 1465 UNTS 85 preamble.

[156] UNGA Res. 41/120 (December 4, 1986) UN Doc. A/RES/41/120.

[157] Addis (n. 149) 425.

[158] Ibid. 425–9.

[159] Carozza (n. 146) 933.

[160] Ibid. (citation and internal quotation marks omitted).

Human dignity thus "serves as a common currency of transnational judicial dialogue and borrowing" that contributes to the development of global human rights.[161] A parallel process is occurring in international criminal law, whereby the universal value of human dignity is being given concrete form through transnational dialogue, thereby developing the *ius commune* of global justice.

If the value that undergirds global prescriptive authority in the criminal law realm is that of human dignity, the associated goal should be to use criminal prohibitions to protect human dignity.[162] This of course assumes that criminal prohibitions are a legitimate way of preventing harm to human dignity. Although this is a debatable proposition, it is widely accepted in the global community at present. If the global community's values change in this regard, for instance through the emergence of a more restorative approach to addressing harm to human dignity, the entire theory of international criminal law would have to be revisited.

Rooting legitimate global prescriptive authority in the protection of human dignity would yield broad parameters for such authority: it would encompass any conduct or omission that is widely viewed around the world as harming or threatening to harm human dignity to such an extent as to give rise to criminal prohibition.[163] Under this approach, gravity would provide a threshold, but only a very low one: it would exclude only conduct that harms human dignity so minimally that it might not deserve criminal sanction at all. If grave crimes are those that shock the conscience of humanity, our collective conscience should be shocked by all meaningful harms and threats to human dignity.

Determining what conduct meaningfully harms human dignity will require the dialogic global process advocated throughout this book for identifying global norms. This process is currently taking place in regard to efforts to develop a treaty prohibiting crimes against humanity.[164] When decision-makers are uncertain as to the existence of a global norm prohibiting conduct, they might do well to avoid global proscription until greater clarity about the norm emerges. The crime of conspiracy provides an example: although some national systems recognize the crime,

---

[161] Ibid. 932.

[162] David Guinn makes an interesting related argument that the interest at the heart of efforts to promote human dignity through human rights law, humanitarian law, and international criminal law is an interest in promoting peace. David Guinn, 'Human Rights as Peacemaker: An Integrative Theory of International Human Rights' (2016) 38 Human Rights Q. 745, 754. Also, although I agree with David Luban that concern for human dignity (what he calls "human rights thinking") was not the sole basis for the development of international humanitarian law, my argument is that it ought to be the focus today. See David Luban, 'Human Rights Thinking and the Laws of War' in Jens David Ohlin (ed.), *Theoretical Boundaries of Armed Conflicts and Human Rights* (Cambridge University Press 2016) 46.

[163] See, e.g., *Law v. Canada (Minister of Employment and Immigration)*, [1999] 1 S.C.R. 497 para. 53 ("Human dignity is harmed when individuals and groups are marginalized, ignored, or devalued.").

[164] See Leila Nadya Sadat, 'A Contextual and Historical Analysis of the International Law Commission's 2017 Draft Articles for a New Global Treaty on Crimes Against Humanity' (2018) 16 J. Intl. Crim. Justice 683, 703–4 (asserting that in codifying crimes against humanity, the ILC should both respect existing international criminal law norms and contribute to their progressive development).

others reject it as akin to punishing intention without action.[165] Under these circumstances, codifying a global crime of conspiracy could threaten the regime's legitimacy.

The gravity threshold does not require absolute global consensus about criminal law values. Such a requirement would preclude many important crimes from global prescription including, for instance, crimes that particularly affect women, some of which are not recognized in all parts of the world. Rather, a substantial portion of the globe must agree that a particular kind of conduct or result harms human dignity in order for the gravity threshold to be met. Although harms to human dignity violate universal moral values, as explained in Chapter 1, no community or group has unique insight into the content of such values. Indeed, history shows that majorities, even global majorities, sometimes fail to identify universal moral values. The treatment of women and minorities around the world continues to attest to this problem. Thus, although majority views can help to identify the minimal gravity threshold, the necessary process of value identification must remain dynamic.

In addition to providing a minimal threshold for global prescription, gravity should be used to identify the crimes that ought to be given priority in the global community's prescriptive efforts. Although the global community has legitimate authority to prescribe all significant harms to human dignity, in light of the limited resources available to the international criminal law regime, it makes sense for that regime to focus on a sub-set of such crimes. As such, the global community can legitimately identify some crimes as "international" and thus worthy of particular global attention. However, to be legitimate, such designation and prioritization must be based on values and goals that are of particular importance to the global community. Reconceptualizing gravity in terms of global values and goals could therefore help to promote the legitimacy of the choice to privilege global prescription of some crimes that harm human dignity over others.

In seeking to express the gravity of particular crimes for purposes of justifying the global community's focus on them, therefore, regime actors should identify the values and goals they seek to pursue. For instance, prescription of aggression can be justified by reference to the importance of preventing armed conflict, which causes various kinds of harm to human dignity, including those associated with the loss of self-determination. As the global community continues to refine the scope of war crimes, such interest articulation is important. For instance, the Rome Statute penalizes the use of certain weapons in international armed conflict, but not in non-international armed conflict. Is the former truly of greater interest to the global

---

[165] See, e.g., Edward M. Wise, 'RICO and Its Analogues: Some Comparative Considerations' (2000) 27 Syracuse J. Intl. L. & Com. 303, 312 (comparing conspiracy laws in the United States with the Italian Penal Code, which rejects the crime of conspiracy, stating: "Except as the law provides otherwise, when two or more persons agree to commit an offense, and it is not committed, none of them shall be punishable for the mere fact of agreement").

community? If so, why? If not, this provision ought to be revised. Likewise, the drafters of the proposed convention on crimes against humanity should explain as clearly as possible the values that animate the convention.[166] To what extent, if any, does quantity of harm matter in elevating the global interest? What kinds of systematic crimes are particularly important subjects of global prescription, and so on. I will not attempt to answer such questions because, as I emphasize throughout this book, what is needed is a dialogic process regarding global values and goals that involves as many members of the global community as possible.

This human dignity approach to international criminality departs from the dominant "atrocity crimes" theory in several respects. First, it rejects the idea that any substantial quantity of harm is necessary to qualify for international criminality. Second, beyond a minimum requirement of global consensus as to criminality, it considers the concept of gravity relevant to justifying the *priority* given to certain kinds of harms to human dignity, not to the legitimacy of prescribing the crimes at all. Third, it conceives of gravity as a vehicle for surfacing values and goals, rather than as a goal-neutral concept. Finally, because global priorities change over time, the human dignity theory suggests that the definitions of international crimes should remain broad and flexible, and global institutions should remain open to including new crimes within their jurisdictions. This has several implications for the operation of international criminal law, particularly at the ICC: The Rome Statute's optional gravity threshold for war crimes should be interpreted as a minimal requirement; states parties should revisit frequently the crimes within the Court's jurisdiction; and the Court's judges should not adopt interpretations of the crimes that exclude harms to human dignity that are of potential current *or future* interest to the global community.

Most of these recommendations align with current decision-making trends, which underscores the mismatch between the dominant rationale for international criminality and the practice of international criminal law discussed. Thus far at the ICC, the optional war crimes threshold has received relatively little attention; the Assembly of States Parties periodically reconsiders the Court's subject matter jurisdiction; and judges fairly consistently adopt broad definitions of international crimes. For instance, the ICC has interpreted broadly the policy element of crimes against humanity;[167] and an investigating judge at the Extraordinary Chambers in the Courts of Cambodia (ECCC) has taken an expansive view of the "civilian

---

[166] See ILC, 'Third Report on Crimes Against Humanity by Sean D. Murphy, Special Rapporteur' 69th Session (May 1–June 2 and July 3–August 4, 2017) UN Doc. A/CN.4/704* (describing discussions surrounding the proposed convention).

[167] *Situation in the Republic of Kenya* (Decision Pursuant to Article 15 of the Rome Statute on the Authorization of an Investigation into the Situation in the Republic of Kenya) (n. 114) para. 84 ("The policy need not be explicitly defined by the organizational group. Indeed, an attack which is planned, directed or organised—as opposed to spontaneous or isolated acts of violence—will satisfy this criterion.").

population" element.[168] In fact, international courts have occasionally cited human dignity as the basis for broad interpretations of international crimes.[169] For instance, in explaining that rape can be committed through oral penetration for purposes of international criminal law even though some national jurisdictions label this conduct "sexual assault,"[170] the ICTY stated:

> The essence of the whole corpus of international humanitarian law as well as human rights law lies in the protection of the human dignity of every person, whatever his or her gender. The general principle of respect for human dignity is the basic underpinning and indeed the very *raison d'être* of international humanitarian law and human rights law; indeed in modern times it has become of such paramount importance as to permeate the whole body of international law. This principle is intended to shield human beings from outrages upon their personal dignity, whether such outrages are carried out by unlawfully attacking the body or by humiliating and debasing the honour, the self-respect or the mental well being of a person.[171]

The Tribunal dismissed objections of unfair stigma associated with a conviction for rape rather than sexual assault by asserting that "any such concern is amply outweighed by the fundamental principle of protecting human dignity, a principle which favors broadening the definition of rape."[172]

A more controversial example is the ICTR's holding that hate speech targeting a population on a discriminatory ground can constitute the crime against humanity of persecution because it "violates the right to respect for the dignity of the members of the targeted group as human beings."[173] This decision has been the subject of a lively scholarly debate.[174] Given the divergent views on hate speech and

---

[168] ECCC Office of the Co-Investigating Judges, 'Notification of the Interpretation of 'Attack Against the Civilian Population' in the Context of Crimes Against Humanity With Regard to a State's or Regime's Own Armed Forces' 003/07-09-2009-ECCC-OCIJ (February 7, 2017).

[169] Heath (n. 147) 258.

[170] *Prosecutor v. Furundzija* (Trial Judgment) IT-95-17/1-T (December 10, 1998) para. 182.

[171] Ibid. para. 183.

[172] Ibid. para. 184. The ICC used similar language in explaining why the "organization" requirement should not be interpreted narrowly, stating that the important question is whether a group is capable of "acts which infringe on basic human values." See *Situation in the Republic of Kenya* (Decision Pursuant to Article 15 of the Rome Statute on the Authorization of an Investigation into the Situation in the Republic of Kenya) (n. 114) para. 90.

[173] *Nahimana et al. v. Prosecutor* (Appeals Judgment) ICTR-99-52-A (November 28, 2007) para. 986.

[174] See, e.g., Diane F. Orentlicher, 'Criminalizing Hate Speech in the Crucible of Trial: *Prosecutor v. Nahimana* (2006) 21 Am. U. Intl. L. Rev. 557, 596 (asserting that the court in *Nahimana* "overstepped its proper role as an international criminal court" and "that a criminal trial is the wrong place to revise the law"); Gregory S. Gordon, 'Hate Speech and Persecution: A Contextual Approach' (2013) 46 Vand. J. Transnational L. 303, 372–3 (agreeing with the Tribunal's "finding that speech can be the basis for persecution charges," but asserting that "it went off track in positing that speech might be considered in granular isolation from other conduct in a CAH attack against civilians . . . . If speech cannot be connected to the broader attack, then the charge has no merit in the first place").

freedom of expression around the world, this debate might be cited as an example of global value pluralism to undermine the claim that a global justice community exists. In my view, however, the debate is precisely the kind of transnational dialogue about values that solidifies the global justice community over time. Although there is currently no global consensus about how to balance the values of expression and dignity, such consensus may be emerging.[175] The crystallization of global values can be relatively rapid, as with the increased recognition of LGBTQ (lesbian, gay, bisexual, transgender, and questioning (or queer)) rights, or more gradual, like the progression toward global respect for women's rights.

Although other scholars have cited human dignity as an important value in international criminal law, none has identified the concept as *the* essential value legitimizing global prescriptive authority. For instance, Massimo Renzo asserts that crimes are international when they constitute "a serious attack on the human dignity of the victims."[176] But Renzo also places significant import on gravity, stating:

> What matters is that the nature of the harm inflicted by certain crimes is so heinous that it cannot be captured by the ordinary categories of criminal law (conceptual point). Moreover, since these crimes are so heinous, we want to make sure that their perpetrators will not go unpunished in case national courts fail to prosecute them (normative point).[177]

This approach blends the human dignity approach with the atrocity rationale. Another important difference between Renzo's account and the one offered here is that Renzo denies that international crimes harm humanity.[178] He argues that international crimes—which he discusses under the rubric of crimes against humanity—are those for which individuals are accountable to the international community, but not because they harm that community.[179] Rather, in his view, crimes against humanity are crimes that deny their victims the status of being human by violating their basic human rights.[180] He says that such crimes *concern* the international community, although they do not necessarily *harm* the international community.[181]

---

[175] Alexander Tsesis, 'Dignity and Speech: The Regulation of Hate Speech in a Democracy' (2009) 44 Wake Forest L. Rev. 497, 531–2 (arguing that democracies around the world generally recognize "the value of preserving human rights" over "bigots' self-determined desire to spread destructive messages").

[176] Massimo Renzo, 'Crimes Against Humanity and the Limits of International Criminal Law' (2012) 31 L. & Philosophy 443, 449.

[177] Massimo Renzo, 'A Criticism of the International Harm Principle' (2010) 4 Crim. L. & Philosophy 267, 276.

[178] Ibid. 267.

[179] Ibid.

[180] Renzo, 'Crimes Against Humanity and the Limits of International Criminal Law' (n. 176) 453.

[181] For this distinction between harm and concern, Renzo draws on the work of Anthony Duff. Renzo, 'A Criticism of the International Harm Principle' (n. 177) 279 (citing Anthony Duff, *Answering for Crime: Responsibility and Liability in the Criminal Law* (Hart 2007) 23).

Renzo's distinction between concern and harm is misplaced. International crimes concern the global community *because* they harm or threaten harm to that community. This harm is sometimes concrete, such as when international crimes cross borders; but it can also be figurative: our common human bond means that all humans are harmed whenever any one of us is harmed.[182]

This notion of harm is linked to the cosmopolitan conception of global community outlined in Chapter 1.[183] Because humans share certain values, including respect for human dignity, attacks on those values constitute attacks on the community itself. As Charles Beitz states: "The doctrine of human rights is the articulation in the public morality of *the idea that each person is a subject of global concern.*"[184] International criminality represents a further articulation of that idea. Harms to human dignity *both concern and harm* the global community because they strike at the heart of that community's identity.

My theory's inclusion of figurative harm distinguishes it from accounts of international crimes that require a collective element, such as group targeting or perpetration.[185] According to Professor Kai Ambos, for instance, "there must always be a collective or group element in international crimes in the sense that the individual victims concerned are not attacked exclusively on the basis of their individuality but also as members or representatives of certain groups or collective entities, which in turn represent humanity."[186] In my view, any crime that harms or threatens the human dignity of any single human has at least the potential to be proscribed as an international crime. The global community's concern over such crimes is rooted in what Andrew Linklater has called "cosmopolitan harm conventions"—an international morality that assumes each person cares about harm to all other persons on the planet.[187]

J. Benton Heath has expressed concern that an emphasis on human dignity as the basis for international criminality will lead to an overly broad international criminal law. He writes that invocations of human dignity "problematize the

---

[182] See, e.g., May, *Crimes Against Humanity* (n. 20) 8 ("[W]hat sets paradigmatic international crimes apart from domestic crimes is that, in some sense, humanity is harmed when these crimes are perpetrated"); Hannah Arendt, *Eichmann In Jerusalem: A Report on the Banality of Evil* (Penguin 1994) 275–6 (arguing that atrocities committed by the Nazis "might be more than crime against the Jewish or the Polish or the Gypsy people, that the international order, and mankind in its entirety, might have been grievously hurt and endangered.").

[183] See Chapter 1, section III.

[184] Charles Beitz, *The Idea of Human Rights* (Oxford University Press 2009) 1 (emphasis added).

[185] See section I.C.

[186] Ambos argues for an interesting notion of international criminality based on a combination of the harm principle and a "Rechtsgut theory." Kai Ambos, 'The Overall Function of International Criminal Law: Striking the Right Balance Between the Rechtsgut and the Harm Principles' (2015) 9 Crim. L. & Philosophy 301.

[187] Andrew Linklater, 'Citizenship, Humanity, and Cosmopolitan Harm Convention' (2001) 22 Intl. Political Science Rev. 261, 261.

self-understanding of international criminal law as a substantially limited regime for the worst crimes facing humanity";[188] and that:

> Dignity pushes the reach of international crimes ever outward to criminalize new forms of conduct perceived as a threat to dignity, potentially disregarding deep national and transnational contestation over those issues.[189]

He concludes that: "international criminal law should take its limits seriously."[190] Heath is correct that dignity pushes the regime outward and that there is a danger of disregard for national and transnational contestation; however, like many other commentators, Heath wrongly assumes that gravity constitutes a moral value that appropriately limits the reach of international criminal law. As discussed throughout this book, this common misperception must be corrected if international criminal law is to build its legitimacy. The best approach to addressing contestation around values associated with dignity is not to use gravity, but rather to adopt a process whereby the global understanding of dignity is shaped by as many diverse perspectives as possible.

Redefining gravity in line with global goals and values is unlikely immediately to bolster the legitimacy of international criminal law. The regime's legal norms will remain contested and subject to various interpretations for the foreseeable future. Indeed, the recommendation that the norms remain flexible may promote such contestation. However, the norms will not be *unstable* in the sense discussed earlier because the discussions around them will address conflicts among values, rather than masking such conflict with ambiguous references to gravity. In other words, the norms' flexibility will facilitate a process of progressive development, rather than simply providing a source of confusion and legitimacy challenges.

In sum, contrary to the conventional view, *all* attacks on human dignity concern the global community. Such attacks need not take place during armed conflict, or as part of a widespread or systematic attack, for global prescriptive authority to be morally justified. Thus, for instance, it is incorrect to assert, as ICTY judges and others have, that "the reason that crimes against humanity so shock the conscience of mankind and warrant intervention by the international community is because they are not isolated, random acts of individuals but rather result from a deliberate attempt to target a civilian population."[191] Rather, even isolated murders, rapes, and tortures render the perpetrator answerable to the global community because he or she has harmed our common humanity. Whether or not such crimes are of sufficient current concern to the global community to warrant global prescription

[188] Heath (n. 147) 279.
[189] Ibid.
[190] Ibid.
[191] *Prosecutor v. Tadić* (Trial Judgment) IT-94-I-T (May 7, 1997) para. 653.

is a question of global goals and priorities. For gravity to distinguish international crimes, therefore, it must be articulated in terms of those goals.

Conclusion

This chapter has shown that most efforts to articulate a moral basis for international criminality rely on gravity in some fashion. Sometimes, they simply assert the shocking or atrocious nature of the crimes as the justification for international prescription. Other theories cite such factors as threats to peace and security, state action or failure, and group-based harm, either as explanations for what makes international crimes grave, or as separate criteria for international criminality. Even in the latter case, however, the theories generally also include a gravity threshold below which international prescription is considered inappropriate. This reliance on undefined gravity as the moral justification for international criminality destabilizes the legal norms governing such crimes. As such, it threatens both the moral and legal legitimacy of international criminal law.

To address this problem, gravity's role as a moral basis for global prescription should be reconceptualized as a function of global values and goals. Because the global community has an interest in preventing all harm to human dignity, gravity should serve as only a minimal threshold for legitimate international prescription. It should exclude only conduct that arguably does not warrant criminal prohibition at all.

Gravity should also be used to help explain the global community's choices about which crimes to proscribe of those that meet the threshold. In this context, gravity should be articulated in terms of the global community's particular crime prevention priorities at a given time. A crime is graver than another if the global community has a greater interest in its prevention. The graver the crime, the more strongly legitimate is its prescription.

Identifying global goals and priorities requires a dialogic process involving courts, advocates, and scholars expressing their views, others responding, adjustments being made, and so forth. This process should take account of as many diverse perspectives as possible, such that, over time, global consensus may emerge. By surfacing and clearly expressing global norms, such a process should improve both the normative and the sociological legitimacy of international criminal law.

Understanding gravity in relation to global values and goals, and acknowledging that the global community has an interest in preventing all harms to human dignity would reduce the importance of the distinction between international and "ordinary" crimes that is central to most theories of international criminality. So-called "ordinary" crimes like murder and rape would no longer be outside the legitimate scope of international criminal law—they would simply not be priorities in light of the global community's greater interest in adjudicating other crimes. This would leave open the possibility that global priorities could change and crimes that are now considered ordinary could become international. Some commentators may object that this approach places insufficient weight on the value of sovereignty. But sovereignty should not be viewed as a limit on legitimate global *prescriptive* authority. Instead, sovereignty should be one of the values that is considered in determining when global *adjudicative* authority ought to be exercised. The next chapter develops this argument.

4

Global Adjudicative Authority

In Chapter 3, I argued that the justification that underpins most theories of global prescriptive authority—the idea that certain crimes meet an unspecified gravity threshold—lacks adequate normative foundation and therefore undermines the regime's legitimacy. The same is true of efforts to justify global adjudicative authority. Global adjudicative authority is the authority that national and supranational institutions exercise when they adjudicate crimes on behalf of the global community. This includes exercises of authority by the International Criminal Court (ICC), but also, at least arguably, by *ad hoc* and hybrid tribunals.[1] It also includes adjudication of international crimes in national courts under the principle of universal jurisdiction.

The most common argument in favor of adjudication in any of these fora is that the crimes at issue are so grave that the international community must seek accountability when the national courts with primary jurisdiction fail to do so. Many commentators combine the prescriptive and adjudicative jurisdiction arguments, asserting that when crimes are sufficiently grave to be called "international," adjudication at the global level is automatically justified. These arguments all rest on the flawed assumption that gravity has sufficient agreed content to justify supranational authority. In fact, the concept of gravity, as currently understood, cannot adequately justify either global prescriptive or adjudicative authority.

Moreover, distinguishing between the two kinds of global authority is important for legitimacy analysis because each has a distinct normative basis. As argued in Chapter 3, the moral justification for global prescription is the global community's interest in preventing harm to human dignity. Global prescription is thus justified for all non-minimal harms to human dignity, and is most strongly legitimate for those in which the global community has the greatest interest. In contrast, the legitimacy of global adjudication depends not only on the strength of the global community's interest in adjudication, but also on whether that interest outweighs any countervailing interests.

There are thus two requirements for legitimate global adjudication: (1) that the case involves harm to human dignity that merits criminal sanction; and (2) that the

---

[1] As I explained in Chapter 1, the extent to which *ad hoc* and hybrid tribunals operate on behalf of the global community is unclear. This makes the applicability to them of the theory of global legitimacy elaborated herein debatable. See Chapter 1, section III.

Shocking the Conscience of Humanity. Margaret M. deGuzman, Oxford University Press (2020). © Margaret M. deGuzman. DOI: 10.1093/oso/9780198786153.001.0001

global community's interest in adjudication outweighs any competing interests, usually national interests. Additionally, global adjudication is *most strongly* legitimate when it concerns situations and cases for which global adjudication is likely to be most effective, that is, likely to achieve efficiently the global community's most important goals.

If gravity is to promote the legitimacy of global adjudication, therefore, it must be reconceptualized as a function of global values and goals. Articulated in this way, gravity can help to ensure that each of the conditions above is met. First, gravity can provide a threshold below which global adjudication is illegitimate because the case does not sufficiently implicate the value of human dignity. Second, gravity can serve as a measure of the global interest in preventing harm to human dignity, excluding cases in which that interest is insufficiently strong to overcome any countervailing interests. Finally, gravity can help decision-makers select among the situations and cases in which global adjudication is legitimate, those for which such adjudication is most strongly legitimate because it will be most effective.

The argument in this chapter unfolds in three stages. First, the chapter critiques current uses of gravity to justify global adjudication, explaining how the failure adequately to link gravity to values and goals undermines the regime's legitimacy. Treating gravity as a goal-independent concept causes decision-makers to neglect the important community-building task of identifying institutional goals and establishing priorities among them. Second, it explains how gravity should be employed to enhance the legitimacy of global adjudication. Finally, it describes how the theory could be implemented by various institutions of international criminal law, including the ICC, *ad hoc* and hybrid tribunals, and national courts asserting universal jurisdiction.

I. Goal-Independent Gravity

When gravity is used to justify global adjudication, it is usually framed as a goal-independent concept, often a threshold. Advocates and commentators assert that a particular case or situation is *sufficiently* grave to warrant global adjudication without explaining how adjudication would promote appropriate values or goals. Yet the real work of justification involves identifying values and goals, and explaining how choices promote them. In this section, I critique the most common invocations of gravity to support the exercise of global adjudicative authority, including to justify decisions: (1) creating tribunals, and referring and admitting situations at the ICC; (2) admitting cases at the ICC and *ad hoc* tribunals; (3) selecting among admissible situations and cases; and (4) adjudicating international crimes in national courts under the principle of universal jurisdiction.

A. Creating Tribunals and Referring and Admitting Situations

Political actors have long relied on claims about gravity, in particular gravity thresholds, to justify decisions to create supranational criminal courts, and, more recently, to refer situations to the ICC. The political leaders who create *ad hoc* tribunals, and the Prosecutors and judges who run them, justify many of their actions by reference to the extreme gravity of the crimes at issue.[2] In opening the Nuremberg Trial, Robert Jackson famously asserted: "The wrongs which we seek to condemn and punish have been so calculated, so malignant, and so devastating, that civilization cannot tolerate their being ignored, because it cannot survive their being repeated."[3] In explaining why the creation of the International Criminal Tribunal for the Former Yugoslavia (ICTY) was a necessary measure to promote peace and security, the UN Security Council:

> express[ed] ... its grave alarm at continuing reports of widespread and flagrant violations of international humanitarian law ... including reports of mass killings, massive, organized and systematic detention and rape of women and the continuance of the practice of "ethnic cleansing."[4]

The Security Council made similar statements in creating the International Criminal Tribunal for Rwanda (ICTR).[5] The ICTY's judges rejected a challenge to the ICTY's legality partly on the grounds that the crimes in question "affect the whole of mankind and shock the conscience of all nations of the world ...."[6] In referring the Libya situation to the ICC, the Security Council stressed the need to hold accountable those responsible for "widespread and systematic attacks ... against the civilian population" that may amount to crimes against humanity.[7]

Such gravity-based justifications rely implicitly, and sometimes explicitly, on the idea that crimes that pass a gravity threshold are the legitimate subjects of global adjudication. When the ICTY Appeals Chamber said in *Prosecutor v. Tadić* that its jurisdiction was appropriate because the crimes "shock the conscience" of the

---

[2] See 'Judgment of the Nuremberg Military Tribunal 1946' (1947) 41 AJIL 172, 186.

[3] Robert H. Jackson, 'Opening Statement Before the International Military Tribunal', International Military Tribunal, Nuremberg, held on November 21, 1945, available at https://www.roberthjackson.org/speech-and-writing/opening-statement-before-the-international-military-tribunal/ (last accessed on July 30, 2019).

[4] Statute of the ICTY (adopted on May 25, 1993) UN Doc. S/RES/827 preamble (stating that the Tribunal has the authority to punish "serious violations of international humanitarian law").

[5] Statute of the ICTR (November 8, 1994) UN Doc. S/RES/955 preamble ("Expressing once again its grave concern at the reports indicating that genocide and other systematic, widespread and flagrant violations of international humanitarian law have been committed in Rwanda").

[6] *Prosecutor v. Tadić* (Decision on the Defence Motion for Interlocutory Appeal on Jurisdiction) IT-94-1 (October 2, 1995) para. 59 (citing *Prosecutor v. Tadić* (Decision on the Defence Motion on Jurisdiction) IT-94-1 (August 10, 1995) para. 42).

[7] UNSC Res. 1970 (February 26, 2011) UN Doc. S/RES/1970 preamble.

world, what it meant was that the crimes passed a gravity threshold above which global adjudication is legitimate. Indeed, like the Security Council resolution in the Libya situation quoted above, such statements sometimes suggest that once the gravity threshold is reached, adjudication is not just permitted, but required. Yet the political actors who create tribunals and refer situations to the ICC rarely specify what they believe makes situations grave enough to warrant international action beyond occasional references to the numbers of people harmed. Gravity in this context has very little agreed content.

In contrast, because the Rome Statute contains an explicit gravity threshold for the admissibility of situations and cases, the ICC's prosecutors and judges have had to grapple with the meaning of gravity. Article 53 of the Statute which governs the initiation of investigations, requires the Prosecutor to ascertain the admissibility of potential cases by, inter alia, determining whether such cases are "of sufficient gravity to justify ... action by the Court" as required by Article 17(d).[8] The Prosecutor has developed policies regarding how to assess whether cases and situations meet the gravity threshold. The ICC's judges have also addressed the meaning of gravity in a number of contexts including when resolving admissibility challenges,[9] deciding whether to confirm charges,[10] and addressing the Prosecutor's requests to open investigations on her own motion.[11]

Two gravity threshold tests have emerged from the ICC's jurisprudence and prosecutorial policies: one related to the admissibility of situations (the situation gravity threshold) and one pertaining to the admissibility of cases (the case gravity threshold). The tests are interrelated because assessing whether a situation meets the gravity threshold requires determining whether the potential cases in the situation are likely to meet the case gravity threshold. Thus, although this section addresses the situation gravity threshold, reserving case gravity for the next section, much of the analysis applies in both contexts. As will be shown, neither test adequately justifies the exercise of adjudicative authority at the ICC.

The ICC's situation gravity threshold, like most gravity tests in the case law and literature, has been interpreted to require consideration of various quantitative and qualitative factors. The case law and prosecutorial policies term the quantitative aspect "scale" and list the qualitative factors as: the nature of the crimes,

---

[8] Rome Statute of the ICC (adopted on July 17, 1998, entered into force on July 1, 2001) arts. 17 and 53. A "situation" is a geographic and sometimes temporal space in which crimes within the jurisdiction of the Court appear to have been committed.

[9] See, e.g., *Prosecutor v. Blé Goudé* (Pre-Trial Chamber Decision on the Defence Challenge to the Admissibility of the Case Against Charles Blé Goudé for Insufficient Gravity) ICC-02/11-02/11 (November 12, 2014) para. 11.

[10] See, e.g., *Prosecutor v. Abu Garda* (Pre-Trial Chamber Decision on the Confirmation of Charges) ICC-02/05-02/09 (February 8, 2010) para. 30.

[11] *Situation in the Republic of Kenya* (Decision Pursuant to Article 15 of the Rome Statute on the Authorization of an Investigation into the Situation in the Republic of Kenya) ICC-01/09-19 (March 31, 2010) para. 62.

the manner in which they were committed, and their impact.[12] The Prosecutor's Office has further clarified its understanding of gravity by elaborating sub-factors to be considered in making determinations about each factor.[13] "Scale" is defined to mean: "*inter alia*, the number of direct and indirect victims, the extent of the damage caused by the crimes, in particular the bodily or psychological harm caused to the victims and their families, or their geographical or temporal spread …."[14] The "nature of the crimes" is elaborated as "the specific elements of each offence such as killings, rapes and other crimes involving sexual or gender violence and crimes committed against children, persecution, or the imposition of conditions of life on a group calculated to bring about its destruction."[15] The "manner of commission of the crimes" is to be assessed by reference to, among other things:

> the means employed to execute the crime, the degree of participation and intent of the perpetrator (if discernible at this stage), the extent to which the crimes were systematic or result from a plan or organised policy or otherwise resulted from the abuse of power or official capacity, and elements of particular cruelty, including the vulnerability of the victims, any motives involving discrimination, or the use of rape and sexual violence as a means of destroying groups.[16]

And "the impact of the crimes" includes "*inter alia*, the sufferings endured by the victims and their increased vulnerability; the terror subsequently instilled, or the social, economic and environmental damage inflicted on the affected communities."[17]

The judges have largely followed the Prosecutor's lead in analyzing and applying the situation gravity threshold, adopting the same four-factor test and similar sub-factors.[18] The Pre-Trial Chamber in the Kenya situation added one requirement, however, holding that the situation gravity threshold is met only if the suspects likely to be investigated in a situation include the persons who bear the greatest responsibility for the crimes alleged.[19] This requirement may constitute

---

[12] See, e.g., Ibid.; Regulations of the Office of the Prosecutor, ICC-OTP Doc. ICC-BD/05-01-09 (April 23, 2009) reg. 29(2); ICC-OTP, 'Policy Paper on Preliminary Examinations' (November 2013) paras. 59–66.

[13] ICC-OTP, 'Policy Paper on Preliminary Examinations' (n. 12) paras. 62–5; ICC Office of the Prosecutor, 'Policy Paper on Case Selection and Prioritisation' (September 15, 2016) paras. 35–41.

[14] ICC-OTP, 'Policy Paper on Preliminary Investigations' (n. 12) para. 62.

[15] Ibid. para. 63.

[16] Ibid. para. 64.

[17] Ibid. para. 65.

[18] See, e.g., *Situation in the Republic of Kenya* (Decision Pursuant to Article 15 of the Rome Statute on the Authorization of an Investigation into the Situation in the Republic of Kenya) (n. 11) para. 62; *Situation on the Register Vessels of the Union of the Comoros* (Decision on the Request of the Union of Comoros to Review the Prosecutor's Decision not to Initiate an Investigation) ICC-01/13 (July 16, 2015) para. 2; *Situation in Georgia* (Decision on the Prosecutor's Request for Authorization of an Investigation) ICC-01/15 (January 27, 2016) para. 51.

[19] See, e.g., *Situation in the Republic of Kenya* (Decision Pursuant to Article 15 of the Rome Statute on the Authorization of an Investigation into the Situation in the Republic of Kenya) (n. 11) para. 60.

an important limit on the Prosecutor's ability to initiate investigations. Prosecutor Fatou Bensouda cited it in explaining why she decided not to open a preliminary examination into the situation of ISIS crimes committed by nationals of states parties to the Rome Statute. She asserted that because "ISIS is a military and political organisation primarily led by nationals of Iraq and Syria," which are not parties to the Rome Statute, "the prospects of [her] Office investigating and prosecuting those most responsible, within the leadership of ISIS, appear limited."[20] She therefore concluded "that the jurisdictional basis for opening a preliminary examination into this situation is too narrow at this stage."[21] This was notwithstanding her finding that: "The atrocities allegedly committed by ISIS undoubtedly constitute serious crimes of concern to the international community and threaten the peace, security and well-being of the region, and the world."[22]

The Prosecutor has cited other aspects of the gravity threshold to justify decisions not to investigate other situations. In the first such decision, Bensouda's predecessor, Luis Moreno-Ocampo, determined that a situation involving war crimes allegedly committed by British soldiers in Iraq did not meet the gravity threshold.[23] Although he found reasonable grounds to believe war crimes were committed, he asserted that the number of willful killings—between four and twelve—was low compared to the other situations before the Court, which involved thousands of deaths.[24]

Bensouda also used the gravity threshold to justify a decision not to investigate a situation referred to the Court by a state party, the Union of the Comoros. The Israeli Defense Forces (IDF) had intercepted a humanitarian flotilla en route to the Gaza strip and boarded the vessels, killing ten people, injuring fifty, and allegedly committing hundreds of instances of outrages upon personal dignity and possibly torture. Although Bensouda found reasonable grounds to believe war crimes were committed, she determined that the situation did not meet the gravity threshold for several reasons. First, mirroring her predecessor's view of the Iraq situation, she found that "the total number of victims ... reached relatively limited proportions as compared, generally, to other cases investigated by the Office."[25] Second, the crimes were not systematic or the result of a plan or policy; and finally, they did not have a significant impact beyond the immediate victims and their families.[26]

---

[20] ICC-OTP 'Statement of the Prosecutor of the International Criminal Court, Fatou Bensouda, on the alleged crimes committed by ISIS' (April 8, 2015), available at https:/www.icc-cpi.int/Pages/item. aspx?name=otp-stat-08-04-2015-1 (last accessed on September 26, 2019).

[21] Ibid.

[22] Ibid.

[23] ICC-OTP 'Letter Concerning the Situation in Iraq' (February 9, 2006) 8–9. The Prosecutor also found that the situation did not appear to meet the permissive threshold of Article 8(1).

[24] Ibid.

[25] *Situation on the Registered Vessels of the Union of Comoros, the Hellenic Republic and the Kingdom of Cambodia* (Article 53(1) Report) ICC-01/13-6-AnxA (November 6, 2014) para. 138.

[26] Ibid. paras. 137 and 141.

The Comoros appealed the Prosecutor's decision, provoking a review by the Pre-Trial Chamber. A majority of the Pre-Trial Chamber judges disagreed with Bensouda's analysis, asserting, inter alia, that the number of victims was sufficiently high, and that a broad impact is not necessary to meet the gravity threshold.[27] The Pre-Trial Chamber therefore requested the Prosecutor to reconsider, as they are permitted to do by Article 53 of the Rome Statute.[28] One judge dissented, opining that the Prosecutor enjoys a "margin of discretion" in determining whether the gravity threshold is met.[29] Upon reconsideration, the Prosecutor issued a 145-page decision, essentially reiterating her original view.[30] The Pre-Trial Chamber then issued a decision asking the Prosecutor to reconsider her decision a second time, this time in accordance with the findings of the Pre-Trial Chamber.[31] The Appeals Chamber resolved the matter, holding that the Prosecutor enjoys a "margin of appreciation" in evaluating gravity for purposes of determining whether to initiate an investigation.[32]

The ICC's judges have yet to find that a situation falls below the gravity threshold, and have several times applied the factor-based approach to hold that situations meet the threshold. In the Kenya situation, for instance, the Pre-Trial Chamber noted that the scale of the crimes involved over 1,000 murders, 900 rapes, and 350,000 displaced persons;[33] the manner in which the crimes were committed included "a degree of brutality" such as cutting off body parts;[34] the impact of the crimes on the victims included psychological trauma and social stigma;[35] and those likely to be prosecuted included people in high-ranking positions who played significant roles in the crimes.[36] Based on these findings, the Court concluded that: "the general gravity threshold under Article 17(1)(d) of the Statute is met."[37]

---

[27] *Situation on the Registered Vessels of the Union of Comoros, the Hellenic Republic and the Kingdom of Cambodia* (Decision on the request of the Union of the Comoros to review the Prosecutor's decision not to initiate an investigation) ICC-01/13-34 (July 16, 2015) para. 49.

[28] Ibid. para. 50

[29] *Situation on the Registered Vessels of the Union of the Comoros, the Hellenic Republic and the Kingdom of Cambodia* (Partly Dissenting Opinion of Judge Peter Kovacs) ICC-01/13-34-Anx (July 16, 2015) para. 8.

[30] *Situation on the Registered Vessels of the Union of Comoros, the Hellenic Republic of Greece and the Kingdom of Cambodia* (Final Decision of the Prosecution concerning the "Article 53(1) Report" (ICC-01/13-6-AnxA), dated November 6, 2014 *with* Public Annexes A-C, E-G and Confidential Annex D) ICC-01/13-57-Anx1 (November 29, 2017) para. 332.

[31] *Situation on the Registered Vessels of the Union of Comoros, the Hellenic Republic of Greece and the Kingdom of Cambodia* (Decision on the "Application for Judicial Review by the Government of the Union of Comoros") ICC-01/13-68 (November 15, 2018) paras. 96–101.

[32] *Situation on the Registered Vessels of the Union of Comoros, the Hellenic Republic of Greece and the Kingdom of Cambodia* (Judgment on the Appeal of the Prosecutor against the Pre-Trial Chamber I's "Decision on the 'Application for Judicial Review by the Government of the Union of Comoros' ") ICC-01/13-98 (September 2, 2019) para. 81.

[33] *Situation in the Republic of Kenya* (Decision Pursuant to Article 15 of the Rome Statute on the Authorization of an Investigation into the Situation in the Republic of Kenya) (n. 11) para. 190.

[34] Ibid. paras. 192–3.

[35] Ibid. para. 194.

[36] Ibid. para. 198.

[37] Ibid. para. 200.

These policies and decisions do not strongly support the legitimacy of ICC decisions to adjudicate situations because they are not clearly grounded in global values and goals. The Prosecutor and judges endeavor to imbue the gravity factors with global values. For instance, the Prosecutor's Policy Paper on Preliminary Examinations asserts that the scale of the crimes will be assessed with particular attention to the "bodily or psychological harm" they cause, implying that these types of harms are more important to the global community, or at least to the ICC, than, for instance, economic harm. With respect to the nature of the crimes, it makes particular mention of certain crimes, including crimes "involving sexual or gender violence and crimes committed against children," implying that a particular goal of the ICC is to address such crimes. Regarding manner of commission, the Policy Paper suggests that crimes involving abuse of power are of particular concern to the Court, among others. In discussing the impact of the crimes, the Policy Paper implies that instillation of terror and damage to the environment are impacts that deserve special attention.

Such value articulation is useful in constructing the global justice community because it facilitates dialogue about the ICC's role in the world. This dialogue has started to take place among scholars, activists, and even states parties to the ICC. Nonetheless, the current process for assessing the situation gravity threshold fails fully to support the ICC's legitimacy because it does not explain how the articulated values affect the threshold—that is, how they determine which situations are appropriate subjects of ICC adjudication. Although values are part of the decision-making process, the decision is not grounded in values. Rather, the various factors, including the values they reflect, are considered in an aggregative way that leaves it unclear which values actually motivate situation gravity decisions.

The current approach to gravity appeals to prosecutors and judges because it purports to avoid subjective judgments about which values and goals are most important to the global community, determinations that often invite criticism. These institutional actors tend to portray their decisions as resting in the "objective" application of law.[38] Both the Policy Paper on Preliminary Examinations and the Prosecutor's Policy Paper on Case Selection discussed below highlight the "objective" nature of the decision-making process.[39] Likewise, the judges present their gravity determinations as involving a simple application of criteria to a factual situation.[40]

---

[38] See, e.g., Louis Moreno-Ocampo, Prosecutor of the International Criminal Court, Informal Meeting of Legal Advisors of Ministers of Foreign Affairs, New York (October 24, 2005) 6.

[39] According to the Policy Paper on Preliminary Examinations, the Office of the Prosecutor (OTP) is "require[d] to focus its efforts objectively on those most responsible for the most serious crimes within the situation ... " (n. 12) para. 66. See also ICC-OTP, 'Policy Paper on Preliminary Examinations' (n. 12) para. 28; ICC-OTP, 'Policy Paper on Case Selection and Prioritisation' (n. 13) para. 19. However, the policy papers also acknowledge that they provide guidelines, rather than clear rules. See, e.g., ICC-OTP, 'Policy Paper on Preliminary Examinations' (n. 12) para 1.

[40] See *Situation in the Republic of Kenya* (Decision Pursuant to Article 15 of the Rome Statute on the Authorization of an Investigation into the Situation in the Republic of Kenya) (n. 11) paras. 197–9.

To better promote the ICC's legitimacy, political actors could take a more active role in determining guiding values and goals, including articulating how
the ICC ought to apply the situation gravity threshold. The Assembly of States
Parties is the most appropriate body to define the Court's mission, including explaining when it should exercise adjudicative authority. Indeed, the Prosecutor
has pleaded with the Assembly to do just that.[41] However, states parties to the
ICC have made little progress in this regard, either at the Rome Conference
where the Statute was adopted, or at the subsequent meetings of the Assembly.[42]
As explained earlier, this may be due to the usefulness of leaving gravity ambiguous, which enabled states with different visions of the Court's mission to
support the institution.

Unfortunately, the current approach to the gravity threshold increasingly
threatens the ICC's legitimacy, making it imperative for the Court to act if the
states parties continue to fail in this regard. The problem is not one of moral legitimacy. As I argue below, the gravity threshold for admissibility ought to be a minimal one that excludes only situations in which criminal punishment is arguably
unwarranted. All of the Court's admissibility decisions to date meet this requirement. However, the legal legitimacy of the decisions is more problematic because
they are not rooted in clear legal norms.

Moreover, the absence of clarity about what motivates gravity threshold decisions threatens the Court's sociological legitimacy. The gravity factors are
highly malleable, and can be used to support most outcomes. There are easy
cases at either end of the spectrum: Most people will consider a situation grave
when it involves a very large number of victims of particularly harmful crimes
like murder and rape, and will deem a situation involving little or no harm to
persons or property not to be very serious. But most situations are in the vast
middle: they inflict very serious harm on a small number of victims; or they impose more modest harm on huge numbers of people; or they affect few victims
directly but a large number indirectly; or they harm no person, but devastate
important property or the environment; and so on. Factors can be cited to label
all such situations grave.

In light of this malleability, observers are often skeptical when prosecutors and
judges claim to have determined gravity "objectively." Because there are so many

---

[41] See Luis Moreno-Ocampo, 'Statement at Informal Meeting of Legal Advisors of Ministries of
Foreign Affairs' 9 (October 24, 2005) 9, available at https://www.icc-cpi.int/NR/rdonlyres/9D70039E-
4BEC-4F32-9D4A-CEA8B6799E37/143836/LMO_20051024_English.pdf (last accessed on November
28, 2019) (asking states parties to reflect on "the desired scope and role of the Court").
[42] Recently, some efforts have been made within the ICC Bureau to encourage states parties to take
a more active role in various aspects of Court management, including case selection. See Bureau of the
Assembly of States Parties, 'Meeting the Challenges of Today for a Stronger Court Tomorrow: Matrix
Over Possible Areas of Strengthening the Court and Rome Statute System' (July 15, 2019) Draft Non-
Paper; Letter from Bureau of the Assembly of States Parties to Bureau Members, ASP/2019/32 (July
15, 2019).

ways to view a situation as grave, determinations that a situation meets the gravity threshold are criticized less often than decisions that they fail to do so. For instance, Moreno-Ocampo's decision that alleged British war crimes in Iraq did not meet the gravity threshold was heavily criticized.[43] Some critics felt the situation was especially grave because it involved international crimes by a major world power,[44] and others opined that the context of illegal armed conflict made the British crimes especially appropriate subjects of global adjudication.[45] Indeed, the Prosecutor's effort to clothe the decision in objectively determined gravity criteria may have fueled suspicions that his real motives were political—to avoid incurring the ire of powerful governments. Bensouda has encountered similar criticism for her decision not to investigate the Comoros situation.[46] Some observers have questioned whether the decision was really based on gravity or on a desire to avoid alienating Israel, and its close ally, the United States.[47]

By linking the gravity threshold more clearly to institutional values and goals, the ICC can promote the legitimacy of its decisions about whether to admit situations. Although some observers will likely criticize whatever threshold the ICC identifies, the debates that ensue will be grounded in views about the ICC's role in the world, rather than in speculation about the true motives behind admissibility decisions. Such dialogue about the ICC's role will help to build the global justice community.

[43] See, e.g., William A. Schabas, 'Prosecutorial Discretion v. Judicial Activism at the International Criminal Court' (2008) 6 J. Intl. Crim. Justice 731, 740–1; Kaveri Vaid, 'Discretion Operationalized Through Law: *Proprio Motu* Decision-Making at the International Criminal Court' (2013) 25 Florida J. Intl. L. 359, 393–4; Ray Murphy, 'Gravity Issues and the International Criminal Court' (2006) 17 Crim. L.F. 281, 311.

[44] See, e.g., Jonathan Hafetz, 'Fairness, Legitimacy, and Selection Decisions in International Criminal Law' (2017) 50 Vanderbilt J. Transnational L. 1133, 1142; Nadia Shamsi, 'The ICC: A Political Tool: How the Rome Statute is Susceptible to the Pressures of More Power States' (2016) 24 Willamette J. Intl. & Dispute Resolution 85, 100–1.

[45] Murat Metin Hakki, 'War Crimes and the War in Iraq: Can George W. Bush and Tony Blair be Held Legally Responsible?' (2006) 10 Intl. J. Human Rights 3, 15–16; See also Schabas (n. 43) 742–3 (criticizing the court for not considering "the 'social alarm' in the international community created by the invasion of Iraq and by the atrocities committed by British troops" and pointing out that there was "more combat-related deaths in Iraq following the British and American invasion than in the DRC and Uganda combined").

[46] See, e.g., Sarah Lazare, 'Outrage as ICC Drops Case Against Israel for Deadly Attack on Humanitarian Flotilla', Common Dreams (November 6, 2014), available at https://www.commondreams.org/news/2014/11/06/outrage-icc-drops-case-against-israel-deadly-attack-humanitarian-flotilla (last accessed on July 31, 2019); Center for Constitutional Rights, 'CCR Outraged by ICC Refusal to Investigate Israel War Crimes in Flotilla Attack that Left Nine Dead', Center for Constitutional Rights, New York (November 6, 2014), available at https://ccrjustice.org/home/press-center/press-releases/ccr-outraged-icc-refusal-investigate-israel-war-crimes-flotilla (last accessed on September 9, 2019).

[47] See, e.g., Hans Köchler, 'Justice and Realpolitik: The Predicament of the International Criminal Court' (2017) Chinese J. Intl. L. 1, 6. The ICC Prosecutor has not entirely avoided investigations involving powerful states, however. The Prosecutor's Office has opened an investigation into the situation in Georgia, which involves potential Russian defendants, and sought to open an investigation into the situation in Afghanistan, which could have involved US defendants.

B. Admitting Cases

Once a situation is admitted before the ICC, the Court's Prosecutor and judges have applied essentially the same factor-based test to determine whether particular cases are sufficiently grave to be admissible: the case gravity threshold. The principal difference between the situation and case gravity thresholds is that the latter occurs at a later stage and no longer requires inquiry into the cases likely to come before the Court, but rather examines a case under adjudication. The Court has held that the Statute's use of the word "case" rather than "crime" means that in addition to the crime being grave, the perpetrator's level of responsibility must be sufficiently significant.[48] However, it held this to be a very low threshold, excluding only levels of responsibility that do not generally give rise to criminal liability.[49]

The most comprehensive effort to explain the case gravity threshold came in an early Pre-Trial decision that was overturned on appeal. In the case against Thomas Lubanga and Bosco Ntaganda, the Pre-Trial Chamber identified substantive requirements for the case gravity threshold and held that the case against Ntaganda did not meet them.[50] The Chamber interpreted the threshold to require that the crimes at issue be large scale or systematic, which they said should be analyzed in part by taking account of the "social alarm" the crimes caused.[51] They also said that the accused must be among the senior leaders most responsible for the crimes.[52] The Chamber reasoned that interpreting the gravity threshold in this way would best promote the Court's central goal of deterring serious crimes.[53] In overturning the decision, the Appeals Chamber noted that interpreting the gravity threshold to require large-scale or systematic conduct is incompatible with the Court's broader subject matter jurisdiction over war crimes; and restricting admissibility to cases involving the most responsible senior leaders would amount to a modification of the Court's personal jurisdiction, and could undermine deterrence.[54] Having rejected the Pre-Trial Chamber's interpretation of the gravity threshold, the Appeals Chamber declined to offer one of its own. However, one judge, writing separately, expressed the view that the threshold should be interpreted as excluding only cases that are "insignificant in themselves; where the criminality on the part of the culprit is wholly marginal; borderline cases."[55] He explained that giving additional

---

[48] *Prosecutor v. Callixte Mbarushimana* (Decision on the Confirmation of Charges) ICC-01/04-01/10 (December 16, 2011) para. 276.

[49] Ibid. para. 277.

[50] *Situation in the Democratic Republic of Congo* (Decision on the Prosecutor's Application for Warrants of Arrest, Article 58) ICC-01/04-01/07 (February 10, 2006) para. 89.

[51] Ibid. para. 46.

[52] Ibid. para. 51.

[53] Ibid. para. 55.

[54] *Situation in the Democratic Republic of Congo* (Judgment on the Prosecutor's Appeal Against the Decision of Pre-Trial Chamber I entitled "Decision on the Prosecutor's Application for Warrants of Arrest, Article 58") ICC-01-04-169 (July 13, 2006) paras. 69–79.

[55] *Situation in the Democratic Republic of the Congo* (Judgment on the Prosecutor's Appeal Against the Decision of Pre-Trial Chamber I entitled "Decision on the Prosecutor's Application for Warrants of

content to the gravity threshold as the Pre-Trial Chamber did would amount to a rewriting of the Court's jurisdiction and would undermine the goal of ending impunity.[56] He opined that if the Statute's drafters had wanted "to limit justiciable crimes under the Statute to the most serious ones, they would have established the necessary criteria for their classification."[57]

As a result of the Appeals Chamber decision, subsequent efforts to apply the gravity threshold to determine the admissibility of cases have failed to endow the provision with much substance.[58] Although the Court has consistently recognized that as a matter of statutory interpretation the gravity threshold for admissibility necessarily requires some gravity beyond that already required by the definitions of crimes within the Court's jurisdiction, the judges have largely avoided specific pronouncements about what this entails.[59] Instead, they apply the same flexible, factor-based method that they do for the situation gravity threshold. They consider quantitative factors, especially the number of victims, and qualitative factors: the nature, manner, and impact of the crimes.[60] In elaborating on the qualitative factors, the judges look to the provision of the Court's Rules of Procedure and Evidence governing gravity for sentencing purposes. This requires consideration of "the extent of the damage caused, in particular the harm caused to the victims and their families, the nature of the unlawful behaviour and the means employed to execute the crime."[61]

The flexibility of this factor-based case gravity test has enabled the Court to conclude that all of the cases it has considered are sufficiently grave to meet the threshold. Two of the more controversial decisions in this regard involved the killing of twelve peacekeepers in the Sudan situation and the destruction of cultural property in the Mali situation. In confirming the charges against Bahar Idriss Abu Garda in the peacekeeper case, the Pre-Trial Chamber held that the gravity threshold was met despite the relatively low number of victims on the grounds that the crime had the broader impact of reducing peacekeeping forces in the area.[62] In the Al Mahdi case, the Court held that the destruction of cultural monuments was sufficient to meet the gravity threshold although it did not involve direct harm to humans.[63]

Arrest, Article 58," Separate and Partly Dissenting Opinion of Judge Georghios M. Pikis) ICC-01/04-169 (February 10, 2006) para. 40.

[56] Ibid. para. 41.
[57] Ibid.
[58] See, e.g., *Prosecutor v. Muthaura et al.* (Decision on the Confirmation of Charges Pursuant to Article 61(7)(a) and (b) of the Rome Statute) ICC-01/09-02/11-382-Red (January 23, 2012) paras. 46–7.
[59] See, e.g., *Situation in the Republic of Kenya* (Decision Pursuant to Article 15 of the Rome Statute on the Authorization of an Investigation into the Situation in the Republic of Kenya) (n. 11) para. 56.
[60] See, e.g., *Abu Garda* (Pre-Trial Chamber Decision on the Confirmation of Charges) (n. 10) para. 31.
[61] ICC Rules of Procedure and Evidence (2002) r. 145(1)(c).
[62] *Abu Garda* (Pre-Trial Chamber Decision on the Confirmation of Charges) (n. 10) paras. 33–4.
[63] *Prosecutor v. Al Mahdi*, (Judgment) ICC-01/12-01/15-171 (September 27, 2016) paras. 77–82.

The ICC Office of the Prosecutor has also used the case gravity threshold to justify prosecuting rebel leaders rather than government forces in situations in which both are believed to have committed serious crimes.[64]

The Court's approach to the case gravity threshold is subject to the same critique as the situation gravity threshold: it undermines legitimacy by failing adequately to link admissibility to the values and goals that ought to guide the ICC's work. Because the gravity threshold ought to be minimal for the reasons I explain below, this failure does not threaten the Court's moral legitimacy: the cases it has admitted all clearly involve harm to human dignity that warrants criminal sanction. However, the absence of clear legal norms guiding admissibility undermines the Court's legal legitimacy; and its inability adequately to justify admissibility threatens its sociological legitimacy. Like decisions applying the factor-based gravity threshold to situations, case gravity threshold decisions have been criticized, often on the grounds that they are motivated by improper considerations, including political power.[65]

Other international courts have applied case gravity thresholds in similar ways, and are subject to similar criticisms. Although the *ad hoc* tribunals had no gravity threshold in their statutes, the concept was central to the tribunals' "completion strategies." In order to facilitate the eventual closure of the tribunals, the Security Council determined that prosecutions should focus on "the most senior leaders suspected of being most responsible" for crimes within the tribunals' jurisdictions, leaving less serious cases to national courts.[66] In response, the tribunals adopted Rule 11*bis*, which required them to transfer to national courts cases that failed to meet the gravity threshold.[67] In this context, as at the ICC, the gravity threshold was factor-based and highly malleable.[68]

---

[64] See, e.g., Luis Moreno-Ocampo, 'Statement by the Chief Prosecutor on the Uganda Arrest Warrants', The Hague (October 14, 2005) 2–3, available at https://www.icc-cpi.int/nr/rdonlyres/3255817D-fd00-4072-9F58-fdb869F9B7cf/143834/lmo_20051014_English1.pdf (last accessed on November 28, 2019).

[65] See, e.g., Matthew Happold, 'The International Criminal Court and the Lord's Resistance Army' (2007) 8 Melbourne J. Intl. L. 159, 170–3 (discussing the ICC Prosecutor's decision not to charge government offenders in Uganda); Hafetz (n. 44) 1135 (stating that, "[i]n practice, the ICC's docket has deepened the perception that the selection of situations and cases for investigation and prosecution remains heavily influenced by structural, strategic, and political considerations …."); Sarah M. H. Nouwen and Wouter G. Werner, 'Doing Justice to the Political: The International Criminal Court in Uganda and Sudan' (2011) 21 Eur. J. Intl. L. 941, 963 (discussing "features of the Court [that] make it … subject to the logic of the political").

[66] UNSC Res 1534 (March 26, 2004) UN Doc. S/RES/1534 para. 5.

[67] ICTY 'Rules of Procedure and Evidence' (adopted on February 11, 1994, amended on July 8, 2015) UN Doc. IT/32/Rev.50 r. 11*bis*; ICTR, 'Rules of Procedure and Evidence' (adopted on June 29, 1995, amended on May 13, 2015) UN Doc. ITR/3/Rev.1 r. 11*bis*.

[68] See, e.g., Lars Waldorf, '"A Mere Pretense": Complementarity, Sham Trials, and Victor's Justice at the Rwanda Tribunal' (2010) 33 Fordham Intl. L.J. 1221, 1258–63; Olympia Bekou, 'Rule 11 *bis*: An Examination of the Process of Referrals to National Courts in ICTY Jurisprudence' (2009) 33 Fordham Intl. L.J. 723, 739–40.

The hybrid tribunals had similar gravity-based limitations built into their jurisdictional structures. The Statute of the Special Court for Sierra Leone (SCSL) limits the court's competence to:

> persons who bear the greatest responsibility for serious violations of international humanitarian law and Sierra Leonean law ... including those leaders who, in committing such crimes, have threatened the establishment of and implementation of the peace process in Sierra Leone.[69]

Likewise, the personal jurisdiction of the Extraordinary Chambers in the Courts of Cambodia (ECCC) is limited to "senior leaders of Democratic Kampuchea and those who were most responsible for the crimes" within the court's temporal jurisdiction.[70]

Like other gravity thresholds, these gravity-based criteria for the courts' exercise of jurisdiction proved difficult to interpret and apply. At the SCSL, the judges debated whether the provision constituted a restriction on the Special Court's jurisdiction or was merely intended as a guide to the prosecutor's discretion.[71] The Appeals Chamber ultimately held in favor of the latter interpretation, thereby avoiding having to interpret the provision.[72] As Charles Jalloh points out, this ruling is dubious as a matter of statutory interpretation,[73] particularly given that the restriction is contained in a provision labeled "competence of the Special Court."[74] At the ECCC, the gravity-based limit on personal jurisdiction provoked intense debates about which suspects should be prosecuted.[75] The controversy pitted the Chambers' international personnel against Cambodian nationals, and remains unresolved.[76]

---

[69] SCSL (signed on January 16, 2002, entered into force on April 12, 2002) 2178 UNTS 145 art. 1.

[70] See Agreement between the United Nations and the Royal Government of Cambodia concerning the prosecution under Cambodian law of crimes committed during the period of Democratic Kampuchea (signed on June 6, 2003, entered into force on April 29, 2005) 2329 UNTS 117 preamble.

[71] Compare *Prosecutor v. Fofana* (Trial Judgment) SCSL-04-14-T-785 (August 2, 2007) para. 91, with *Prosecutor v. Brima et al.* (Trial Judgment) SCSL-04-16-T-613 (June 20, 2007) para. 653.

[72] *Prosecutor v. Brima et al.* (Appeals Judgment) SCSL-04-16-A-675 (February 22, 2008) para. 282.

[73] Charles C. Jalloh, 'Prosecuting Those Bearing "Greatest Responsibility": The Lessons of the Special Court for Sierra Leone' (2013) 96 Marquette L. Rev. 863, 892–3.

[74] SCSL Statute (n. 69) art. 1.

[75] ECCC Office of the Co-Prosecutors, 'Statement of the Co-Prosecutors' (January 5, 2009), available at https://www.eccc.gov.kh/sites/default/files/media/Statement_OCP_05-01-09_EN.pdf (last accessed on August 1, 2019); ECCC Pre-Trial Chamber, 'Considerations of the Pre-Trial Chamber Regarding the Disagreement Between the Co-Prosecutors Pursuant to Internal Rule 71' 001/18-11/2008-ECCC/PTC (August 18, 2009). See also Seth Mydans, 'Cambodia Trial Dispute Runs Deeper' *New York Times* (February 7, 2009), available at www.nytimes.com/2009/01/27/world/asia/27iht-cambo.1.19708207.html (last accessed on August 1, 2019) (detailing the contradictory submissions of the co-prosecutors and failing to come to the required super-majority of justices to make a binding ruling under ECCC rules).

[76] See Open Society Justice Initiative, 'Recent Developments at the Extraordinary Chambers in the Courts of Cambodia' (August 2019) Briefing Paper 6, available at https://www.justiceinitiative.org/uploads/db1828f3-d7ea-4b7b-96bd-1e4e5f46876a/briefing-eccc-recent-developments-20190829.pdf (last accessed on September 9, 2019) (detailing the ongoing conflict).

One case gravity threshold stands out as relatively easy to apply: The jurisdiction of the Special Tribunal for Lebanon (STL) is limited essentially to the killing of a single person, former Prime Minister Rafik Hariri.[77] This is the clearest use of a gravity-based restriction to date. The Security Council found that this particular act of terrorism posed a special threat to international peace and security because it targeted an important political leader.[78] This special threat made the case sufficiently grave to warrant a special tribunal. The clarity of the restriction to the Lebanon Tribunal's mandate helps to illustrate, by contrast, why the gravity-based limitations at the other institutions are problematic.

First, the STL's jurisdiction is unambiguous. Its Statute states: "The Special Tribunal shall have jurisdiction over persons responsible for the attack of 14 February 2005 resulting in the death of former Lebanese Prime Minister Rafik Hariri and in the death or injury of other persons."[79] Additionally, the values and goals that undergird the Lebanon Tribunal's jurisdiction are relatively clear: the goal is to punish those responsible for an important political assassination, thus upholding the value of political self-determination. In contrast, the ICC's gravity threshold lacks a clear indication of animating values and goals.

The ICC's ambiguous gravity threshold poses a greater threat to the legitimacy of that Court than do the limits at the other courts and tribunals due to the ICC's complementarity regime. The other courts and tribunals were either embedded in national court systems or had "primacy" over them, meaning that they had the first right to adjudicate cases within their jurisdictions. In contrast, the ICC is to complement national courts, limiting admissible situations and cases to those over which no national court with jurisdiction is genuinely exercising jurisdiction. When the ICC determines that a case would be admissible because no national court is adjudicating genuinely, but nonetheless fails to meet the gravity threshold, it is suggesting that the case is not appropriate for any form of global adjudication. Such a determination may set a precedent that is applied to exclude similar cases in other situations. In contrast, a determination that a case is insufficiently grave for adjudication at an *ad hoc* tribunal or hybrid court simply suggests that it is more appropriately adjudicated in a national court. Such a ruling is less likely to be applied beyond the particular situation. Because the ICC's interpretation of its gravity threshold has the potential to create impunity gaps and cause far-reaching consequences, it is a particularly serious threat to the ICC's, and indeed the regime's, legitimacy.

---

[77] Agreement between the United Nations and the Lebanese Republic on the Establishment of a STL (with Statute) (signed on January 22, 2007 in Beirut and February 6, 2007 in New York, entered into force on June 10, 2007) 2461 UNTS 257, art. 1.

[78] UNSC Res. 1757 (May 30, 2007) UN Doc. S/RES/1757 preamble ("Reaffirming its determination that this terrorist act and its implications constitute a threat to international peace and security.").

[79] STL Statute (n. 77) art. 1.

C. Discretionary Selection Decisions

In addition to statutory gravity limits, international prosecutors invoke gravity to justify discretionary selection decisions. The ICC Prosecutor has issued a Policy Paper on Case Selection and Prioritisation that establishes gravity, including the perpetrator's level of responsibility, as the central consideration for case selection.[80] The Policy Paper states that the criteria the office uses for discretionary case selection gravity are similar to those used in assessing gravity for purposes of admissibility, except that the test may be stricter in this context in light of limited resources. The Policy Paper then discusses the usual criteria of scale, nature, manner of commission, and impact.

In elaborating the gravity criteria, the Policy Paper largely mirrors the earlier Policy Paper on Preliminary examinations. One notable addition, however, is that with regard to the impact of the crimes, this Policy Paper states that "the Office will give particular consideration to prosecuting Rome Statute crimes that are committed by means of, or that result in, inter alia, the destruction of the environment, the illegal exploitation of natural resources or the illegal dispossession of land."[81] This is a further effort to identify global values and goals for the Court to pursue, and is remarkable because it seeks to bring within the Court's ambit cases that cause harms that are not elements of crimes in the Rome Statute.

With respect to degree of responsibility, the Policy Paper notes that the Office may need to focus on "a limited number of mid- and high-level perpetrators" in order to build cases against those most responsible.[82] The degree of responsibility of an alleged perpetrator is assessed, inter alia, with reference to the nature of their behavior, degree of participation, intent, discrimination, and abuse of power or position.[83] In its Strategic Plan for 2019-21, the Office of the Prosecutor suggested that it may adopt a strategy of building cases up, starting with lower-level perpetrators.[84] The *ad hoc* tribunals adopted similar factor-based processes for determination of case selection gravity.[85]

Unlike the gravity thresholds, for which relative gravity analysis is inappropriate as explained above, in this context, international prosecutors correctly use gravity to measure the relative seriousness of admissible cases. Although not required by law, the use of gravity to select among admissible cases is uncontroversial. International courts and tribunals have limited resources and usually address

---

[80] ICC-OTP, 'Policy Paper on Case Selection and Prioritisation' (n. 13) para. 6.

[81] Ibid. para. 40.

[82] Ibid. para. 42.

[83] Ibid. para. 43.

[84] ICC-OTP, 'Strategic Plan 2019-2021' (July 17, 2019) para. 24.

[85] See, e.g., *Prosecutor v. Jankovic* (Decision on Referral of Case under Rule 11*bis*) IT-96-23/2-PT (July 22, 2005) para. 19 (considering factors in determining gravity such as geographic and temporal scope, number of victims affected, and whether the accused held a leadership role).

situations involving large number of potential cases. There is widespread agreement that prosecutors should use gravity as a central criterion for allocating institutional resources among admissible cases.

Perhaps because this discretionary use of gravity is uncontroversial, international prosecutors have been more willing to explicitly ground their decisions in global values and goals. The ICC Prosecutor has issued policy papers stating some of the values the Prosecutor believes should be given priority. These include a Policy Paper on Sexual and Gender-Based Crimes, which states that such crimes "are among the gravest under the Statute," and that the Prosecutor's Office "pays particular attention" to such crimes "at all stages of its work";[86] and a Policy on Children, which affirms that "whenever the evidence permits" the Prosecutor will seek to charge crimes that particularly affect children.[87] In explaining the choice to prosecute Thomas Lubanga for recruiting and using child soldiers, the ICC Prosecutor noted the importance of expressing the global value of protecting children, asserting that: "Forcing children to be killers jeopardises the future of mankind."[88] Likewise, in explaining the decision to pursue a case involving the destruction of historic monuments, the Prosecutor stated:

> Such attacks affect humanity as a whole. We must stand up to the destruction and defacing of our common heritage ... We will continue to do our part to highlight the severity of such war crimes with the hopes that such efforts will deter the commission of similar crimes in the future.[89]

Likewise, with regard to the case involving the killing of twelve peacekeepers in Sudan, the Prosecutor linked the gravity of the crime to the importance of protecting peacekeepers around the world.[90] In each of these cases, the Prosecutor explained the gravity of the case, and thus justified selecting it, on the basis of the importance to the global community of particular values—protecting children, historic monuments, and peacekeepers—and related preventive goals.

Although these decisions have been criticized, the criticisms do not threaten the ICC's legitimacy in the same way as gravity decisions that are unmoored from global values and goals. In fact, they generate a dialogue about such values and goals that should enhance the Court's legitimacy over time. For instance, in

---

[86] ICC-OTP, 'Policy Paper on Sexual and Gender-Based Crimes' (June 2014) para. 45.

[87] ICC-OTP, 'Policy on Children' (November 2016) para. 95.

[88] ICC-OTP 'Statement by Luis Moreno-Ocampo, Press Conference in relation with the surrender to the Court of Mr. Thomas Lubanga Dyilo' (March 18, 2006) (emphasis omitted).

[89] ICC-OTP, 'Statement of the Prosecutor of the International Criminal Court, following the transfer of the first suspect in the Mali investigation: "Intentional attacks against historic monuments and buildings dedicated to religion are grave crimes"' (September 26, 2015).

[90] ICC-OTP 'Eighth Report of the Prosecutor of the International Criminal Court to the UN Security Council Pursuant to UNSCR 1593' (2005) (December 3, 2008) para 56.

response to the charges against Lubanga, some critics argued that the Prosecutor should have also charged him with crimes of sexual violence.[91] They asserted that preventing such crimes is a particularly important global goal.[92] This critique generated discussions within and outside the Court that may have helped to ensure the inclusion of such charges in later cases.

Other international courts and tribunals have also asserted values and goals as the bases for selection decisions, thereby promoting a dialogic process. For instance, the Prosecutor of the Special Court for Sierra Leone stated that his case selections were based in part on the importance of demonstrating that each of the parties to the conflict had committed international crimes.[93] This generated discussions among participants in, and observers of, international criminal law about whether such distribution of responsibility promotes important goals, such as national reconciliation, or instead, creates a false sense of moral equivalency in situations where responsibility is not equally distributed.[94] As elaborated below, such discussions are an important part of building the global justice community.

The ICC Prosecutor has denied having discretion to select among admissible situations, citing article 53's statement that the Prosecutor "*shall* ... initiate an investigation unless ... she determines that there is no reasonable basis to proceed ...."[95] However, as discussed earlier, when the Prosecutor has declined to investigate situations on the grounds that they do not meet the gravity *threshold* she has justified the decisions in part by reference to the relative gravity of the situation in relation to other situations before the Court. Because determining the gravity threshold does not require a relative analysis, this appears to be an effort to exercise situation selection discretion under the guise of a statutory constraint. This threatens the ICC's legitimacy for the reasons explained earlier: the gravity threshold is currently unmoored from values and goals.

---

[91] See, e.g., Human Rights Watch, 'Joint Letter from Avocats Sans Frontières et al. to the Chief Prosecutor of the International Criminal Court' (July 31, 2006), available at https://www.hrw.org/news/2006/07/31/dr-congo-icc-charges-raise-concern (last accessed on September 9, 2019).

[92] Gloria Gaggioli, 'Sexual Violence in Armed Conflicts: A Violation of International Humanitarian Law and Human Rights Law' (2015) 96 Intl. Rev. Red Cross 503, 505.

[93] See Charles Jalloh, 'Special Court for Sierra Leone: Achieving Justice' (2011) 32 Mich. J. Intl. L. 395, 419.

[94] Compare Matthew Happold, 'The International Criminal Court and the Lord's Resistance Army' (2007) 8 Melbourne J. Intl. L. 159, 172 (discussing the impunity gap that may arise when only one side of a conflict is prosecuted), with Martin Imbleau, 'Initial Truth Establishment' in William Schabas and Shane Darcy (eds.), *Truth Commissions and Courts: The Tension Between Criminal Justice and the Search for Truth* (Springer 2007) 175–6 (discussing the issue of moral equivalency).

[95] Rome Statute (n. 8) art. 53(1) (emphasis added). See also ICC-OTP, 'Policy Paper on the Interests of Justice' (September 2007) 1. The Appeals Chamber has affirmed that the Prosecutor enjoys a "margin of appreciation" in deciding whether to initiate an investigation. See *Situation on the Register Vessels of the Union of the Comoros, the Hellenic Republic of Greece and the Kingdom of Cambodia* (Judgment on the appeal of the Prosecutor against Pre-Trial Chamber I's "Decision on the 'Application for Judicial Review by the Government of the Union of the Comoros'") ICC-01/13-98 (September 2, 2019) para. 81.

D. Exercising Universal Jurisdiction

Gravity is also used to justify the exercise of universal jurisdiction over international crimes by national courts. According to a state representative speaking at the United Nations, universal jurisdiction applies to the "gravest crimes of universal concern."[96] The Princeton Principles on Universal Jurisdiction apply, in the words of one commentator, to: "crimes of such exceptional gravity that they affect the fundamental interests of the international community as a whole."[97] Several judges of the International Court of Justice have opined that universal jurisdiction is permitted for "those crimes regarded as the most heinous by the international community."[98] Many scholars concur. According to Leila Sadat: "The application of universal jurisdiction is predicated largely on the notion that some crimes are so heinous that they offend the interest of all humanity, and, indeed, imperil civilization itself."[99] Noah Feldman justifies universal jurisdiction by reference to a duty of all morally legitimate legal systems to punish "heinous crimes."[100] Alejandro Chehtman argues that universal jurisdiction is morally justified over crimes that are "widespread or systematic," criteria often associated with gravity.[101]

In this context, as in most of those discussed earlier, gravity has little agreed content. Indeed, the scope of universal jurisdiction is even more undertheorized than the jurisdiction of global courts. It is widely acknowledged that universal jurisdiction is not limited to the crimes that are typically considered to most offend humanity—genocide, crimes against humanity, and war crimes—but extends also to crimes like piracy that are not uniformly considered grave.[102] Various treaties require states to extradite or prosecute persons suspected of certain crimes on their territories without limiting the obligation to particularly serious instances of the crimes. The requirements of *aut dedere aut judicare* in the Convention Against Torture and the Geneva Conventions, for instance, extend to single instances of such crimes.[103]

This ambiguity about the nature of crimes eligible for universal jurisdiction was evident when the British House of Lords disagreed in the Pinochet case about

---

[96] UNGA Sixth Committee (67th Session) 'The Scope and Application of the Principle of Universal Jurisdiction' (November 9, 2012) UN Doc. A/C.6/67/SR.12 para. 58.

[97] Stephen Macedo (ed.), *The Princeton Principles on Universal Jurisdiction* (Princeton Project on Universal Jurisdiction 2001) 23.

[98] *Arrest Warrant of 11 April 2000 (Democratic Republic of Congo v. Belgium)* Joint Separate Opinion of Judge Higgins, Kooijmans, & Buergenthal, ICJ Reports 2002 para. 60. See also *Arrest Warrant of 11 April 2000 (Democratic Republic of Congo v. Belgium)* Dissenting Opinion of Judge Van Den Wyngaert, ICJ Reports 2002 para. 46.

[99] Leila Nadya Sadat, 'Exile, Amnesty and International Law' (2006) 81 Notre Dame L. Rev. 955, 975.

[100] Noah Feldman, 'Cosmopolitan Law?' (2007) 116 Yale L.J. 1022, 1063.

[101] Alejandro Chehtman, *The Philosophical Foundations of Extraterritorial Jurisdiction* (Oxford University Press 2010) 119.

[102] For discussion, see Chapter 2, section I.

[103] Convention against Torture and Other Cruel, Inhuman, or Degrading Treatment or Punishment (adopted on December 10, 1984, entered into force on June 26, 1987) 1465 UNTS 85, 113 art. 1.

whether universal jurisdiction over torture is limited to cases involving widespread or systematic torture.[104] National Statutes adopting the doctrine of universal jurisdiction likewise reveal different views as to the meaning of gravity in this context. For instance, Swedish courts are permitted to prosecute any crime, wherever committed, that is punishable by more than four years' imprisonment under Swedish law.[105] In contrast, German law limits universal jurisdiction to genocide, crimes against humanity, and serious war crimes.[106]

When courts exercise universal jurisdiction over international crimes on behalf of the global community, they can be considered part of the international criminal law regime. As such, the confusion surrounding gravity's role in legitimizing the exercise of such jurisdiction can negatively impact upon the regime's legitimacy. When the rhetoric that universal jurisdiction applies to the most serious crimes of concern to the whole international community fails to match the reality of the kinds of crimes and defendants prosecuted, the moral foundations of the system are called into question and perceptions of the regime's legitimacy suffer. Many states have voiced concerns about the potential misuse of universal jurisdiction for political purposes. A decision of the African Union Assembly states:

> The political nature and abuse of the principle of universal jurisdiction by judges from some non-African States against African leaders, particularly Rwanda, is a clear violation of the sovereignty and territorial integrity of these States;
>   The abuse and misuse of indictments against African leaders have a destabilizing effect that will negatively impact on the political, social, and economic development of the States and their ability to conduct international relations.[107]

Failing to clarify the role of gravity in justifying universal jurisdiction can exacerbate such fears by providing a purportedly neutral basis for decision that masks political considerations.

---

[104] Compare *R v. Bow Street Metropolitan Stipendiary Magistrate and others, ex parte Pinochet Ugarte* (No. 3) [2000] 1 AC 147, 273–4 (Lord Millet) ("Significantly, however, the court also held that the scale and international character of the atrocities of which the accused has been convicted fully justified the application of universal jurisdiction."), with *R v. Bow Street Metropolitan Stipendiary Magistrate and others, ex parte Pinochet Ugarte* (No. 3) [2000] 1 AC 147, 264 (Lord Hutton) ("Therefore I consider that a single act of torture carried out or instigated by a public official ... constitutes a crime against international law, and that torture does not become an international crime only when it is committed or instigated on a large scale.").

[105] See Swedish Penal Code, 1962:700 Brottsbalken, Chapter 2, s. 3, art. 7.

[106] Criminal Code in the version promulgated on November 13, 1998, *Bundesgesetzblatt* [Federal Law Gazette] I p. 3322, last amended by Article 1 of the Law of September 24, 2013, Federal Law Gazette I p. 3671 and with the text of Article 6(18) of the Law of October 10, 2013, Federal Law Gazette I p. 3799, s. 6.

[107] See, e.g., Assembly of the African Union Eleventh Ordinary Session 'Decision on the Report of the Commission on the Abuse of the Principle of Universal Jurisdiction' (June 30–July 1, 2008) Assembly/AU/Dec.199 (XI) para. 5(ii) and (iii).

In sum, while gravity is frequently invoked to justify adjudicating crimes on behalf of the global community, whether at global courts or in national courts exercising universal jurisdiction, the concept's meaning is unclear. Even at the ICC, which has examined the idea of gravity in greatest detail, many gravity decisions remain unmoored from consideration of institutional values and goals. Gravity is usually treated as a threshold consideration, but without adequate explanation for the location of the threshold, making gravity-based determinations easy to criticize. This must change if gravity is to promote, rather than detract from, the legitimacy of international criminal law.

II. A New Theory of Gravity to Legitimize Global Adjudication

To best support the legitimacy of international criminal law, gravity should play three roles in decisions about when to exercise global adjudicative authority. First, it should function as a minimal threshold below which global adjudication is not legitimate. This threshold should apply to cases at all global courts, cases brought under the doctrine of universal jurisdiction, and to situations at the ICC. Second, gravity should be used to determine whether global interests in adjudication outweigh countervailing interests, particularly those of relevant national communities. Global adjudication is only legitimate if this requirement is met. Finally, gravity should continue to function as a relative measure to help decide which cases should be adjudicated at global courts, and this relative gravity discretion should also be extended to determinations of which situations should be adjudicated at the global level. Used in this way, gravity can help determine when global adjudicative authority is *most strongly* legitimate.

In each of these roles, gravity should be understood as a measure of the global community's interest in adjudication, that is, the value to the global community of pursuing its adjudicative goals and priorities. Below the gravity threshold, the global community has no interest in adjudication because the conduct does not affect human dignity sufficiently to warrant criminal sanction. Once the threshold is met, the global community's interest in adjudication must be weighed against countervailing interests, especially national interests. Global adjudication is only legitimate when the value of adjudication to the global community is stronger than the value to national communities of non-adjudication, or of other accountability mechanisms. The final step is to compare the relative global interests in adjudicating various situations and cases to determine how to allocate resources.

Using gravity in these ways would enhance the legitimacy of the international criminal law regime. Applying a minimal gravity threshold linked to the protection of human dignity would promote legitimacy by ensuring that global institutions do not adjudicate cases that are unworthy of criminal sanction. Moreover, rejecting a more stringent gravity threshold ensures that the regime's scope is not limited in ways that undermine its goals. In the second role, gravity would contribute to legitimacy by ensuring that the global community's interests are not pursued in the face of more important interests, in particular national interests, and perhaps eventually regional or sub-regional interests. Finally, by properly informing selection decisions, gravity would help to ensure the regime's effectiveness, which is an important aspect of legitimacy.

A. The Minimal Gravity Threshold

Global adjudication should be subject to a gravity threshold, but not in the sense in which the term is typically used. As explained earlier, commentators often assert that global adjudication, particularly at the ICC, requires a level of gravity beyond that inherent in the definitions of international crimes. As I argued in Chapter 3, however, the global community has an interest in seeking to prevent all harms to human dignity through adjudication by virtue of our common humanity. Nonetheless, for global adjudication to be legitimate, the harm to human dignity that a crime causes or threatens, as well as the actor's culpability, must be sufficient to warrant criminal adjudication. The gravity threshold for legitimate global *prescription* advocated in Chapter 3 would ensure that only the kinds of conduct that cause or threaten non-minimal harm to human dignity are proscribed as international crimes. The gravity threshold for legitimate global *adjudication* would exclude from such adjudication instances of the proscribed conduct that cause minor harms or where the offender's culpability is minimal.

For instance, imagine that a soldier, knowing that the army for which he fights is engaged in a widespread attack against a civilian population, slaps a member of the persecuted group and insults them based on their identity. Assume that the assault caused non-minimal harm to the victim. This might qualify as a crime against humanity of "persecution," or as an "other inhumane act"[108] under some definitions. Nonetheless, the conduct would not be worthy of criminal prosecution if the harm it caused was minor. Indeed, the Rome Statute's definition of crimes against humanity excludes this conduct by requiring that persecution be committed in connection with another prohibited act, and that "other inhumane acts" be "of a similar character [to the other acts listed in the definition] causing great suffering, or serious injury to body or to mental or physical health."[109] For definitions that do not contain such restrictions, however, such as those in the Statutes of the *ad hoc* tribunals, the gravity threshold for adjudication would ensure that global institutions do not adjudicate conduct causing such minor harms.

---

[108] See, e.g., Rome Statute (n. 8) art. 7; ICTY Statute (n. 4) art. 5; ICTR Statute (n. 5) art. 3.
[109] Rome Statute (n. 8) art. 7(k).

The gravity threshold would also exclude crimes involving minimal moral culpability, even if they cause significant harm. For instance, it would exclude the conduct of a soldier who negligently killed a civilian in combat. Assuming that the conduct was not grossly negligent—she was merely unaware of a risk that many others would have recognized—her culpability is insufficient to warrant criminal accountability.[110] Indeed, even gross negligence is probably insufficient to warrant criminal liability for certain harms. The Rome Statute excludes negligent conduct by requiring a *mens rea* of intent and knowledge, but this requirement is not contained in other international courts' Statutes.

As these examples illustrate, the kinds of conduct that the minimal gravity threshold would exclude are unlikely to come before international courts in any event. Indeed, national courts generally do not prosecute these kinds of cases—at least as crimes. Such conduct sometimes bears other labels, such as "violation," or "contravention."[111] Offenders are not incarcerated for such conduct, although they may be subject to other sanctions, such as fines or required community service.

Nonetheless, adopting a minimal gravity threshold is important for two reasons. First, international criminal law is likely to continue to expand, and it is necessary to mark a lower boundary beyond which it cannot legitimately reach. Second, the idea that international criminal law is subject to a gravity threshold is firmly embedded in the regime's discourse, and is enshrined in the ICC's Rome Statute. Clarifying that the threshold is a minimal one will ensure that courts do not seek to endow the threshold with content that would be detrimental to the regime's legitimacy.

A substantial gravity threshold would threaten the legitimacy of international criminal law by limiting its ability to accomplish its central goal of crime prevention. If the Lubanga Trial Chamber had succeeded in defining the threshold to include only crimes that are large scale or systematic and perpetrators who are senior leaders, a vast array of criminal conduct would have been beyond the ICC's reach. This would have greatly restricted the Court's ability to prevent crimes through individual and general deterrence, and through the expression of global norms.

Indeed, as the Appeals Chamber pointed out in that case, a restrictive gravity threshold would undermine the ICC's jurisdictional regime. The concept of admissibility is "quasi-jurisdictional."[112] The admissibility requirements, including the

[110] The Rome Statute excludes such crimes by requiring a mental element of intent and knowledge. See Ibid. art. 30.

[111] See, e.g., Model Penal Code s. 1.04(5), American Law Institute (2019) ("An offense defined by this Code or by any other statute of this State constitutes a violation if it is so designated in this Code or in the law defining the offense or if no other sentence than a fine, or fine and forfeiture or other civil penalty is authorized upon conviction."); Richard Frase, 'Sentencing Laws & Practice in France' (1995) 7 Fed. Sentencing Reporter 275, 276 ("In France, a very large number of minor offenses ... are not subject to incarceration. These *contraventions* are punishable by a fine, forfeiture of objects or privileges, or up to 120 hours of community service.").

[112] Leila Nadya Sadat, *The International Criminal Court and the Transformation of International Law: Justice for the New Millennium* (Transnational Publishers 2002) 125.

gravity threshold, delineate the scope of the ICC's legitimate exercise of authority. In fact, when the gravity threshold was first added to the ILC Draft Statute, it was described as a limit on the Court's ability to exercise its jurisdiction.[113] Imbuing the gravity threshold with significant content would thus effectively restrict the Court's jurisdiction.

The position the ICC Prosecutor took in the Comoros situation illustrates this problem. In asserting that the situation failed to meet the gravity threshold because it involved a relatively low number of victims of war crimes, the prosecutor was effectively arguing that situations with that profile are inadmissible, which is akin to restricting the Court's jurisdiction over such situations.[114] Some might argue that such a limit is supported by the Statute's war crimes provision, which grants the Court jurisdiction over war crimes "in particular when committed as part of a plan or policy or as part of a large-scale commission of such crimes."[115] However, the Court has recognized that this is merely a guide to the exercise of discretion.[116]

The Pre-Trial Chamber's ruling that the situation gravity threshold is met only when an investigation includes the people who bear greatest responsibility for the crimes is also akin to a jurisdictional requirement.[117] If situations where the prosecutor is unable to investigate those most responsible are inadmissible, they are beyond the institution's reach. It matters little whether this is called admissibility or jurisdiction, the effect is the same.

The minimal gravity threshold I advocate is akin to the one Judge Pikis endorsed in his dissent in the Lubanga Arrest Warrant decision. Judge Pikis asserted that the gravity threshold should exclude only:

> Cases [that are] insignificant in themselves; where the criminality on the part of the culprit is wholly marginal; borderline cases. A crime is insignificant in itself if, notwithstanding the fact that it satisfies the formalities of the law, i.e. the insignia of the crime, bound up with the mens rea and the actus reus, the acts constituting the crime are wholly peripheral to the objects of the law in criminalizing the conduct. Both, the inception and the consequences of the crime must be negligible .... The subject-matter must be minimal, so much so that it can be ignored by the Court.[118]

---

[113] ILC, 'Report on the Work of Its Forty-Sixth Session' (May 2–July 22, 1994) UN Doc. A/49/10 22 para. 50.

[114] *Situation on the Registered Vessels of the Union of Comoros, the Hellenic Republic of Greece and the Kingdom of Cambodia* (Final Decision of the Prosecution concerning the "Article 53(1) Report") (n. 30) paras. 77–9.

[115] Rome Statute (n. 8) art. 8(1).

[116] *Prosecutor v. Bemba Gombo* (Decision Pursuant to Article 61(7)(a) and (b) of the Rome Statute) ICC-01/05-01/08 (June 15, 2009) para. 211.

[117] See *Situation in the Republic of Kenya* (Decision Pursuant to Article 15 of the Rome Statute on the Authorization of an Investigation into the Situation in the Republic of Kenya) (n. 11) para. 60.

[118] *Situation in the Democratic Republic of the Congo* (Judgment on the Prosecutor's appeal against the decision of Pre-Trial Chamber I entitled "Decision on the Prosecutor's Application for Warrants of Arrest, Article 58," Separate and Partly Dissenting Opinion of Judge Georghios M. Pikis) (n. 55)

To determine which harms and levels of culpability are "wholly peripheral to the objects of the law" will require the same process as this book advocates for identifying other global norms: a dialogue involving as many sectors of the global community as possible. When international criminal law decision-makers face decisions about the gravity threshold they should seek guidance from the broadest possible sources, and articulate their conclusions transparently, inviting responses that will help guide future decisions. With respect to borderline cases for which international criminal courts have difficulty identifying global norms of criminality, legitimacy is best fostered by refraining from adjudication. This approach respects the principle of legality, which requires clear prior law for criminal adjudication.

The recommendation of a minimal gravity threshold does not mean that international courts ought to adjudicate all situations and cases involving crimes that meet the threshold. The next section explains how gravity can help ensure that global adjudication takes place only when the global community's interests outweigh other community interests.

B. Balancing Global and National Interests

To be legitimate, global adjudication must produce a net positive effect in the world. For that reason, it should be pursued only when the global interest in adjudication outweighs any competing interests. In this context, legitimacy is an absolute, rather than a scalar concept. When there is no global interest in adjudication, or the global interest is not sufficiently strong to outweigh competing interests, global adjudication is not legitimate.

Various communities have interests that could be considered in determining whether global adjudication is legitimate. For instance, regional communities may be emerging as important in this regard. Of particular note is the proposed addition of criminal jurisdiction to the work of the African Court on Human and Peoples' Rights.[119] If this proposal is implemented, or the African continent otherwise develops stronger regional norms of criminal justice, those norms would have to be factored into any proposed uses of global criminal justice mechanisms.[120]

---

para. 40. See also *Situation in the Republic of Kenya* (Decision Pursuant to Article 15 of the Rome Statute on the Authorization of an Investigation into the Situation in the Republic of Kenya) (n. 11) para. 56 (arguing that the reference to insufficiency of gravity is an additional protection against pursuing "peripheral cases").

[119] African Union, 'Protocol on Amendments to the Protocol on the Statute of the African Court of Justice and Human Rights' (June 27, 2014), available at www.africancourtcoalition.org/images/docs/legal-texts/Protocol_on_amendments_to_the_Protocol_on_the_Statute_of_the_African_Court_of_Justice_and_Human_Rights%20.pdf (last accessed on September 27, 2019).

[120] I explore the potential relationship between the proposed African Criminal Court and the ICC in Margaret M. deGuzman 'Complementarity at the African Court' in Charles C. Jalloh et al (eds.), *The*

Currently, however, the communities whose interests are most important to balance against global interests are the national communities most directly affected by the crimes at issue in potential situations and cases before international courts and tribunals. Until recently, national communities had largely unfettered discretion to decide what conduct to proscribe and under what circumstances to adjudicate and punish violations of those criminal proscriptions. The idea that so-called "atrocity" crimes require criminal prosecution emerged only after the creation of the *ad hoc* tribunals,[121] and only in the last decade or so has international human rights law been interpreted as requiring criminal adjudication for some human rights violations.[122] Although these developments limit the discretion of national courts, national communities retain the most substantial interests in criminal adjudication, alongside the global community.

The important question of how national interests should be ascertained is beyond the scope of this project. Just as the global community is a useful but artificial construct, no monolithic national community with undifferentiated interests exists. Moreover, even when the values and priorities of a majority of people in a national setting can be determined, the question of how to address minority views remains. Additionally, it is far from clear that national governments adequately represent even majority interests, let alone those of minorities. This problem exists in democracies, and is even more pronounced in many non-democratic systems. The question of how to determine national interests thus requires greater attention. For the sake of developing a gravity theory, however, this chapter assumes that national interests can be identified and that national governments seek to pursue them.

The claim that global interests can sometimes defeat national interests departs from the prevailing view that international courts, particularly the ICC, are "courts of last resort."[123] The last resort narrative assumes that national communities always have superior interests in adjudicating crimes that affect them, and that national proceedings should therefore always take priority over international adjudication. Supporters of this view often assert that limiting international adjudication to situations where national courts are unable or unwilling genuinely to act encourages states to fulfill their obligations to protect their populations.[124]

African Court of Justice and Human and Peoples' Rights in Context (Cambridge University Press 2019) 645–79.

---

[121] See Diane F. Orentlicher, 'Settling Accounts: The Duty to Prosecute Human Rights Violations of a Prior Regime' (1991) 100 Yale L.J. 2537, 2586.

[122] Alexandra Huneeus, 'International Criminal Law by Other Means: The Quasi-Criminal Jurisdiction of the Human Rights Courts' (2013) 107 AJIL 1, 2.

[123] See, e.g., E. Mendes, *Peace and Justice at the International Criminal Court: A Court of Last Resort* (Edward Elgar Publishing 2010); P. Kirsch, 'The Role of the International Criminal Court in Enforcing International Criminal Law' (2007) 22 Am. U. Intl. L. Rev. 539, 543.

[124] Carsten Stahn, 'Complementarity: A Tale of Two Notions' (2008) 19 Crim. L.F. 87, 92.

The Rome Statute's complementarity provision is often cited in support of the "last resort" approach to legitimate global adjudication. Article 17(1)(a) of the Statute states that a case is inadmissible when it "is being investigated or prosecuted by a State which has jurisdiction over it, unless the State is unwilling or unable genuinely to carry out the investigation or prosecution."[125] This complementarity provision, along with the gravity threshold and *ne bis in idem*, comprise the Court's "admissibility" regime. Canadian diplomat John Holmes, who chaired the committee that drafted the complementarity provision, describes the complementarity system as creating a mechanism "to fill the gap where States could not or failed to comply with" their obligations to prosecute international crimes.[126]

Yet the "last resort" narrative does not reflect how international criminal jurisdiction is being exercised, either at the ICC or at other international courts and tribunals. The ICC's judges have interpreted the complementarity provision to mean that the Court may exercise its jurisdiction whenever no national court with jurisdiction is actively investigating or prosecuting the same case.[127] To be active on the same "case," state authorities must be investigating or prosecuting the same defendants for substantially the same conduct.[128] Although the crimes charged need not mirror the ICC charges—the state can charge murder rather than crimes against humanity, for instance—they must cover similar incidents of criminality.[129]

The ICC examined the requirements of complementarity in the Kenya situation. There, the state objected to the ICC's exercise of jurisdiction on the grounds that Kenya was in the process of amending its laws to include international crimes and planned to investigate the crimes.[130] The Court held that such assurances of future investigation or prosecution did not render the situation inadmissible.[131] It determined that complementarity must be measured at the time of the admissibility challenge, and Kenya was not investigating or prosecuting the same defendants for substantially the same conduct as the ICC at the relevant time.[132] Although it was far from clear that Kenya was willing genuinely to adjudicate, the Court did not

[125] Rome Statute (n. 8) art. 17(1)(a).

[126] J. T. Holmes, 'Principle of Complementarity', in R. S. Lee (ed.), *ICC: The Making of the Rome Statute* (Kluwer Law International 1999) 74.

[127] *Prosecutor v. Muthaura et al.* (Judgment on the Appeal of the Republic of Kenya Against the Decision of Pre-Trial Chamber II of 30 May 2011 entitled "Decision on the Application by the Government of Kenya Challenging the Admissibility of the Case Pursuant to Article 19(2)(b) of the Statute") ICC-01/09-02/11 OA (August 30, 2011) para. 39.

[128] Ibid. For a discussion of this decision, see Rod Rastan, 'What is "Substantially the Same Conduct"?' (2017) 15 JICJ 1.

[129] See *Prosecutor v. Al Senussi* (Judgment on the Appeal of Mr. Abdullah Al-Senussi Against the Decision of Pre-Trial Chamber I of 11 October 2013 entitled "Decision on the Admissibility of the Case Against Abdullah Al-Senussi") ICC-01/11-01/11-565 OA6 (July 24, 2014) para. 119.

[130] *Situation in the Republic of Kenya* (Decision on the Application by the Government of Kenya Challenging the Admissibility of the Case Pursuant to Article 19(2)(b) of the Statute) ICC-01/09-01/11-101 (May 30, 2011) para. 13.

[131] Ibid. para. 70.

[132] Ibid. para. 68.

reach the issue. The Court has thus interpreted its complementarity regime as permitting it to adjudicate whenever a state is not adjudicating the same persons for substantially the same conduct at the time the admissibility challenge is brought, regardless of the state's willingness and ability to do so in the future.

ICC policies and practice further undermine the last resort narrative. The ICC has accepted "self-referrals"—referrals of situations on the states' own territory— from states that appeared both willing and able to prosecute the cases. The Court's first defendant was transferred to The Hague by the Democratic Republic of Congo, which had charged him with genocide and crimes against humanity, crimes that were arguably more serious than those for which he was prosecuted at the ICC.[133] With regard to the Uganda situation, Mahnoush Arsanjani and Michael Reisman noted that "there is no evidence that a total or substantial collapse of the national judicial system of Uganda has occurred or that its national judicial system is unavailable."[134]

The Office of the Prosecutor has also adopted a "burden sharing" policy that is incompatible with the last resort narrative. The Office's Policy Paper on Case Selection and Prioritisation states that if relevant national authorities are investigating the same person for substantially the same conduct as the ICC, the Office may turn its attention to "other perpetrators that form part of the same or a different case theory, in line with a burden-sharing approach."[135] The burden-sharing approach is also evident in the Prosecutor's policy of "positive complementarity." From the early days of the Court's operation, the Office of the Prosecutor interpreted its role to include assisting national courts in fulfilling their obligations to investigate and prosecute international crimes.[136] One way the Prosecutor does this is by sharing evidence and intelligence related to situations the Court is investigating with national authorities when appropriate.[137] The goal is not for the national system to take over from the ICC entirely, but to share the burden. In particular, the Office of the Prosecutor has suggested that it may prosecute some of the highest-level perpetrators and leave lower-level accused to national courts.[138]

The ICC's rejection of the last resort narrative is appropriate in light of the varied circumstances in which global adjudication may be legitimate. The last resort

---

[133] *Prosecutor v. Lubanga* (Decision on the Prosecutor's Application for a warrant of arrest. Article 58) ICC 01/04-01/06-1-Corr-Red (February 10, 2006) para. 33.

[134] Mahnoush H. Arsanjani and W. Michael Reisman, 'The Law-in-Action of the International Criminal Court' (2005) 99 AJIL 2, 395 (internal quotation marks omitted). See also William A. Schabas, 'Complementarity in Practice: Some Uncomplimentary Thoughts' (2008) 19 Crim. L.F. 5, 18 (noting that Uganda's referral "did not allege that the national courts were unable to prosecute. Everything would indicate, in fact, that Uganda has one of Africa's better criminal justice systems, and that its courts are more than able to prosecute the leaders of the Lord's Resistance Army.").

[135] ICC-OTP, 'Policy Paper on Case Selection and Prioritisation' (n. 13) para. 31.

[136] ICC-OTP, 'Paper on Some Policy Issues before the Office of the Prosecutor' (September 2003) 2–3, 5.

[137] ICC-OTP, 'Prosecutorial Strategy, 2009–2012' (February 1, 2010) para. 17.

[138] ICC-OTP, 'Paper on Some Policy Issues before the Office of the Prosecutor' (n. 136) 7.

narrative erroneously assumes: (1) that national proceedings are always better able to promote national interests than international prosecution; and (2) that global interests never outweigh national interests. In fact, sometimes global adjudication can best promote national interests, and even when this is not the case, global interests should sometimes be given priority.

There are various possible combinations of national and global interests, and gravity's role differs depending on how these interests align. The first possibility is that national and global interests coincide. When there is no conflict of interest, there is no need to use gravity to help balance interests and ensure legitimacy. If the minimal gravity threshold is met, global adjudication is legitimate—assuming of course that any non-gravity-related legitimacy criteria, such as fairness of proceedings, are met.

Such interest alignment can occur under various conditions. First, national courts may be willing and able to prosecute, but the national community may view global prosecution as preferable for any number of reasons. For instance, global prosecution may bring desirable attention to a situation; signal global commitment to assisting a population; or enable national communities to secure some measure of justice without disrupting a fragile peace. The first situations to come before the ICC fall into this category. The governments of both Uganda and the Democratic Republic of Congo referred their own situations to the ICC even though they were almost certainly willing and able to adjudicate the crimes. As noted earlier, the Democratic Republic of Congo arrested and charged Lubanga before sending him to the ICC. The primary impediment to trial in Uganda was the government's inability to capture the defendants.

As Sarah Nouwen has documented, the governments likely had motivations for these referrals that were not rooted in optimizing the well-being of their populations.[139] Uganda's referral, for instance, sought to involve the ICC only in prosecuting crimes committed by the Lord's Resistance Army (LRA), not by government forces, suggesting an effort to gain international support for the government's efforts against the LRA. Even if the referrals were not strongly legitimate, however, the ICC's decision to adjudicate was legitimate as long as it was in service of global goals, and the national communities either supported, or were at least unopposed to global adjudication.

Another situation in which national and global interests align is when national courts are unable or unwilling to prosecute, and national communities either support or are indifferent to global adjudication. This may arise, for instance, when a post-conflict community has lost its judicial infrastructure or, more drastically, the

---

[139] Sarah M. Nouwen, *Complementarity in the Line of Fire: The Catalysing Effect of the International Criminal Court in Uganda and Sudan* (Cambridge University Press 2013) 171 (explaining how the referral of the LRA to the ICC, although "[c]overed in a legal cloak ... fitted neatly into the [Government of Uganda's] military strategy").

entire state has collapsed. Communities in these circumstances may support global efforts at justice, or may be too focused on securing life necessities to pay much attention to criminal justice issues, whether national or global. Again, because there is no conflict of interests, there is no need for gravity, beyond the minimal gravity threshold discussed above.

In many situations, however, there is at least some tension between national and global interests. National interests, like global, exist on a spectrum. At one end, national communities have a slight preference against global adjudication, while at the other, global adjudication may actually harm national community interests. The most widely cited example of the latter is when global prosecution risks undermining a peace process or fueling or reigniting a conflict.

The relationship between peace and justice has received significant attention in the literature, with some scholars arguing that lasting peace is impossible without justice,[140] and others supporting the view more commonly held outside academia that the pursuit of justice sometimes undermines efforts toward peace.[141] For global adjudication to be legitimate in the midst of conflict or an unstable peace, it would have to be true either that accountability is required for peace, or that accountability is more important than peace in the particular circumstances.

Global and national interests may also conflict because the national community prefers responses other than international adjudication. These may include non-adjudicatory responses, such as truth commissions, or restorative or traditional justice mechanisms. Alternatively, the national community may prefer adjudication in national courts or no reckoning at all, for example, through amnesties. In each of these circumstances, global adjudication will be legitimate only if global interests outweigh national.

When such conflicts exist, the concept of gravity can be used to help resolve the question of whether global adjudication is legitimate if it is understood and articulated in relation to the global community's interests and related goals. In this context, gravity represents the extent of the global community's interest in preventing future harms by adjudicating a particular situation or case.[142] It is this value that must outweigh the national community's conflicting interests for global adjudication to be legitimate.

---

[140] M. Cherif Bassiouni, 'Perspectives on International Criminal Justice' (2010) 50 Va. J. Intl. L. 269, 293–4 (stating that "[j]ustice is ... an essential component of peace"); William Zartman, 'Negotiating Forward and Backward-Looking Outcomes' in William Zartman and Viktor Kremeniuk (eds.), *Peace versus Justice* (Rowman & Littlefield 2005) 6 (stating that "[p]roperly conceived, there is no peace without justice ... ").

[141] Samuel P. Huntington, *The Third Wave: Democratization in the late Twentieth Century* (University of Oklahoma Press 1993) 230–1 (arguing that justice may sometimes threaten democracy and stating that "on the issue of 'prosecute and punish vs. forgive and forget', each alternative presents grave problems, and that the least unsatisfactory course may well be: do not prosecute, do not punish, do not forgive, and, above all, do not forget").

[142] As explained in Chapter 1, the book rejects retributive rationales for global adjudication and adopts a utilitarian theory focused on crimes prevention.

To measure the value of global adjudication to the global community two questions must be answered: (1) how important are the goals the global community seeks to advance through adjudication?; and (2) how likely is adjudication to advance those goals? Because the central goal of global adjudication is crime prevention, the answer to the first question depends on the importance of preventing particular crimes, or crimes in a particular situation. The importance of prevention depends on the kinds of factors typically used in gravity analyses: the scale of harm, the nature and manner of commission, and the impact of the crimes. However, contrary to current practice, it is not sufficient to employ an aggregative analysis that considers all of the factors abstractly. Instead, decision-makers should identify preventive priorities, and give special attention to the factors relevant to those priorities. For instance, the quantity of harm in a given situation standing alone does not warrant global adjudication; but such adjudication may be an important priority if it will serve to prevent similarly large-scale crimes in the future. A case that involved the use of particularly dangerous weapons, but caused no concrete harm, might be given priority on the same basis: deterring the use of such weapons is important to preventing future crimes. A crime that occurs frequently around the world but is under-prosecuted may also warrant special attention at the global level. This applies, for example, to crimes of sexual and gender-based violence. A situation involving ongoing conflict might legitimately be given priority on the grounds that stopping particular harms by particularly dangerous perpetrators is an important goal.

Although, as explained earlier, the conventional wisdom that the "core international crimes" always merit adjudication is flawed, their definitions include elements that often give rise to strong global preventive interests. For example, the global community has a very strong interest in preventing the crime of aggression, which undermines the right to national self-determination and causes large-scale harm to human dignity in many cases. Likewise, crimes that target a particular category of victims also often give rise to a particularly strong global interest because they affect and endanger the well-being of all people in that category around the world. This is part of what motivated the creation of the crime of genocide. Rafael Lemkin had in mind crimes that threaten the actual, physical annihilation of a group, but other crimes motivated by discrimination can also cause special concern to the global community. Crimes that particularly target women or children, immigrants, members of a political group, racial group, gender group, or many other kinds of human groups can raise global concerns about the wellbeing of the group and also about the normalization of an ethos of prejudice that harms all of humanity.

Crimes that are not currently labeled "core international crimes" can also have characteristics that make them particularly important to prevent at the global level. Terrorist crimes can be said to affect the global community in a special way because they cause fear well beyond their immediate victims. Crimes related to the deterioration of the natural environment, as well as crimes associated with corruption and the misuse of natural resources, have broad impacts that make their prevention important to the global community.

The identity and role of the perpetrator can also increase the importance of global prevention. The global community has a particular interest in preventing crimes committed by, or with the support of, members of governments or quasi-government organizations. Governments are an essential building block of the global community. When they attack populations, rather than protecting them, they threaten the entire global structure. Moreover, leadership crimes have the potential to cause greater quantities of harm than crimes committed by individuals, which increases the importance of their prevention. Thus, a variety of factors can affect the importance of global adjudication. To ensure legitimacy, decision-makers must assess the factors in relation to the particular preventive goals they seek to accomplish, especially deterrence and norm promotion.

Assuming that an important global goal is identified, the second consideration for determining the strength of the global community's interest in global adjudication is the likelihood that adjudication will promote that goal. Determining the relationship between prosecution and crime prevention is a notoriously difficult task because it requires counter-factual analysis. To know whether punishment deters, for instance, we must determine whether crimes that did not occur would have occurred but for the threat of punishment. Some empirical studies purport to show that global adjudication promotes deterrence,[143] but the value of such studies is disputed.[144] Measuring the preventive effect of norm expression is even more challenging. It requires not only evaluating the extent to which a norm has penetrated a community, but also how significantly it has affected behavior within the community. In light of these measurement difficulties, decision-makers can be expected to do little more than make educated guesses about the likelihood that adjudication in a given situation or case will promote prevention—at least until more compelling empirical evidence is available.

One aspect of the likelihood of success that may be more readily ascertainable, at least in some cases, is the probability that adjudication will yield conviction. Global adjudication can promote general prevention even in the absence of convictions

---

[143] See, e.g., Hyeran Jo and Beth A. Simmons, 'Can the International Criminal Court Deter Atrocity?' (2016) 70(3) International Organization 443 (finding that "the ICC can deter some governments and those rebel groups that seek legitimacy"); Benjamin J. Appel, 'In the Shadow of the International Criminal Court: Does the ICC Deter Human Rights Violations?' (2018) 62 J. Conflict Resolution 3 (comparing changes in human rights protections in ratifying states to non-ratifying states to show that ratification of the Rome Statute is associated with improvements in governmental protection of human rights).

[144] See, e.g., Padraig McAuliffe, 'Suspended Disbelief: The Curious Endurance of the Deterrence Rationale in International Criminal Law' (2012) 10 New Zealand J. of Public and Int'l L. 227, 254–61 (arguing that the use of empirical research to prove deterrence works in international criminal law is "dubious" and suggesting that a commitment to advocacy has led many proponents of ICL to compromise empirical research by relying on single case analysis and "cherry-picking").

by signaling the global community's condemnation of particular kinds of conduct. For instance, the ICC Prosecutor's decision to seek custody of Sudan's president signaled that even state leaders are not beyond the reach of the law. Nonetheless, punishment and the threat of punishment are important components of crime prevention. To convict and punish offenders, courts must obtain custody of the offender, and obtain the evidence necessary for conviction. The likelihood of accomplishing these tasks should factor into the determination of the importance of pursuing global adjudication. When there is no reasonable chance of obtaining a conviction the importance of global adjudication is low and such adjudication is thus illegitimate.

Once the importance of global adjudication to the global community is determined, the final step in assessing whether such adjudication is legitimate is to balance the global community's interest in adjudication against any competing interests, especially those of the most affected national communities. This kind of balancing is a common feature of legal analysis, although no scientific method exists for valuing competing interests.[145] American jurist Rosco Pound asserted the futility of seeking to develop an "absolute formula" ensuring that the "intrinsically weightier" of various interests prevails.[146] What is important, therefore, is for decision-makers to be clear and explicit about how they assign weight to competing interests. This will enable the kind of dialogic process this book advocates wherein constituents react to decisions based on the articulated bases for those decisions, and those reactions inform future decisions.

This balancing, as well as the assessment of likelihood of success, could be framed as part of the gravity analysis for determining when global adjudication is legitimate. The gravity analysis would then include determining: (1) how important adjudication is to the global community; (2) how likely adjudication is to achieve the global community's goals; and (3) whether the global community's interests outweigh competing interests. Alternatively, the latter two considerations could be assessed independently of gravity, restricting gravity to the importance of adjudication to the global community. For instance, at the ICC, questions about the likelihood of success and the balance of national and global interests could be considered under the "interests of justice," as explained in the section III, below.

In sum, gravity can help to legitimize decisions about whether to exercise global adjudicative authority by providing a measure of global interest to be balanced with competing interests, particularly national interests. Global adjudication, whether at international courts or national courts exercising universal jurisdiction, is only legitimate when global and national interests align, or when global interests outweigh national.

---

[145] See T. Alexander Aleinikoff, 'Constitutional Law in the Age of Balancing' (1987) 96 Yale L.J. 943, 973.

[146] Ibid. (citing Roscoe Pound, *Jurisprudence*, Vol. 3 (West Publishing Co. 1959) 330–1).

C. Discretionary Selection Gravity

Gravity's final role in helping to legitimize global adjudication is to guide decisions about which situations and cases global courts ought to adjudicate from among all those that meet both the minimal gravity threshold and the interest balancing test. Choosing among cases within a situation is largely in the discretion of prosecutors, although their decisions are sometimes subject to judicial review. Selecting situations, on the other hand, can sometimes devolve to political actors, such as when they decide whether to support a Security Council referral to the ICC; sometimes to bureaucrats at the UN, such as when they create *ad hoc* or hybrid tribunals; and sometimes to prosecutors, such as when they seek to initiate investigations on their own motion (*proprio motu*) at the ICC. In each of these circumstances, the relative gravity of the crimes at issue in the situation should be considered in determining whether to pursue global adjudication.

Selecting the gravest situations and cases—those that best promote the global community's most important goals—will enhance the legitimacy of the international criminal law regime by maximizing its effectiveness. Effectiveness, like legitimacy, is a contested concept;[147] and the relationship between legitimacy and effectiveness is a matter of debate.[148] This book uses effectiveness to mean the efficient achievement of morally appropriate goals. Effectiveness enhances legitimacy because the efficient achievement of morally appropriate goals helps to justify the exercise of authority—the book's definition of legitimacy.[149] The more important the goals, and the more efficiently they are achieved, the more they help to promote the regime's legitimacy.

Determining the relative importance of various goals—relative gravity—for purposes of selecting among situations and cases requires inquiry into the same kinds of factors as discussed earlier with regard to identifying the absolute importance of global goals for purposes of balancing them against competing goals. The difference is that for this purpose, the gravity of a case or situation is assessed in relation to that of other potential cases or situations, rather than in absolute terms.

As for absolute gravity, to assess relative gravity, decision-makers should first consider the importance of the goals that could be pursued in each potential

---

[147] See, e.g., Yuval Shany, 'Assessing the Effectiveness of International Courts: A Goal-Based Approach' (2012) 106 AJIL 225, 226–7 (discussing literature on effectiveness of international courts).

[148] Some scholars cite effectiveness as a criterion of legitimacy and others claim that legitimacy is a source of effectiveness. Compare G. C. A. Junne, 'International Organizations in a Period of Globalization: New (Problems of) Legitimacy' in Jean-Marc Coicaud and Veijo Heiskanen (eds.), *The Legitimacy of International Organizations* (United Nations University Press 2001) 195 (using effectiveness as one of four categories to analyze legitimacy of international organizations), with Yuval Shany, 'Stronger Together? Legitimacy and Effectiveness of International Courts as Mutually Reinforcing or Undermining Notions' in Nienke Grossman et al. (eds.), *Legitimacy and International Courts* (Cambridge University Press 2018) 365 (noting "that legitimacy—especially, sociological legitimacy—helps international courts in sustaining judicial effectiveness").

[149] See Chapter 1, section I.

situation or case—here, the relative importance—and, second, compare the efficiency with which the goals are likely to be achieved in each—here, the relative efficiency. As discussed earlier, the ICC Office of the Prosecutor is already doing much of this analysis when it selects cases. It has articulated criteria to guide such decisions that are linked to specific global values, such as the need to prevent crimes that particularly affect women, children, and the environment.[150] Moreover, it has explained at least some of its case selections as related to global goals, such as preventing the recruitment and use of child soldiers.

In contrast, the ICC has declined to exercise such relative gravity discretion with regard to decisions to open investigations in situations. Instead, it has sought to ground decisions not to open investigations in the gravity threshold, an approach I critiqued earlier.[151] Using relative gravity reasoning, and linking gravity to goals, would better promote the ICC's legitimacy because it would require decision-makers to articulate priorities and invite feedback from constituents that could inform future decisions. In the Comoros situation, for instance, instead of claiming that the situation did not meet the gravity threshold based on a purportedly objective goal-neutral analysis, the Office of the Prosecutor could have explained why adjudicating that situation would not promote the ICC's goals as well as other situations. As further elaborated below, she could have grounded this claim in the "interests of justice," arguing that because prevention is more important in situations involving greater harm, it is not in the interests of justice to pursue the situation. The judges reviewing her decision could then have expressed their disagreement in terms of their vision of the appropriate priorities. Over time, this process would help to develop greater clarity about the Court's mission.

The Pre-Trial Chamber adopted an approach akin to that recommended here in its decision rejecting the Prosecutor's request to open an investigation in the Afghanistan situation. The Chamber accepted the Prosecutor's conclusions that there were reasonable grounds to believe that the Taliban, Afghan government, and US military and CIA leaders committed crimes within the Court's jurisdiction. It further agreed that the crimes met the gravity threshold for admissibility based on an "objective" application of factors like the scale, nature, and impact of the crimes. However, the Chamber invoked the interests of justice to reject the request to investigate, holding that an investigation would not serve justice because there is no substantial likelihood that evidence necessary to secure convictions can be obtained. Importantly, the Chamber stressed that the purposes of the ICC would not be served by an investigation that is unlikely to lead to convictions and that the

---

[150] See section I.A.
[151] See nn. 23–32 and accompanying text.

Court's resources should instead be put toward situations that are more likely to yield convictions.[152]

This decision appropriately grounds situation selection discretion in the interests of justice provision, and appeals to the ICC's goals in exercising that discretion. However, there are several flaws in the Chamber's analysis. First, it considered only the efficiency question, not the relative importance of the goals at stake. If the goals that could be pursued in adjudicating the situation are especially important to the global community, adjudication could be appropriate even if the likelihood of success is relatively low. The goals of adjudication in the Afghanistan situation are arguably more important to the global community than those in at least some other situations the ICC is considering pursuing. One of the most important values that the Court can express is that of equality before the law. This is especially important in light of the charges that have been leveled at the Court of invidious selectivity against offenders from Africa, and in favor of powerful government actors. For the Court to investigate US crimes in Afghanistan would express the principle that even powerful actors are subject to global justice. Indeed, some measure of expression could be obtained even in the absence of convictions.

Another flaw in the Court's reasoning is its emphasis on the possibility that a failed investigation would disappoint victims.[153] This reasoning is problematic for two reasons. First, as explained in Chapter 1, the primarily goal of global adjudication should not be satisfaction of victims' needs for justice.[154] The global justice system is simply not equipped to accomplish that task. As such, victims' expectations ought to be moderated in all situations before the Court. Additionally, failing to investigate may disappoint victim expectations at least as much, if not more, than investigating and failing to secure adequate evidence for convictions, particularly if the inability to convict results from the lack of cooperation of relevant authorities, rather than the Court's own failure.

Finally, the decision to decline the Prosecutor's request based on the low likelihood of obtaining convictions erroneously assumes the judges have access to the information necessary to make such a prediction. Yet the Prosecutor had engaged in an eleven-year preliminary examination and had reached the opposite conclusion. Indeed, it is advisable to leave the efficiency evaluation to the Prosecutor in most circumstances. Although the judges are correct that investigations should generally not be opened when there is *no* chance of success, the Prosecutor has ample incentives not to request authorization to investigate under such circumstances.

Exercising discretionary relative gravity in selecting situations would increase the effectiveness of the ICC, and thus promote its legitimacy. It would focus the

---

[152] *Situation in the Islamic Republic of Afghanistan* (Decision Pursuant to Article 15 of the Rome Statute on the Authorisation of an Investigation into the Situation in the Islamic Republic of Afghanistan) ICC-02/17 (April 12, 2019) para. 96.
[153] Ibid.
[154] See Chapter 1, section II.

ICC's limited resources on situations where the Court is best able to advance its most important goals. By articulating what they believe those goals to be, the Court's Prosecutor and judges can stimulate dialogue about the ICC's role in the world that will build consensus on that question over time, and thus help to solidify the global justice community. Relative gravity discretion should also inform global decisions about whether to invest resources in *ad hoc* tribunals or other global criminal justice mechanisms for the same reasons.

In sum, to maximize the legitimacy of global adjudication, decision-makers should clarify their uses of gravity, distinguishing between the concept's role as an admissibility threshold, which ought to be minimal; as an aid in balancing global and national interests; and as a tool for selecting the situations and cases that most strongly promote global interests. In each of these contexts, decision-makers should seek to identify the goals and values underlying their decisions, and should communicate them as clearly as possible to relevant audiences. The next section provides suggestions regarding the procedural mechanisms that can be used to help ensure the most productive uses of gravity in justifying global adjudication.

III. Operationalizing Gravity for Legitimate Global Adjudicative Authority

For international courts and tribunals to employ gravity in the ways suggested here, they will have to adopt policies and procedures that facilitate this kind of decision-making. These will differ depending on the institution. The next section provides some thoughts about how to operationalize gravity-based adjudicative decision-making at international criminal law's principal institutions.

A. The ICC

The Rome Statute contains an express gravity threshold, so the recommendation to apply such a threshold, albeit a minimal one, poses no procedural challenges for that court. Moreover, it is widely accepted that the Prosecutor may use relative gravity in exercising case selection discretion. However, the proposals that gravity should function as an aid in balancing global and national interests, and in selecting situations require an implementing mechanism. I suggest using the "interests of justice" provision in Article 53 of the Rome Statute for these purposes.

Article 53 states that the Prosecutor "shall ... initiate an investigation unless he or she determines that there is no reasonable basis to proceed ...."[155]

---

[155] Rome Statute (n. 8) art. 53(1).

To determine whether there is a reasonable basis to proceed, the prosecutor must consider whether a situation involves admissible cases, including whether the potential cases reach the gravity threshold and meet the requirements of complementarity. In addition, Article 53 instructs the Prosecutor to consider whether: "[t]aking into account the gravity of the crime and the interests of the victims, there are nonetheless substantial reasons to believe that an investigation would not serve the interests of justice."[156] Any decision not to proceed based on the interests of justice is subject to judicial review, including on the initiative of the judges.[157]

Despite the breadth of the "interests of justice" language, the Office of the Prosecutor's policy statements to date have adopted a narrow interpretation of the provision. In a 2007 Policy Paper, the Office of the Prosecutor asserted that the prosecutor's discretion under the interests of justice provision "is exceptional in its nature" and stated "that there is a presumption in favour of investigation or prosecution" of admissible cases within the Court's jurisdiction.[158] The Policy Paper asserts in particular that the interests of justice do not include the interests of peace.[159]

This restrictive interpretation of the interests of justice is not supported by the provision's drafting history. The provision was introduced by the United Kingdom and was "intended to reflect a wide discretion on the part of the Prosecutor to decide not to investigate comparable to that in (some) domestic systems ...."[160] The provision seems to have received relatively little attention at the Rome Conference where the Statute was adopted, probably because its inclusion was relatively uncontroversial. Indeed, like the ambiguity surrounding the gravity threshold, the lack of clarity about the meaning of "interests of justice" may have been a strategic decision on the part of at least some of the conference's participants. Some delegations envisioned the interests of justice as justifying non-prosecution in situations, such as that in South Africa after apartheid, where a state opts for other forms of transitional justice.[161] Leaving the provision ambiguous enabled agreement between those delegations and others that believed that lasting peace after atrocities always requires criminal accountability.[162]

---

[156] Ibid.

[157] Ibid. art. 53(3)(b).

[158] ICC-OTP, 'Policy Paper on the Interests of Justice' (September 2007) 1.

[159] Ibid. 8–9.

[160] William Schabas, *The International Criminal Court: A Commentary on the Rome Statute* (Oxford University Press 2010) 663, citing UK Discussion Paper, "International Criminal Court, Complementarity" (March 29, 1996) para. 30, also available at http://www.iccnow.org/documents/UKPaperComplementarity.pdf (last accessed on September 27, 2019).

[161] See Antonio Cassese, 'Round Table: Prospects for the Functioning of the International Criminal Court', in Mauro Politi and Giuseppe Nesi (eds.), *The Rome Statute of the International Criminal Court: A Challenge to Impunity* (Ashgate 2001) 300.

[162] Darryl Robinson, 'Serving the Interests of Justice: Amnesties, Truth Commissions and the International Criminal Court' (2003) 14 Eur. J. Intl. L. 481, 488–9.

The interests of justice provision ought to be interpreted broadly to afford the Prosecutor discretion both to conduct the global/national balancing test advocated earlier, and to select the gravest situations from among admissible situations. This is admittedly not the most intuitive reading of the provision. The use of the word "nonetheless" appears to set the gravity of the crimes and interests of victims on the one hand, against separate unnamed considerations on the other. But there are many factors that can help to determine the interests of justice. The interests of victims and gravity of crimes are two such factors, but they are not the only ones; and they do not always pull in the same direction. As explained above, the gravity of the crimes, understood in terms of the extent of the global interest in adjudication, will not always align with national interests, including those of victims. Because the interests of justice are not served by global adjudication when national interests outweigh global interests, that provision should be interpreted to require the balancing test advocated above.

The Court should also interpret the Statute to afford the Prosecutor discretion to select the gravest situations for adjudication—those where the global community can most efficiently pursue its most important goals. This is easiest with regard to *proprio motu* situations. The Prosecutor's role in this regard is governed by Article 15, which unlike Article 53's mandatory language, states that the Prosecutor "*may* initiate investigations *proprio motu*" after she "analyze[s] the seriousness of the information received."[163] This suggests that the Prosecutor has discretion to decline to investigate *proprio motu* based on the relative seriousness of potential situations.

Extending such discretion to referred situations requires a broad reading of the interests of justice provision, and is likely to be more controversial. Some supporters of the Court, including delegates from states parties, may argue that the Prosecutor should not be permitted such discretion because it would elevate her judgment over that of the referring entity, whether a state party or the Security Council. But allowing the Prosecutor to select among referred situations makes sense for a number of reasons. As explained above, in a world of limited resources, the Court's legitimacy is maximized when it pursues the situations that best promote global interests. States and the Security Council refer situations for various reasons that may not account for the global interest in resource maximization. Even if referring entities were motivated to help the Court maximize the use of its resources, state actors do not have access to the information they would need to make relative gravity determinations because they lack access to complete information about available evidence, which is often confidential; and they rarely have a complete picture of the ICC's goals in the various actual and potential situations before the Court.

---

[163]   Rome Statute (n. 8) art. 15(1)–(2) (emphasis added).

With regard to situations referred by the Security Council, the Prosecutor should be particularly judicious in exercising her discretion to decline to investigate based on the interests of justice. Security Council referrals are based on a finding that ICC adjudication serves international peace and security. Because the promotion of peace and security is one of the global community's most important goals, it will rarely be the case that this goal is outweighed by other goals in other situations. Nonetheless, in some circumstances, such as when the Court lacks adequate resources to open a new investigation, it may be important for it to decline to investigate even a situation referred by the Security Council. Not only will this enable the Court to promote its legitimacy by pursuing situations where it is best able to pursue its goals, but it may motivate the Security Council, or the states parties, to increase the Court's resources to enable the additional prosecutions.

As with all gravity-related decisions, it is important that ICC decision-makers express their reasoning clearly to facilitate productive reactions from relevant communities. Decision-makers should then take the feedback they receive into account in making future decisions. The ICC is already engaged in this process with regard to some of its decisions about whether to adjudicate situations and cases. For instance, the Court's decisions about whether to open investigations into the Comoros and Afghanistan situations have promoted important conversations about the ICC's role in the world, including the part that gravity ought to play. For instance, with regard to the Comoros situation, the Prosecutor and judges have exchanged views about whether the situation meets the gravity threshold.[164] This has precipitated commentary from observers and state actors.[165] As explained earlier, those discussions ought to have concerned discretionary *relative* gravity rather than the gravity threshold. Nonetheless, the exchange of prosecutorial and judicial views has stimulated productive conversation among constituents about the ICC's goals. This is precisely the kind of dialogue that, over time, will help the ICC to hone its mission and thus bolster its legitimacy.

To ensure that such discussions support the ICC's long-term legitimacy, the Prosecutor and judges should assess gravity, both absolute and relative, in relation to the institution's values and goals, and the appropriate priorities among them.

---

[164] See nn. 25–32 and accompanying text.

[165] See, e.g., Kevin Jon Heller 'The Pre-Trial Chamber's Dangerous Comoros Review Decision' in Opinio Juris, July 17, 2015, available at http://opiniojuris.org/2015/07/17/the-pre-trial-chambers-problematic-comoros-review-decision/ (last accessed on September 27, 2019) (asserting that the Office of the Prosecutor's (OTP's) approach to "potential perpetrator gravity" is superior to the Pre-Trial Chamber's (PTC's) approach because the OTP focuses on "the importance of perpetrators relative to the hierarchy of their state or organization"); Marco Longobardo 'Everything Is Relative, Even Gravity: Remarks on the Assessment of Gravity in ICC Preliminary Examinations, and the Mavi Marmara Affair' (2016) 14 J. Intl. Crim. Justice 1011, 1030 (concluding that the OTP's evaluation of gravity was flawed because the admissibility threshold at the preliminary examination stage is less strict than under Article 53(2)).

They should articulate their analysis as clearly as possible, so that the resulting dialogue centers on values and goals, rather than on accusations or speculation about the motives for decisions.

B. Hybrid and *Ad Hoc* Courts and Tribunals

How gravity ought to factor into adjudication decisions at *ad hoc* and hybrid courts and tribunals depends on the purposes of each institution, including the extent to which the institution is intended to serve national and global goals. This book has defined gravity in relation to global interests, and has argued that global institutions, in particular the ICC, ought to privilege such interests. This is a controversial proposition with respect to the ICC, and it is even more so for *ad hoc* and hybrid tribunals. Those institutions were created to address specific situations, inevitably raising expectations in the relevant communities that the interests of those communities would be privileged. The structures of the institutions support such expectations. Hybrid tribunals are comprised in part of national personnel and apply a mix of national and international law. In fact, one *ad hoc* tribunal, the Special Tribunal for Lebanon, applies exclusively national law. On the other hand, the institutions were created under international law, either by the Security Council or by treaty between the state and the United Nations. Moreover, decision-makers at each institution have made clear that they consider the institutions to be international in important respects. For instance, the Special Court for Sierra Leone asserted its status as an international court to justify refusing to recognize a national amnesty;[166] and the Special Tribunal for Lebanon cited its international nature in employing international law to interpret the Lebanese law defining terrorism.[167]

To improve the normative and sociological legitimacy of these institutions, it will be important for them, and any future *ad hoc* and hybrid courts and tribunals, to clarify the goals they seek to achieve, and the priorities among them, especially the extent to which they serve global and national goals. Without greater clarity in this regard, it is difficult to determine the role that gravity ought to play in adjudicative decisions. For instance, an institution created entirely to serve a particular national community would not need even a minimal gravity threshold, because it would simply apply the criminal law norms of that community. Nor would it need to use gravity as part of an interest balancing test. For such a court, gravity would thus serve simply to guide decisions about which cases to prioritize when resources are limited; and gravity would be defined largely in terms of national

---

[166] *Prosecutor v. Kallon* (Appeals Judgment) SCSL-2004-15-AR72(E) (March 13, 2004) para. 85.

[167] *Interlocutory Decision on the Applicable Law: Terrorism, Conspiracy, Homicide, Perpetration, Cumulative Charging*, STL-11-01/I (February 16, 2011) para. 124.

community goals. For instance, if the community has a serious problem with theft, it might privilege prosecution of theft, perhaps even at the expense of prosecuting some killings. In other words, such an institution would function essentially like a national court.

Even for a court pursuing exclusively national law goals, however, gravity arguably requires some attention to global norms in case prioritization. Human rights law increasingly requires national courts to prosecute certain crimes. Certain treaties, such as the Convention Against Torture, require states to extradite or prosecute persons suspected of those crime found on their territories. Moreover, the European and Inter-American Courts of Human Rights have held that states must prosecute certain additional crimes including rape and disappearance.[168] If a national court chose to privilege prosecution of other crimes at the expense of those that must be prosecuted under human rights law, such decision would likely be illegitimate, and could undermine the court's legitimacy. As such, even in courts with exclusively national goals, gravity for purposes of case selection must take universal human rights norms into account.

For hybrid and *ad hoc* courts and tribunals with a mix of national and global goals, the best use of gravity in decisions about adjudication depends on which goals are being privileged in a given situation. Ideally, the Statutes of future courts and tribunals will provide greater clarity in this regard than have those created to date. This could take the form of preambular language in their Statutes explaining their institutional objectives in greater detail, and perhaps jurisdictional provisions with more specificity about the kinds of cases the courts should prioritize. Statutes should also contain a minimal gravity threshold, and should recognize a significant degree of prosecutorial discretion in case selection, perhaps with some judicial review. In exercising selection discretion, decision-makers should assess gravity in relation to the goals and priorities identified as most appropriate for the particular institution in the particular situation. For instance, a hybrid institution might select some cases because they are of particular importance to the global community and others that especially concern the national community. Such decisions would be normatively legitimate if they align with the institution's mandate. To ensure strong sociological legitimacy, the institution should strive for the kind of clarity of expression advocated above for the ICC. They should explain which goals they are choosing to privilege and why, thereby promoting productive dialogue with constituent communities.

---

[168] Karen Engle, 'Anti-Impunity and the Turn to Criminal Law in Human Rights' (2015) 100 Cornell L. Rev. 1069, 1080; Alexandra Huneeus, 'International Criminal Law by Other Means: The Quasi-Criminal Jurisdiction of the Human Rights Courts' (2013) 107 AJIL 1, 8.

C. Universal Jurisdiction

Often, national courts exercising universal jurisdiction claim to act on behalf of the global community.[169] Under such circumstances, gravity plays a similar role in legitimizing such adjudication as it does for global adjudication. Currently, there is no treaty or other positive law governing the exercise of universal jurisdiction, although scholars and non-governmental organizations have suggested some rules and standards.[170] As the law in this area continues to develop, it should clarify that a minimal gravity threshold applies, similar to that advocated earlier for global adjudication. Adjudication under universal jurisdiction is only legitimate when the case concerns harms and levels of culpability that warrant criminal accountability. Thus, for instance, it may not be legitimate to use universal jurisdiction to prosecute the crime of conspiracy or a defendant who was merely negligent.

Additionally, gravity should be used to help balance global and national interests in determining when it is legitimate to exercise universal jurisdiction. As with the exercise of jurisdiction at global courts like the ICC, national courts should not exercise universal jurisdiction when national interests in avoiding such adjudication outweigh the global interests in adjudication. Thus, for instance, when the national community most affected by the crimes has a strong interest in employing alternative justice mechanisms, or even amnesty, the global interest in adjudication would have to be very strong for the exercise of universal jurisdiction to be legitimate. This might be the case, for instance, when on-going crimes have significant effects beyond the national community.

Finally, gravity should be used to guide national prosecutors in determining when to privilege universal jurisdiction cases as a matter of resource allocation. The global community's interest in such cases should be understood in terms of the goals adjudication is expected to promote, in particular crime prevention through norm expression and deterrence. These global interests should be weighed against the interests of the national community in adjudicating other cases to determine when adjudication using universal jurisdiction is most strongly legitimate.

---

[169] ICJ, 'Arrest Warrant of 11 April 2000' (*Democratic Republic of Congo v. Belgium*) I.C.J. 3, 78 (February 14, 2002).

[170] See, e.g., Diane Orentlicher, 'Striking a Balance: Mixed Law Tribunals and Conflicts of Jurisdiction' in Mark Lattimer and Phillippe Sands (eds.) *Justice for Crimes Against Humanity* (Hart Publishing 2006) 233–4 (arguing that giving priority to the claims of states most directly linked to the crimes in question will "mitigate the hubris associated with universal jurisdiction" and "enhance the legitimacy of prosecutions in fora outside the territorial state"); Steven R. Ratner, 'Belgium's War Crimes Statute: A Postmortem' (2003) 97 AJIL 888, 893–5 (proposing factors); Stephen Macedo (ed.), *The Princeton Principles on Universal Jurisdiction* (Princeton Project on Universal Jurisdiction 2001) 24 (proposing principles).

Conclusion

This chapter has argued that current efforts to justify the exercise of global adjudicative authority by reference to gravity generally fail to produce the desired legitimizing effect because they do not articulate gravity in relation to the goals and priorities of such adjudication. It has proposed a new theory of gravity that can better promote the legitimacy of international criminal law by aligning with the regime's essential purpose of preventing crimes that harm human dignity, and encouraging decision-makers to explain decisions about when to adjudicate in terms of both the balance of global and national interests, and the need to make the most efficient use of global resources. This can promote a dialogic process of mission-refinement, providing constituents with information with which to evaluate the regime, and enabling regime decision-makers to continually re-evaluate priorities.

5

Defendants' Rights and Defenses

In addition to invoking gravity to support international prescriptive and adjudicative authority, courts and commentators sometimes use the concept to justify limiting defendants' rights and rejecting defenses. In this context, as in those
already discussed, gravity is usually insufficiently explained, and is treated as a
threshold above which rights and defenses should be limited. A common narrative is that because international crimes are "atrocities," those accused of such
crimes should not be given the same kinds of protections, or have access to the
same defenses, as other criminal defendants. This narrative has influenced even
some of the most ardent supporters of defendants' rights. For instance, Human
Rights Watch, an organization that has long promoted the rights of criminal defendants, asserts that: "truth commissions, amnesties, or traditional justice processes, regarding the types of crimes covered by the Rome Statute, should not be
regarded as alternatives to international prosecution and the trend is that they
contravene international law."[1] Amnesty International, despite a name that reflects its historical agenda of seeking amnesty for prisoners, rejects amnesty for
international crimes.[2] Such positions reflect the power of the global movement to
prevent impunity for "atrocity crimes."

The idea that rights and defenses can be limited for atrocity crimes is not of recent vintage. A seventeenth century Latin maxim holds that *in delictis atrocissimis
jura transgredi liceat*—for atrocious crimes, legal rules can be relaxed.[3] Nor is the
narrative likely to change anytime soon. Even if the international criminal law regime adopts the goal-based understanding of gravity advocated herein, many
international crimes will continue to involve large-scale harm, tempting decision-
makers to generalize based on their "atrocious nature."

Such uses of gravity threaten the legitimacy of international criminal law because they limit protections of defendants on the basis of an unclear countervailing value: undefined gravity. This chapter exposes this problem and proposes
an alternative way for decision-makers to navigate tensions between the values
of global adjudication and of protecting defendants. Like the proposal regarding

---

[1] Human Rights Watch, 'Policy Paper: The Meaning of "The Interests of Justice" in Article 53 of the
Rome Statute' (2005) para. II(B).
[2] Amnesty International, 'The International Criminal Court: 16 Fundamental Principles for a Just,
Fair and Effective International Criminal Court' (1998) IOR 40/12/98 para. 10.
[3] Mirjan Damaska, 'The Competing Visions of Fairness: The Basic Choice for International Criminal
Tribunals' (2011) 36 N.C.J. Intl. L. & Com. Reg. 365, 370–1.

Shocking the Conscience of Humanity. Margaret M. deGuzman, Oxford University Press (2020). © Margaret M. deGuzman.
DOI: 10.1093/oso/9780198786153.001.0001

legitimate adjudicative jurisdiction, this proposal involves surfacing the values that vague invocations of gravity mask, and balancing them against countervailing values.

As in the contexts already discussed, gravity should be understood here as representing the strength of the global community's interest in global adjudication. This is a function of the goals it seeks to achieve: the more important the global community's objectives in a given situation or case, the greater the gravity of the crime. The value of global adjudication sometimes comes into conflict with values associated with the protection of the persons accused of the crimes. When this happens, decision-makers must first ensure they respect baseline human rights. Such *jus cogens* norms are not subject to derogation, and thus balancing them against other values is not appropriate. However, like many values, those related to the protection of the accused exist on a spectrum with minimum protections at one end, and the highest possible levels of protection at the other. Above the required baseline, decision-makers should balance the values associated with protecting defendants against those related to global adjudication. The greater the importance of global adjudication—gravity—the more legitimate it is to limit protections of defendants.

Engaging in a transparent process of value balancing will enhance the regime's legitimacy for reasons similar to those discussed in the prior chapters: it will highlight the values at stake rather than obscuring them with opaque claims about gravity; and it will also encourage a process of norm articulation, reaction, adjustment, response, and so on, that will help the regime hone its mission over time. This should improve the regime's normative and sociological legitimacy in the long-run. The chapter begins by describing some of the major ways in which decision-makers use vague references to gravity to limit defendants' rights and defenses, before outlining a more legitimacy-enhancing approach to these issues.

I. Restricting Defendants' Rights

The importance of international criminal courts respecting defendants' rights is widely acknowledged in the jurisprudence and literature. Because these courts work on behalf of the global community, for them to undermine the norms of that community would harm their legitimacy. Moreover, in light of the important role international courts play in affirming global norms, failure to respect defendants' rights can damage respect for such rights around the world. Nonetheless, arguments are frequently made that certain rights ought to be limited or disregarded based on the undefined gravity of international crimes. These include arguments that international courts can, and perhaps should: (1) dilute fair trial rights, (2) limit habeas corpus, and (3) de-emphasize the right to a speedy trial.

A. Fair Trial

The right to a fair trial is a universally recognized human right. It is enshrined in numerous international human rights instruments, including the Universal Declaration of Human Rights and the International Covenant on Civil and Political Rights (ICCPR), as well as in the Statutes of international criminal courts.[4] An important tenet of the right to a fair trial is that a defendant's guilt must be proven to a high degree of certainty for a conviction to be legitimate. Common law systems generally require that guilt be proven "beyond a reasonable doubt," while in civil law systems judges must be "intimately convicted" of the defendant's guilt.[5] The International Committee of the Red Cross has determined that customary international law requires application of one of these standards;[6] and international criminal courts have generally adopted the common law's "beyond a reasonable doubt" standard.[7]

Despite global agreement that criminal conviction requires a high burden of proof to ensure fairness, international courts sometimes cite gravity as a justification for accepting evidence that would normally be considered unreliable. In an important study of several international criminal courts and tribunals, Nancy Combs discovered that such courts sometimes make factual determinations based on evidence that would not be considered reliable in many domestic courts.[8] In particular, courts rely on witnesses who lack credibility, or whose veracity or accuracy is at least highly questionable.[9] She writes:

> [T]he testimony of international witnesses often is vague, unclear, and lacking in the information necessary for fact finders to make reasoned factual assessments. Moreover, what clear information witnesses do provide in court often conflicts

---

[4] Universal Declaration of Human Rights (UDHR) (adopted on December 10, 1948) UNGA Res 217 A(III) (UDHR) art. 10; ICCPR (adopted on December 16, 1966, entered into force on March 23, 1976) 999 UNTS 171 (ICCPR) art. 14(1); Rome Statute of the ICC (adopted on July 17, 1998, entered into force on July 1, 2002) arts. 64(2) and 67(1); Statute for the ICTR (adopted on November 8, 1994) UN Doc. S/RES/955 art. 19(1); Statute of the ICTY (adopted on May 25, 1993) UN Doc. S/RES/827 art. 19(2); Statute of the Special Court for Sierra Leone (signed on January 6, 2002) art. 17(2); Agreement between the United Nations and the Lebanese Republic on the Establishment of a Special Tribunal for Lebanon (signed on January 22, 2007 in Beirut and February 6, 2007 in New York, entered into force on June 10, 2007) art. 16(2).

[5] See Kevin M. Clermont and Emily Sherwin, 'A Comparative View of Standards of Proof' (2002) 50 Am. J. Intl. Comparative L. 243.

[6] International Committee of the Red Cross (ICRC), 'Customary IHL Database—Rule 100. Fair Trial Guarantees', available at https://ihl-databases.icrc.org/customary-ihl/eng/docs/v1_rul_rule100#refFN_2751A 976_00042) (last accessed on June 3, 2019).

[7] Rome Statute (n. 4) art. 66(3); STL Statute (n. 4) art. 16(3)(c); ICTY, 'Rules of Procedure and Evidence' (amended on July 10, 1997) UN Doc. IT/32/Rev 50 r. 87(A); ICTR, 'Rules of Procedure and Evidence,' UN Doc. MICT/1/Rev. 1 r. 87(A).

[8] See Nancy A. Combs, *Fact-Finding Without Facts: The Uncertain Evidentiary Foundations of International Criminal Convictions* (Cambridge University Press 2010).

[9] Ibid. 6–7.

with the information that the witnesses previously provided in their pre-trial statements.[10]

In the sample of cases she studied, more than 50 percent of prosecution witnesses testified in ways that were seriously inconsistent with their previous pretrial statements.[11] Many international criminal prosecutions rely heavily on witness testimony due to the absence of documentary or other material evidence, making low standards of reliability particularly troubling. Combs concludes that the gravity of the crimes helps to account for judges' willingness to accept unreliable evidence.[12]

International judges have explicitly cited gravity as a reason to allow witnesses to testify anonymously, a practice that can undermine fairness. In the *Tadić* case, the International Criminal Tribunal for the Former Yugoslavia (ICTY) justified anonymous witness testimony in part by asserting that the usual fair trial rights apply to "ordinary" crimes, whereas "the International Tribunal is adjudicating crimes which are considered so horrific as to warrant universal jurisdiction."[13] Likewise, some scholars cite gravity to justify expansive admissibility rules. For instance, Mirjan Damaška has argued that minor rights violations like "illegal electronic intercepts" can be tolerated when adjudicating grave international crimes.[14] In his view, excluding reliable evidence illegally obtained could be perceived as "grossly insensitive to victims of mass atrocity …."[15] Neither scholars like Damaška, nor international judges, have proposed a definition of gravity to substantiate the claim that grave crimes warrant such divergences from commonly accepted procedures aimed at protecting defendants.

B. Habeas Corpus

Another well-recognized right is that of habeas corpus—the right to be free from illegal arrest and detention. This right is also enshrined in international human rights instruments and customary international law,[16] and in the Rome Statute of

---

[10] Ibid. 5.

[11] Ibid.

[12] Ibid. 224–34.

[13] *Prosecutor v. Tadić* (Decision) ICTY-IT-94-1-T (August 10, 1995) para. 28.

[14] Mirjan Damaska, 'Reflections on Fairness in International Criminal Justice' (2012) 10 J. Intl Crim. Justice 611, 618–19.

[15] Ibid.

[16] UDHR (n. 4) art. 9; Convention for the Protection of Human Rights and Fundamental Freedoms (European Convention on Human Rights, as amended) (ECHR) art. 5; American Convention on Human Rights (ACHR) (adopted on November 22, 1969, entered into force on July 19,1978) 1144 UNTS 123 (ACHR) art. 7(3); African Charter on Human and Peoples' Rights (adopted on June 27, 1981, entered into force on October 21, 1986) (1982) 21 ILM 58 (African Charter) art. 6. The ICRC has found this to be part of customary international law. See ICRC, 'Customary IHL Database—Rule 99. Deprivation of Liberty,' available at https://ihl-databases.icrc.org/customary-ihl/eng/docs/v1_rul_rule99 (last accessed on June 3, 2019).

the International Criminal Court (ICC).[17] Abduction and other forms of illegal detention thus violate human rights law. In some national systems, the remedy for such violations is dismissal, while others provide for less drastic remedies.[18] But, as Dragana Radosavljevic has pointed out, "in cases of egregious international crimes, the illegal arrest may be [treated as] a mere mitigating sentencing factor."[19]

In the *Eichmann* case, the Israeli government abducted the defendant from Argentina and brought him to Israel to stand trial for his role in the Holocaust. The Israeli court rejected Eichmann's motion challenging his illegal arrest, reasoning in part that the crimes with which he was charged, including war crimes and crimes against humanity, were so serious that accountability was imperative.[20] In the *Nikolić* case, the ICTY followed the *Eichmann* precedent to find that the Tribunal had jurisdiction to adjudicate the case despite the defendant's illegal arrest.[21] Nikolić was abducted from the Federal Republic of Yugoslavia by unknown persons and transported in the trunk of a car to Bosnia and Herzegovina where he was arrested and sent to the ICTY.[22] When he challenged the Tribunal's jurisdiction in light of his illegal arrest, the Trial Chamber held that the violation of his rights were not sufficiently egregious to warrant dismissing the case.[23] The Appeals Chamber upheld the ruling after balancing "the fundamental rights of the accused and the essential interests of the international community in the prosecution of persons charged with serious violations of international humanitarian law."[24] It held that for "universally condemned offenses," illegal abduction does not warrant dismissal.[25] The gravity of international crimes thus tipped the balance in favor of adjudication. Although the Chamber engaged in a balancing analysis, it did not elucidate how gravity contributed to that analysis.[26] The International Criminal Tribunal for Rwanda (ICTR) used similar reasoning to reject a motion to dismiss after an illegal detention in the *Kajelijeli* case.[27] Some commentators support the view that international crimes are so serious as to warrant trials after illegal arrest or detention.

[17]   Rome Statute (n. 4) art. 55(1)(d).

[18]   Robert J. Currie, 'Abducted Fugitives Before the International Criminal Court: Problems and Prospects' (2007) 18 Crim. L.F. 349, 352–60.

[19]   Dragana Radosavljevic, 'Mala Captus Bene Detentus and the Right to Challenge the Legality of Arrests Under the ICC Statute' (2008) 29 Liverpool L. Rev. 269, 270.

[20]   *The Attorney-General of the Government of Israel v. Eichmann* (1962) Criminal Appeal No. 336/61.

[21]   *Prosecutor v. Nikolić* (Decision on Interlocutory Appeal Concerning Legality of Arrest) IT-94-2-AR73 (June 5, 2003) para. 23.

[22]   Ibid. para. 2.

[23]   *Prosecutor v. Nikolić* (Judgment) ICTY-94-2-PT (October 9, 2002) para. 114.

[24]   *Nikolić* (Decision on Interlocutory Appeal Concerning Legality of Arrest) (n. 21) para. 30.

[25]   Ibid. para. 26.

[26]   Ibid.

[27]   *Kajelijeli v. Prosecutor* (Appeals Judgment) ICTR-98-44A-A (May 23, 2005) para. 206 (finding the detention did not rise to the "requisite level of egregiousness amounting to the Tribunal's loss of personal jurisdiction").

Abraham Mohit, for instance, has argued that the importance of accountability for "violators of jus cogens norms" justifies trials after illegal captures.[28]

Gravity is also often used to justify subjecting international defendants to lengthy pre-trial detention and denying them provisional release.[29] The *ad hoc* tribunals have held that, in light of the gravity of the crimes they adjudicate, pre-trial detention ought to be the norm, with release justified only in exceptional circumstances.[30] The ICTY has limited such circumstances to situations in which the defendant's health is "incompatible with any form of detention."[31] The ICTY has also held that the gravity of international crimes justifies shifting the burden to the accused to show exceptional circumstances justifying provisional release.[32] In other words, there is a presumption of detention that the accused must overcome. Some scholars have voiced support for this use of gravity to restrict pre-trial release.[33]

C. Right to an Expeditious Trial

The right of every defendant to a hearing within a reasonable time is also enshrined in international human rights law,[34] as well as in the Statutes of international courts and tribunals.[35] Yet courts and commentators often support significant limitations on this right based on claims about the gravity of international crimes, and the concomitant complexity of international trials.[36] International trials often last many years, during which time almost all defendants are incarcerated.

Additionally, some international courts and tribunals have adopted procedural mechanisms that contribute to lengthy trials. In particular, the ICC, Extraordinary Chambers in the Courts of Cambodia (ECCC), and Special Tribunal for Lebanon (STL) allow victims to participate in trials,[37] which greatly increases the time

---

[28] Abraham Mohit, 'The Customary Law of International Abductions: Limits and Boundaries' (2003) 11 Asian Y.B. Intl. L. 123, 145–6.

[29] Caroline Davidson, 'No Shortcut on Human Rights: Bail and the International Criminal Trial' (2010) 60 Am. U. L. Rev. 1, 32.

[30] *Prosecutor v. Blaškić* (Order Denying a Motion for Provision Release) IT-95-14-T (December 20, 1996).

[31] *Prosecutor v. Blaškić* (Press Release) AMcD/PIO/066-E (April 25, 1996).

[32] *Prosecutor v. Delalić* (Decision on Motion for Provisional Release Filed by the Accused Zejnil Delalić) IT-96-21-A (September 25, 1996) para. 20.

[33] See, e.g., Johan David Michels, 'Compensating Acquitted Defendants for Detention before International Criminal Courts' (2010) 8 J. Intl. Crim. Justice 407, 414–15.

[34] See, e.g., ICCPR (n. 4) art. 14(3)(c); ECHR (n. 16) art. 6(1).

[35] Rome Statute (n. 4) art. 64(2); ICTR Statute (n. 4) art. 20(1); ICTY Statute (n. 4) art. 19(1).

[36] See, e.g., *Prosecutor v. Mugiraneza* (Decision) ICTR-99-50-I (October 2, 2003) para. 12; Patrick L. Robinson, 'Ensuring fair and expeditious trials at the International Criminal Tribunal for the former Yugoslavia' (2000) 11(3) Eur. J. Intl. L. 569, 588.

[37] Rome Statute (n. 4) art. 68; Law on the Establishment of Extraordinary Chambers in the Courts of Cambodia for the Prosecution of Crimes Committed During the Period of Democratic Kampuchea (entered into force on October 27, 2004) NS/RKM/1004/006 art. 33; STL Statute (n. 4) art. 17.

required for trials.[38] Time is needed to process victim applications, enable victims' attorneys to question witnesses, facilitate communication between victims' attorneys and prosecutors, and ensure protective measures for participating victims.[39] For its first trial, the ECCC received more than 8,200 victim participation applications,[40] and ninety victims represented by eight attorneys participated in the court's first case.[41] Each of these attorneys was permitted to question witnesses, making questioning repetitive and time-consuming.[42] The ECCC ultimately recognized the impact of this process on defendants' rights and eventually implemented time limits for questioning.[43] Nonetheless, the question of how to balance defendants' right to an expeditious trial with the requirements of victim participation remains unresolved.

II. Limiting Defenses

In addition to restrictions related to the fairness of trials and punishment, unexplained gravity claims are frequently made in support of rejecting defenses that might otherwise apply. Among the most commonly espoused limitations are the unavailability of immunity and amnesty, dilution of the principle of legality, and the rejection of the defenses of duress and superior orders.

A. Immunity

One of the most important ways that international criminal law limits defenses based on gravity claims is by denying defendants immunity. Generally, international law provides two kinds of immunity from criminal prosecution. First, personal immunity, or immunity *ratione personae*, protects certain people from criminal prosecution based on their professional positions. This applies to heads of state and certain other high government officials. This immunity is connected to state immunity—heads of state are viewed as embodying the state and thus entitled to its immunity.[44] This kind of immunity no longer applies once the official is out of office.

---

[38] Bridie McAsey, 'Victim Participation at the International Criminal Court and Its Impact on Procedural Fairness' (2011) 18 Australian Intl L.J. 105, 122.

[39] Ibid.

[40] Thorsten Bonacker and Christoph Safferling, *Victims of International Crimes: An Interdisciplinary Discourse* (Springer Science & Business Media 2013) 351.

[41] Johanna Herman, 'Realities of Victim Participation: The Civil Party System in Practice at the Extraordinary Chambers in the Courts of Cambodia (ECCC)' (2013) 16 Contemporary Justice Rev. 461, 465.

[42] Ibid.

[43] Ibid.

[44] Salvatore Zappala, 'Do Heads of State in Office Enjoy Immunity from Jurisdiction for International Crimes? The Ghaddafi Case Before the French Cour de Cassation' (2001) 12 Eur. J. Intl. L. 595, 599.

The second kind of immunity is functional or *ratione materiae*. This protects certain kinds of government officials from prosecution based on their official functions. This kind of immunity persists even after the official has left the government position.

The Statutes of international criminal courts and tribunals, as well as some treaties prohibiting international crimes, reject both kinds of immunities. The Statutes of the *ad hoc* tribunals,[45] Special Court for Sierra Leone (SCSL),[46] and even the Nuremberg Tribunal[47] exclude immunity defenses. Article IV of Genocide Convention asserts that even "constitutionally responsible rulers" are punishable for genocide;[48] the International Law Commission (ILC) has rejected immunity for the core international crimes;[49] and the ICTY has held that no immunity agreement can bind an international criminal court.[50]

The Rome Statute asserts that its provisions "apply equally to all persons without any distinction based on official capacity" and that no immunities, whether under national or international law, apply.[51] The ICC Appeals Chamber has held that the immunity provision applies even to non-party states when the Security Council refers a situation.[52] The decision came in response to the refusal by Jordan, a state party, to arrest Sudan's president, Omar Al Bashir, who was wanted by the ICC. The Court rejected Jordan's argument that Bashir enjoys immunity because Sudan is not a party to the ICC, noting:

> The obligation to cooperate with the Court reinforces the obligation *erga omnes* to prevent, investigate and punish *crimes that shock the conscience of humanity*, including in particular those under the jurisdiction of the Court and it is this *erga omnes* character that makes the obligation of States Parties to cooperate with the Court so fundamental.[53]

Likewise, a Trial Chamber in the same case asserted that respecting immunity, even that of a head of a non-party state, would contravene the ICC's goal of ending impunity for the most serious crimes of concern to the international community.[54]

---

[45] ICTY Statute (n. 4) art. 7(2); ICTR Statute (n. 4) art. 6(2).

[46] SCSL Statute (n. 4) art. 6(2).

[47] Charter of the International Military Tribunal (adopted on August 8, 1945, entered into force on August 8, 1945) 82 UNTS 279 art. 7.

[48] Convention on the Prevention and Punishment of the Crime of Genocide (adopted on December 9, 1948, entered into force on January 12, 1951) 72 UNTS 277 art. IV.

[49] United Nations General Assembly (UNGA), 'Sixth Report on Immunity of State Officials from Foreign Criminal Jurisdiction, by Concepción Escobar Hernandez, Special Rapporteur' (2018) UN Doc. A/CN.4/722, Annex art. 7.

[50] *Prosecutor v. Karadžić* (Judgment) IT-95-5/18-PT (December 17, 2008) para. 25.

[51] Rome Statute (n. 4) art. 27.

[52] *Prosecutor v. Al-Bashir* (Judgment in the Jordan Referral re Al-Bashir Appeal) ICC-02/05-01/09 OA2 (May 6, 2019) para. 7.

[53] Ibid. para. 123 (emphasis added).

[54] *Prosecutor v. Al-Bashir* (Decision on the Prosecution's Application for a Warrant of Arrest against Omar Hassan Ahmad Al Bashir) ICC-02/05-01/09-3 (March 4, 2009) paras. 40–5.

The International Court of Justice has held that certain incumbent government officials have immunity from prosecution before national courts, even for international crimes, but has suggested that this immunity may not apply to the prosecution of international crimes at international courts. In the *Yerodia* case, Belgium had issued a warrant for the arrest of the incumbent foreign minister of the Congo who was accused of war crimes and crimes against humanity. The International Court of Justice upheld the minister's immunity from prosecution in Belgium, but also stated that such immunity does not mean there can be no accountability for crimes "irrespective of their gravity." The judges thus implied that accountability should be available for grave crimes.[55] The decision goes on to note that incumbent foreign ministers have no immunity "before certain international criminal courts, where they have jurisdiction," giving as examples, the ICTY, ICTR, and ICC.[56] In a separate opinion, three judges were even more explicit about the role of gravity in overcoming immunities. Although they acknowledged that immunities will sometimes apply, even to "perpetrators of grave and inhuman international crimes," they also noted that "the worldwide aversion to these crimes" means that "immunities have to be recognized with restraint."[57]

The Special Court of Sierra Leone (SCSL) rejected the immunity defense of Liberia's former president Charles Taylor, relying in part on the "nature" of the offenses at issue—an implicit reference to gravity.[58] As Professor Charles Jalloh has written, the Taylor decision is seen as proof that the "long arm of international criminal law [can] extend to reach the most powerful state official, so long as that person commits crimes that shock the conscience of the international community."[59] In rejecting a similar claim in the case of former Yugoslav president Slobodan Milošević, the ICTY stated: "In future those who commit *atrocities* against civilian populations must expect to be called to account if fundamental human rights are to be properly protected."[60]

Some national courts have also held that immunities do not apply for international crimes based on their gravity, at least with respect to former heads of state. In the ground-breaking Pinochet case, the British House of Lords decided that the

[55] *Democratic Republic of the Congo v. Belgium* (Judgment) ICJ GL No 121 (February 14, 2002) para. 60.

[56] Ibid. 61.

[57] *Democratic Republic of the Congo v. Belgium* (Joint Separate Opinion of Judges Higgins, Kooijmans and Buergenthal) ICJ GL No. 121 (February 14, 2002) para. 79.

[58] *Prosecutor v. Taylor* (Decision on Immunity from Jurisdiction) SCSL-03-01-I (May 31, 2004) para. 49.

[59] Charles Jalloh, 'Immunity from Prosecution for International Crimes: The Case of Charles Taylor at the Special Court for Sierra Leone' 8(21) ASIL Insights, available at www.asil.org/insights/volume/8/issue/21/immunity-prosecution-international-crimes-case-charles-taylor-special (last accessed on September 14, 2019).

[60] *Prosecutor v. Milošević* (Decision on Preliminary Motions) IT-02-54 (November 8, 2001) para. 33 (emphasis added).

former ruler of Chile was not immune from prosecution for torture in part because of the gravity of that crime.[61] In Lord Hutton's words:

> [S]ince the end of the second world war there has been a clear recognition by the international community that certain crimes are so grave and so inhuman that they constitute crimes against international law and that the international community is under a duty to bring to justice a person who commits such crimes.[62]

A French court in the Ghaddafi case also found that no immunity is available with respect to certain international crimes.[63]

B. Amnesty

Throughout history, amnesties have been an important tool for ending conflicts. Protocol 2 to the Geneva Conventions encourages authorities in charge at the end of non-international armed conflicts to "grant the broadest possible amnesty."[64] However, in recent decades, some authorities have asserted that amnesties may not be granted for international crimes. This claim is usually based on the notion that such crimes are so grave that the international community has an interest in their prosecution that outweighs the state's interest.[65] For instance, a resolution of the UN Human Rights Commission states that "amnesties should not be granted to those who commit violations of international humanitarian and human rights law that constitute serious crimes";[66] and the UN General Assembly has called on states not to grant amnesties for violations of human rights and international humanitarian law.[67] Some authorities claim amnesties are ineffective for international crimes because without accountability for such grave crimes, no lasting peace can be achieved.[68] According to former UN Secretary General Kofi A. Annan,

---

[61] *R. v. Bow Street Metropolitan Stipendiary Magistrate and others, ex parte Pinochet Ugarte* (No. 3) (March 24, 1999) 1 AC 147, para. 242 (Lord Hutton).

[62] Ibid.

[63] *Prosecutor v. Gaddafi* (Fr. Court of Cass. Appeal) 125 ILR 490 (March 13, 2001) para. 9 (holding that "while the immunity of foreign heads of State was still accepted by international society, including France, no immunity could cover the facts of complicity in the destruction of property using an explosive substance leading to the deaths of others, in relation with a terrorist enterprise").

[64] Protocol Additional to the Geneva Conventions of August 12, 1949, and Relating to the Protection of Victims of Non-International Armed Conflicts (adopted on June 8, 1977, entered into force on December 7, 1978) 1125 UNTS 3 art. 6(5).

[65] See Naomi Roht-Arriaza, 'The Developing Jurisprudence on Amnesty' (1998) 20 Hum. Rts. Q. 843, 866; Ronald C. Slye, 'The Legitimacy of Amnesties Under International Law and General Principles of Anglo-American Law: Is a Legitimate Amnesty Possible?' (2002) 43 Va. J. Intl. L. 173, 178–80.

[66] UNCHR Res. 2002/79 (2002) para. 2.

[67] UNGA Res. 58/157 (March 9, 2004) para. 8.

[68] See, e.g., M. Cherif Bassiouni, 'Searching for Peace and Achieving Justice: The Need for Accountability' (1996) 59 L. & Contemp. Probs. 9, 13 (asserting that "[i]f peace is not intended to be a brief interlude between conflicts, then in order to avoid future conflict, it must encompass what justice is intended to accomplish: prevent, deter, punish, and rehabilitate").

amnesties for serious violations of humanitarian and criminal law "do not bring about lasting peace and reconciliation."[69] The International Committee of the Red Cross has identified a customary rule prohibiting amnesty for war crimes and crimes against humanity.[70]

The Statutes of several international tribunals, including the SCSL,[71] ECCC,[72] and the STL,[73] explicitly invalidate amnesties granted for criminal conduct within their jurisdictions; and other international courts and tribunals have refused to apply national amnesties. In the *Furundžija* case, the ICTY declared that the *jus cogens* nature of the prohibition of torture invalidates any amnesty for that crime.[74] The SCSL declared the existence of a "crystallizing international norm that a government cannot grant amnesty for serious violations of crimes under international law . . . ."[75] The ECCC also adopted this view.[76]

The ICC Statute, on the other hand, is silent on the question of amnesties because its drafters did not agree about whether amnesties should be categorically prohibited for international crimes.[77] Some commentators interpret the Rome Statute's provision allowing situations and cases to be declared inadmissible "in the interests of justice" to permit the Court to decline to investigate or prosecute a situation where a national amnesty has been granted.[78] Others disagree with this interpretation.[79] The ICC's Office of the Prosecutor has stated that the interests of justice are not determined by reference to the "interests of peace," suggesting it would not defer to a national amnesty in making determinations about when to investigate a situation.[80]

None of the sources cited earlier that categorically reject amnesties for international crimes based on their gravity adequately explains what gravity means in this context. They generally acknowledge that amnesty is appropriate for some non-international crimes; but they fail to identify values that distinguish international crimes in ways that account for the unavailability of amnesty as to those

---

[69] UN Secretary-General, 'Report on the Protection of Civilians in Armed Conflict' (2001) UN Doc. S/2001/331 para. 10.

[70] ICRC, 'Customary IHL Database—Rule 159. Amnesty,' available at https://ihl-databases.icrc.org/customary-ihl/eng/docs/v1_rul_rule159 (last accessed on June 5, 2019).

[71] SCSL Statute (n. 4) art. 10.

[72] ECCC Statute (n. 4) art. 11(1).

[73] STL Statute (n. 4) art. 6.

[74] *Prosecutor v. Furundžija* (Trial Judgment) IT-95-17/1-T (December 10, 1998) para. 155.

[75] *Prosecutor v. Kallon*, (Jurisdiction) Case No. SCSL-04-15-AR72(E) (March 13, 2004) para. 82.

[76] *Co-Prosecutors v. Nuon* (Decision) 002/19-09-2007/ECCC/TC (November 3, 2011) para. 53.

[77] See Darryl Robinson, 'Serving the Interests of Justice: Amnesties, Truth Commissions and the International Criminal Court' (2003) 14 Eur. J. Intl. L. 481, 483.

[78] See, e.g., Ibid, 505; Richard J. Goldstone and Nicole Fritz, 'In the Interests of Justice and Independent Referral: The ICC Prosecutor's Unprecedented Powers' (2000) 13 Leiden J. Intl. L. 655, 667.

[79] Claudia Angermaier, 'The ICC and Amnesty: Can the Court Accommodate a Model of Restorative Justice' (2004) 1 Eyes on the ICC 131, 144–5; Kenneth A. Rodman, 'Is Peace in the Interests of Justice? The Case for Broad Prosecutorial Discretion at the International Criminal Court' (2009) 21 Leiden J. Intl. L. 105–6.

[80] ICC, 'Policy Paper on the Interests of Justice' (2007) ICC-OTP-2007 1.

crimes. Probably the most common argument is Kofi Annan's claim, cited above, that accountability for international crimes is a requisite for lasting peace and security. However, as explained in Chapter 3, not all international crimes threaten international peace and security, except in a highly figurative sense that could be applied to many non-international crimes as well.

C. Principle of Legality

The principle of legality, or *nullum crimen sine lege*, holds that no one should be tried or convicted for conduct that was not criminal when it took place. That principle is designed to provide notice to defendants of the types of conduct that are punishable and thus to ensure the fair application of the law. A related principle, *nulla poena sine lege*, prohibits retroactive punishment. These principles are enshrined in human rights law.[81] Nonetheless, international courts sometimes cite the gravity of international crimes to reject defenses based on the principle of legality. The first modern international criminal tribunals, the International Military Tribunal at Nuremberg (IMT) and International Tribunal for the Far East (IMTFE), rejected defense arguments that convictions of crimes against peace and crimes against humanity would violate the principle of legality because neither of those crimes existed at the time the defendants acted.[82] The IMT held that the defendants ought to have known their actions were wrong and thus punishable.[83] As Shane Darcy has noted, "[i]mplicit in the judgment is the idea that justice demands the punishment of atrocities and this must take precedence over the rule against retroactivity."[84]

Other international courts have followed this precedent. For instance, in its first case, the ICTY held that the defendant could be held liable under a new theory of participation, which it called "joint criminal enterprise," in part because the "moral gravity of such participation is often no less—or indeed no different—from that of those actually carrying out the acts in question."[85] The court was clear about its gravity-based motivation, stating that "all those who have engaged in serious violations of international humanitarian law, whatever the manner in which they may have perpetrated, or participated in the perpetration of those violations, must be brought to justice."[86] Although the decision purports to find support for the doctrine in customary international law, many commentators disagree; and one

---

[81] ICCPR (n. 4) art. 15(1); UDHR (n. 4) art. 11(2); ECHR (n. 16) art. 7.
[82] Judgment of the Nuremberg Military Tribunal 1946 (1947) 41 AJIL 172, 216–17.
[83] Ibid.
[84] Shane Darcy, 'The Principle of Legality at the Crossroads of Human Rights and International Criminal Law' in Margaret M. deGuzman and Diane Marie Amann (eds.), *Arcs of Global Justice: Essays in Honour of William A. Schabas* (Oxford University Press 2018) 209.
[85] *Prosecutor v. Dusko Tadić* (Judgment) ICTY-94-1-A (July 15, 1999) para. 191.
[86] Ibid. para. 190.

of the judges responsible for the decision has since admitted that the doctrine was not part of customary international law.[87] Other ICTY Chambers considering the legality of joint criminal enterprise have likewise relied on gravity. One Chamber noted that "the egregious nature of the crimes charged would have provided notice to anyone that the acts committed by the accused in 1999 would have engaged criminal responsibility on the basis of participation in a joint criminal enterprise."[88]

When the doctrine was applied in non-international armed conflict for the first time, the tribunals again rejected defense arguments based on the principle of legality, asserting that "any potential perpetrator was able to understand that the criminalization of acts of such gravity did not depend on the international or internal nature of the armed conflict."[89] Similarly, the SCSL found that defendants could be convicted of the newly minted crime of conscripting child soldiers based on the international community's widespread rejection of the use of child soldiers since 1994 and the gravity of the conduct.[90] In such cases, gravity is generally used without definition.

D. Superior Orders and Duress

Respondeat superior, or superior orders, has long been recognized as a defense to war crimes.[91] According to Oppenheim's treatise on international law, "[i]f members of the armed forces commit violations by order of their Government, they are not war criminals and may not be punished by the enemy."[92] However, the Statutes of many international courts and tribunals reject the defense.[93] Some international conventions also preclude the defense for crimes such as torture and forced disappearance.[94] Such legal provisions are sometimes based on the assumption that international crimes, particularly those adjudicated at international courts, are categorically more serious than other crimes.

---

[87] Darcy (n. 84) 214.

[88] See, e.g., *Prosecutor v. Ojdanić*, (Jurisdiction) ICTY-99-37-AR72 (May 21, 2003) para. 43.

[89] *Prosecutor v. Karemera*, (Jurisdiction) ICTR-98-44-1271/1 (May 11, 2004) paras. 44.

[90] *Prosecutor v. Norman* (Decision on Preliminary Motion Based on Lack of Jurisdiction (Child Recruitment)) SCSL-2004-14-AR72(E) (March 13, 2004) paras. 52–3 and 39.

[91] Yoram Dinstein, *The Defense of "Obedience of Superior Orders" in International Law* (Oxford University Press 2012) 8.

[92] Lasa Oppenheim, *International Law, A Treatise: War and Neutrality*, Vol. II, 2nd edn. (Longmans, Green, and Co. 1912) 310. For an overview of the history of this defense, see Matthew R. Lippman, 'Humanitarian Law: The Development and Scope of the Superior Orders Defense' (2001) 20 Penn. St. Intl. L. Rev. 153.

[93] SCSL Statute (n. 4) art. 6(4); STL (n. 4) art. 3(3); ICTY Statute (n. 4) art. 7(4); IMT Charter (n. 47) art. 8; ICTR Statute (n. 4) art. 6(4).

[94] Convention against Torture and Other Cruel, Inhuman or Degrading Treatment or Punishment (adopted on December 10, 1984, entered into force on June 26, 1987) 1465 UNTS 85 (Torture Convention) art. 2(3); Inter-American Convention on Forced Disappearance of Persons (entered into force on March 28, 1996) 33 ILM 1429 art. 8.

In contrast, the Rome Statute of the ICC permits the defense of superior orders for war crimes only. To be eligible for the defense, a defendant must have been under a legal obligation to obey the order and must not have known the order was unlawful.[95] Orders to commit crimes against humanity and genocide are deemed to be manifestly unlawful.[96] This provision suggests that war crimes are categorically less serious than crimes against humanity and genocide.[97]

Some scholars support the rejection of the superior orders defense for all international crimes. For instance, Professor Paola Gaeta finds fault with the Rome Statute's inclusion of the defense for war crimes on the ground that this undermines the drafters' determination " 'to put an end to impunity for the perpetrators' of 'the most serious crimes of concern to the international community as a whole,' " and contravenes customary international law.[98] Micaela Frulli likewise criticizes the Statute for effectively drawing an arbitrary distinction between the gravity of war crimes on the one hand, and that of crimes against humanity and genocide on the other.[99]

Duress has also been excluded as a defense to international crimes in some contexts. The ICTY has held that duress is not a defense to murder as a crime against humanity, even when the perpetrator would himself have been killed had he not complied.[100] The judges reasoned in part that such a defense is inappropriate for international crimes due to their gravity. In their joint and separate opinion, two judges noted that some national laws deny duress as a defense to murder and reasoned that "international law can do no less than match that policy since it deals with murders often of far greater magnitude."[101] The judges did not explain how the "often ... far greater magnitude" of international crimes justifies a categorical rejection of the defense. The decision was controversial;[102] and the Rome Statute's drafters rejected it, instead permitting the duress defense to all crimes.[103]

[95] Rome Statute (n. 4) art. 33(1).

[96] Ibid. art. 33(2).

[97] Micaela Frulli, 'Are Crimes against Humanity More Serious than War Crimes?' (2001) 12 Eur. J. Intl. L. 329, 340.

[98] Paola Gaeta, 'The Defence of Superior Orders: The Statute of the International Criminal Court versus Customary International Law' (1999) 10 Eur. J. Intl. L. 185–65 (quoting Rome Statute).

[99] Frulli (n. 97) 340.

[100] *Prosecutor v. Erdemović*, (Sentencing Judgment) IT-96-22T*bis* (March 5, 1998) para. 17.

[101] *Prosecutor v. Erdemović*, (Joint Separate Opinion of Judge McDonald and Judge Vohrah) IT-96-22-A (October 7, 1997) para. 75.

[102] Compare Miriam Gur-Arye, 'Should Duress Be Treated Differently Under ICL?' (March 17, 2012) 22–3, available at https://ssrn.com/abstract=2025368 (last accessed on September 24, 2019) (arguing that the gravity of international crimes should preclude recognizing duress as a defense) with Luis E Chiesa, 'Duress, Demanding Heroism, and Proportionality' (2008) 41 Vand. J. Transnat'l L. 741, 773 (arguing that it was unfair to convict Erdemović "[b]ecause he could not have prevented the deaths of his victims even if he had resisted coercion").

[103] Rome Statute (n. 4) art. 31(1)(d).

E. Statutes of Limitations

Statutes of limitations exist in most criminal justice systems to ensure that defendants are not prejudiced by stale evidence and lapsed memories. Yet international criminal law generally prohibits Statutes of limitations on the grounds that international crimes are too serious to warrant this protection of defendants. A convention prohibiting the application of Statutes of limitations to war crimes and crimes against humanity has been ratified by fifty-five states.[104] The convention's justification for excluding this defense is that:

> [W]ar crimes and crimes against humanity are among the gravest crimes in international law [and] the effective punishment of war crimes and crimes against humanity is an important element in the prevention of such crimes, the protection of human rights and fundamental freedoms, the encouragement of confidence, the furtherance of co-operation among peoples and the promotion of international peace and security.[105]

The Statutes of some international courts also reject Statutes of limitations;[106] national courts have held that the non-applicability of Statutes of limitations to international crimes is a general principle of international law;[107] and the International Committee of the Red Cross has found it to be a norm of customary international law.[108] The Inter-American Court of Human Rights held that the prohibition on Statutes of limitations for crimes against humanity is a "norm of General International Law."[109] It asserted that such crimes: "are intolerable in the eyes of the international community and offend humanity as a whole,"[110] and that:

> the damage caused by these crimes still prevails in the national society and the international community, both of which demand that those responsible be investigated and punished regardless of the time that has passed.[111]

---

[104] The Convention on the Non-Applicability of Statutory Limitations to War Crimes and Crimes Against Humanity (adopted on November 26, 1968, entered into force on November 11, 1970) 754 UNTS 73. For the status of the ratifications, see the Convention, available at https://treaties.un.org/Pages/ViewDetails.aspx?src=TREATY&mtdsg_no=IV-6&chapter=4&clang=_en (last accessed on December 3, 2019).

[105] Ibid. Preamble.

[106] ECCC Statute (n. 4) art. 5(3), 6(3); Rome Statute (n. 4) art. 29.

[107] See, e.g., Court of Appeals of Santiago, Fifth Chamber, *María Barros Perelman Case*, Case No. 24.471-2005 (September 5, 2009) para. 19.

[108] ICRC, (n. 6) 'Customary IHL Database—Rule 160. Statutes of Limitations' https://ihl-databases.icrc.org/customary-ihl/eng/docs/v1_rul_rule160 (last accessed on January 18, 2019).

[109] *Almonacid Arellano et al. v. Chile* (Judgment) IACHR Series C No. 154 (September 26, 2006) para. 153.

[110] Ibid. para. 152.

[111] Ibid.

Gravity is thus the fundamental basis for the exclusion of Statutes of limitations for international crimes; but, as in the other contexts discussed herein, the categorical distinction has gone unexamined.

III. Categorical Gravity-Based Limits on Rights and Defenses Threaten Legitimacy

As these examples demonstrate, there is a tendency in international criminal law to rely on the concept of gravity, with little elaboration as to its content, to restrict defendants' rights and defenses. The claim is usually categorical—that *all* international crimes, by their nature, are so serious that there must be accountability. This approach obscures the values that are in tension in particular contexts, thus discouraging decision-makers from engaging in the value balancing necessary to reach optimal results—results that would best enhance the regime's legitimacy.

The reasoning in the *Erdemović* case discussed earlier illustrates this problem. The judges asserted that duress should *never* be a defense to killing as a crime against humanity because such crimes are *often* very grave.[112] This kind of analysis creates precedents that are applied to all international crimes, risking unfairness to defendants who commit international crimes that are no more serious than crimes typically adjudicated in national systems. The ICTY arguably reached the right result in *Erdemović*, at least if one accepts that accountability is particularly important for large-scale harms—Erdemović killed approximately 100 people;[113] but it is far less clear that Erdemović should have been precluded from pleading duress if he had killed only one innocent civilian under threat of death.

The same problem exists with respect to the other rights and defenses discussed earlier. It may sometimes make sense for international courts to adopt different evidentiary standards than would be acceptable in most other courts. For instance, when the defendant is a leader of a group that indisputably committed large-scale crimes, a conviction might legitimately rest on evidence that is less specific than usual about what happened, when, and where.[114] But not all international crimes are committed by leaders of criminal groups. Likewise, it is sometimes a good idea for courts to refuse to recognize immunities and amnesties based on the nature of the crimes at issues, but in some cases there are countervailing values, such as a local population's goal of achieving or maintaining peace, that ought to be given priority. It may generally be fair for international courts to exclude defenses based on the principle of legality or superior orders because the crimes are so serious as to be obviously wrong, but that is not true in all cases. For instance, a defendant who

---

[112] *Erdemović* (Joint Separate Opinion of Judge McDonald and Judge Vohrah) (n. 101) para. 75.
[113] *Erdemović* (Sentencing Judgment) (n. 100) para. 15.
[114] See Combs, *Fact-Finding Without Facts* (n. 8).

recruited a child soldier in a community where children often engage in adult work may not have had sufficient notice of the illegality or immorality of the conduct to justify criminal conviction—at least until the recent international convictions for such crimes.

The problem of legal categorization creating risks of unfairness in particular cases is not unique to international criminal law; it is pervasive in law, especially criminal law. For instance, a law creating a separate offense for assault when committed with a deadly weapon inevitably captures some conduct that does not warrant the additional stigma or penalty associated with the more serious offence. Various circumstances can mitigate the seriousness of assault with a deadly weapon such that it is less, or no more, serious than regular assault. These include the intent of the perpetrator, the nature of the weapon, and the way in which the weapon was used. Nonetheless, as scholars and judges have long acknowledged, legal categorization is necessary to the efficient administration of justice.

However, categorical restrictions of rights and defenses based on the supposed gravity of international crimes are particularly problematic for several reasons. First, unlike many such legal categorizations, the values underlying the gravity label are highly uncertain. Offenders who use deadly weapons to commit assault generally pose a special danger to their victims and to the larger community that justifies increased punishment. Such punishment is necessary to accomplish the purposes of the criminal law, such as deterrence, reform, and incapacitation. In contrast, as explained in the previous chapters, the gravity label is generally applied using a multi-factor analysis without relating the results to particular regime values or goals. Consequently, values associated with protecting defendants are sacrificed without any clear gain in terms of countervailing values.

Moreover, the risk of unfairness associated with categorical invocations of gravity to restrict rights and defenses is increasing because the regime is expanding. The development of international criminal law over the past several decades has seen a steady growth in the types of crimes considered "international." War crimes have expanded to include crimes committed in internal armed conflict; crimes against humanity have been interpreted to extend to crimes committed in limited geographic and temporal spaces and affecting limited numbers of victims; and genocide has been held to apply to the acts of a lone madman.[115] The types of acts that can constitute crimes against humanity have also expanded to include, for instance, the theft or destruction of various kinds of property.[116] International

---

[115] The argument that the scope of international crimes is expanding is developed in more detail in Margaret M. deGuzman, 'How Serious are International Crimes? The Gravity Problem in International Criminal Law' (2012) 51 Columbia J. Transitional L. 18.

[116] See *Prosecutor v. Kordić* (Appeals Judgment) IT-95-14/2-A (December 17, 2004) para. 108 (holding "that the destruction of property, depending on the nature and extent of the destruction, may constitute a crime of persecutions of equal gravity to other crimes listed in Article 5 of the Statue").

courts have adopted increasingly broad doctrines regarding *mens rea* and modes of liability.[117]

Such expansion is likely to continue in light of the identities and incentives of international judges and prosecutors. As Darryl Robinson has persuasively argued, these regime actors often see their work as part of a broader human rights promotion agenda.[118] Judges therefore employ interpretive approaches borrowed from the human rights context to justify expansive doctrines and conflate international criminal law norms with human rights norms.[119] International judges and prosecutors are also connected to human rights advocacy networks that encourage regime expansion. For example, human rights organizations pushed strongly for the crimes in Darfur to be labeled genocide,[120] even though many international law experts, including an international commission of inquiry, asserted that the requirement of intent to destroy a group was not met.[121] This may have contributed to the ICC Prosecutor's decision to charge Sudan's president with genocide.

As I argued in Chapter 3, expansive norms of international criminal law are a normatively positive development. International crimes ought to be broadly defined in light of the global community's interest in protecting human dignity. However, the more international criminal law expands, the more problematic it becomes for the regime's legitimacy for decision-makers to use categorical gravity claims to justify limits to defendants' rights and defenses. It is one thing to say that the defendants at Nuremberg should have known what they were doing was criminal, and another to say the same of a soldier who made improper use of a flag of truce. Wayne Jordash and Tim Parker have predicted "a gradual erosion of the accused's rights" that will threaten the true goal of international criminal courts: "the application of principles of law based on the highest international standards of criminal justice."[122] To avoid this outcome, it is important to develop a new approach to addressing the tension between accountability and protecting defendants.

---

[117] Jenia Iontcheva Turner, 'Defense Perspectives on Law and Politics in International Criminal Trials' (2008) 48 Va. J. Intl. L. 529, 552, 561.

[118] Darryl Robinson, 'The Identity Crisis of International Criminal Law' (2008) 21 Leiden J. Intl. L. 925, 939.

[119] Ibid. 946–7.

[120] See Eric A. Heinze, 'The Rhetoric of Genocide in U.S. Foreign Policy: Rwanda and Darfur Compared' (2007) 122 Academy of Political Science 359, 361.

[121] International Commission of Inquiry on Darfur, Report of the International Commission of Inquiry on Darfur to the United Nations Secretary General, (January 25, 2005) 4, available at http://news.bbc.co.uk/1/shared/bsp/hi/pdfs/02_02_05drafur_report.pdf (last accessed on December 5, 2019).

[122] Wayne Jordash and Tim Parker, 'Trials in *Absentia* at the Special Tribunal for Lebanon: Incompatibility with International Human Rights Law' (2010) 8 J. Intl. Crim. Justice 487, 508.

IV. Finding the Right Balance

Any discussion of how international courts and tribunals should address the tension between protecting defendants and securing accountability should start with the recognition that such institutions must always respect fundamental human rights. However, it is also important to acknowledge that protection of defendants exists on a spectrum, with respect for fundamental rights at one end and maximum rights protection at the other. For instance, criminal courts implement the value of fairness by adopting various standards of proof, which yield different levels of protection for defendants, depending on the values at stake.

Some commentators argue that international courts and tribunals should adhere to the highest standards of protection in order to serve as models of justice for other courts.[123] But serving as models of justice does not always mean privileging protection of defendants over other values, in particular values associated with accountability. Preventing crime through accountability is very important to the global community, and pursuit of that goal can justify limiting the protections afforded to defendants in some circumstances. To do so in a way that enhances, rather than detracts from, the regime's legitimacy requires an analysis that takes account of all relevant values.

It is beyond the scope of this project to develop a theory about how courts should balance the values of accountability and protecting defendants in determining applicable rights and defenses. That is a very complex endeavour, which deserves significant scholarly and judicial attention. Even in the best of circumstances, judicial value-balancing is fraught with challenges. As Jenia Turner has pointed out, although balancing has important advantages, including flexibility and the promotion of transparency, it also involves risks.[124] These include the danger that judges will infringe on the legislative realm, and that their efforts to take account of other values will dilute defendants' rights over time.[125]

There are reasons to be less concerned about the first risk in the context of international criminal law, than in other judicial systems. First, the international criminal law regime has no legislature that regularly makes policy decisions. Its closest analog is the ICC's Assembly of States Parties, which meets once a year, and has difficulty reaching policy decisions in light of the diversity of its membership. For courts created under the auspices of the United Nations it is even more difficult to obtain policy guidance. As such, value-balancing in international criminal law

---

[123] Joanna Nicholson '"Too High," "Too Low," or "Just Fair Enough"?' (2019) 17 J. Intl. Crim, Justice 351, 351.

[124] Jenia Turner, 'Policing International Prosecutors' (2012) 45 Intl. L. & Politics 175, 213; Farhad Makekian, 'Emasculating the Philosophy of International Criminal Justice in the Iraqi Special Tribunal' (2005) 38 Cornell Intl. L.J. 673, 694 (asserting with regard to the ICTY that "we would expect that the judges of the Tribunal are delivering the highest standard of international justice regarding the investigations, proceedings, and conclusions of the case").

[125] Turner (n. 124) 213.

inevitably falls to prosecutors and judges to a greater extent than it does in many other criminal justice systems.

To address the second challenge, Turner suggests that international criminal courts follow the proportionality approach that is often used to resolve conflicts between individual rights and public interests in national and international human rights courts.[126] This approach includes ensuring that the social interests to be balanced against the defendant's rights are sufficiently important, that there is a strong enough connection between the interests and the restriction, that there is no better option, and that the benefit to society outweighs the loss to the defendant.[127]

Although Turner advocates this approach with respect to judicial remedies for prosecutorial violations of defendants' rights, something similar makes sense in the broader context discussed in this chapter. Defendants' rights and defenses should only be limited when there is a sufficiently strong countervailing global interest. That global interest can be understood in terms of gravity: the extent of the global community's interest in adjudicating a case to pursue its most important goals, especially crime prevention. Categorical claims based on undefined gravity should thus be replaced with a balancing of values that weighs the extent of the global interest in accountability against the importance of providing the defendant a right or defense under the particular circumstances of each case.

Consider for instance the question of what kinds of proof should be accepted in international criminal trials. To protect innocent persons and ensure proportionate punishment, it is generally essential to have highly reliable evidence of the facts—usually, of who did what to whom, where, and when. As Nancy Combs has demonstrated, however, international tribunals do not always adhere to a high level of reliability and detail in the evidence they accept.[128] This necessarily restricts protection of defendants—they are not being shielded from wrongful conviction to the greatest possible extent. However, features of *certain* international crimes may justify admitting evidence that should not be admitted in other criminal trials. In her book, Combs ultimately countenances the looser evidentiary standards of international courts compared to many national courts in part based on the nature of the crimes at issue. She writes that:

> We may be justifiably less concerned about preventing the wrongful conviction of a defendant accused of an international crime because the nature of international crimes, their perpetration, and their subsequent investigation are apt to put the defendant's innocence in a different light from the innocence of a typical domestic defendant.[129]

---

[126] Ibid. 182.
[127] Ibid. 215.
[128] See Combs, *Fact-Finding Without Facts* (n. 8).
[129] Ibid. 353.

This reference to the "nature of international crimes" appears to be the kind of general gravity claim against which this book warns; but Combs goes on to argue that reliance on a standard below "beyond a reasonable doubt" may be justified by the fact that international courts often prosecute leaders of organizations that are widely known to be engaged in widespread criminality.[130] She thus elaborates on the features of *some* international cases that may justify the looser standard: that the crimes are widespread, notorious, and committed by organizations; and that the defendants are leaders of the organizations.[131] She notes that such cases often give rise to "an amorphous, common sense understanding that the defendant could not have held the position she did without playing *some* role in the atrocities." It is thus the particular features of certain international crimes that justify reducing the evidentiary requirements, rather than the nature of all international crimes. The features in question—the widespread and notorious nature of the crimes, and the defendants' positions as organizational leaders—are factors that can increase the importance of global adjudication—the gravity—of crimes. The value of accountability for crimes of such gravity thus mitigates the value of ensuring defendants the highest levels of protection sufficiently to justify a lower evidentiary burden.

Similar balancing is appropriate with regard to many of the rights and defenses discussed earlier. The rights to be free from illegal capture and to an expeditious trial may be restricted on the basis of compelling countervailing values in some circumstances. For instance, the trial of a high government official responsible for a policy of widespread criminality may be sufficiently important to the global community's preventive goal to warrant a trial after illegal capture. Likewise, when a defendant's guilt is easily established, a lengthy trial may nonetheless be warranted because it would serve global prevention by establishing a historical record of events.[132] Under such circumstances, the global community's preventive goal may outweigh the defendant's interest in an expeditious trial both because the goal is an important one, and because the defendant is unlikely to suffer unnecessary detention. The longer-than-usual trial might also serve global efficiency goals if the historical record created in the trial obviates the need for global trials of other defendants in the situation.

---

[130] Ibid. 244.

[131] Ibid.

[132] Compare Nancy Combs 'Copping a Plea to Genocide: The Plea Bargaining of International Crimes' (2002) 151 U. Penn. L. Rev. 1, 104 (stating that "unlike any domestic criminal justice system, the Tribunals also were established to 'contribute to the restoration and maintenance of peace' .... One way that the Tribunals try to do this is by creating a historical record, which is designed to thwart later attempts at revisionism and to help promote reconciliation and healing"), with Jose Alvarez, 'Rush to Closure: Lessons of the Tadic Judgment' (June 1998) Michigan L. Rev. 2031, 2100 (stating that "criminal proceedings may not ... facilitate the rendering of an accurate account of the scope and nature of a massacre as a whole"); and Mark Osiel, 'Ever Again: Remembrance of Administrative Massacre' (1995) 144 U. Penn. L. Rev. 463, 466–7 (arguing that the goal of creating a historical record can compromise the rights of the defendant).

Likewise, rejecting defenses based on amnesties, immunities, and Statutes of limitations will be appropriate in some cases of international crimes, but not all. Courts should generally disregard the self-granted amnesty of a high-level government official; but it may be appropriate to apply a general amnesty to a low-level soldier accused of small-scale war crimes. Immunities should be unavailable for heads of state who orchestrate systematic policies of extermination, but not necessarily for government officials accused of single war crimes or acts of persecution— at least until they are out of office. While such officials are in office, the values of facilitating inter-state relations may outweigh those associated with accountability.[133] Likewise, the value of protecting defendants will sometimes mitigate in favor of accepting defenses like duress and superior orders, and at other times the value of accountability will prevail.[134] Finally, as Beth Van Schaack and other commentators have noted, international courts must balance these same values in deciding how to apply the principle of legality.[135] In this context as well, blanket assertions of gravity should be replaced with more fine-tuned considerations of countervailing values.

Conclusion

The value balancing advocated herein is a complex endeavor, as the substantial literature cited earlier attests; and further exploration of this process must be left to future projects. The central argument of this chapter is that any such exploration should begin by rejecting the common narrative that categorizes all international crimes as sufficiently grave to justify restrictions on defendants' rights and defenses. Moreover, until the power of gravity rhetoric in international criminal law diminishes, decision-makers should be cautious about valuing accountability over the protection of defendants. Unexamined rhetorics like the gravity narrative can be dangerous because they "narrow the range of discursive space and interpretive possibility."[136] Gravity rhetoric performs this narrowing by categorically asserting

---

[133] Zappala (n. 44) 599 (explaining that heads of state receive immunity while in office because of their position as a representative of their state and out of respect and courtesy for the state within the international community).

[134] For a discussion of superior orders as a defense at the ICC, see Charles Garraway, 'Superior Orders and the International Criminal Court: Justice Delivered or Justice Denied' (1999) 81 Intl. Rev. Red Cross 785, 793–4 (arguing that if the ICC were to exclude superior orders as a defense, it would be inconsistent with its quest for international justice).

[135] Beth Van Schaack, 'The Principle of Legality in International Criminal Law' (2009) 103 ASIL Proc. 101, 102 (stating that courts balance "considerations of fairness ... against other objectives: the condemnation of brutal acts, ensuring individual accountability, victim satisfaction and rehabilitation, the preservation of world order, and deterrence" in applying the principle of legality); Darcy (n. 84) 225 (discussing "the almost inevitable tension that arises between the prosecution and punishment of past atrocities and the rule against retroactivity").

[136] See, e.g., Anthony Amsterdam and Jerome Brunder *Minding the Law* (Harvard University Press 2000) 193. For a related discussion, see Alice Ristroph, 'Criminal Law in the Shadow of Violence' (2011)

the superiority of accountability over other values. To resist the influence of this rhetoric, decision-makers should err on the side of protecting defendants when they are in doubt as to the right balance to strike between that value and others. A judge of the SCSL made an argument along these lines in dissenting from the judgment denying a legality defense for the crime of recruiting child soldiers. He asserted that: "[I]t is precisely when the acts are abhorrent and deeply shocking that the principle of legality must be most stringently applied, to ensure that a defendant is not convicted out of disgust rather than evidence, or of a non-existent crime."[137] When decision-makers have strong emotional reactions to crimes, it is important for them to examine those reactions and to ensure that any restrictions on defendants' rights they endorse are adequately grounded in global values.

As with the prescriptive arguments made in Chapters 3 and 4, to address the challenges gravity poses for protection of defendants, decision-makers must conduct their analysis in an open and transparent manner, promoting dialogue that can enhance the regime's legitimacy over time. Courts should be transparent about the values they are balancing and about how they balance them. This will promote the regime's long-term legitimacy by enabling various audiences, especially the courts' oversight bodies, to provide the institutions with feedback about their decisions. This dialogic process is the best way to ensure that the regime is identifying universal values and implementing them in ways that most people in the world support.

---

62 Alaska L. Rev. 571, 575. (exposing the limiting effects of "violence" rhetoric on efforts at criminal law reform in the United States).

[137] Dissenting Opinion of Justice Robertson, *Prosecutor v. Sam Hinga Norman* (Jurisdiction) SCSL2004-14-Ar72(e) (May 31, 2004) paras. 10–13.

6
Sentencing

A final context in which gravity plays an important role in determining the legitimacy of international criminal law is sentencing. Gravity is a central concept—often *the* central concept—that international criminal courts invoke in justifying sentencing decisions. Although courts consider a variety of factors in determining appropriate sentences, they place particular emphasis on the gravity of the crime, and the role and circumstance of the offender. This chapter refers to all of these factors taken together—crime gravity and the defendant's role and circumstances—as "sentencing gravity," since each is an aspect of seriousness relevant to sentencing. In this context, as in those already discussed, courts have not given the concept of gravity clear and consistent meaning. This ambiguity detracts from the normative and sociological legitimacy of their sentencing decisions. Normatively, relying on ambiguous invocations of gravity to justify decisions results in potential unfairness to defendants and detracts from the ability of courts to effectuate their goals. Sociologically, this practice contributes to perceptions among important audiences that sentences are inconsistent and unfair.

The chapter begins by demonstrating how gravity is typically used in international sentencing decisions, focusing particular attention on the *ad hoc* tribunals and the International Criminal Court (ICC), and also discussing two hybrid tribunals—the Special Court for Sierra Leone (SCSL) and the Extraordinary Chambers in the Courts of Cambodia (ECCC). It shows that gravity is treated as a multi-factor sentencing criterion, with judges emphasizing different factors in different decisions. Although some consistent themes emerge in the jurisprudence, there is a high degree of inconsistency in the courts' application of the gravity criterion. The chapter then explains how these inconsistencies threaten to undermine the normative and sociological legitimacy of international sentencing decisions. Finally, the chapter proposes a theory of sentencing gravity, arguing that gravity as a sentencing criterion at international courts ought to be conceptualized in relation to the goals of punishment that are most appropriate for those institutions. For some international courts, such as hybrid courts, it may be appropriate to consider the punishment values and goals of the national communities most affected by the crimes at issue. Global courts like the ICC, however, should seek to develop global sentencing goals and practices to help build a global justice community.

As explained in Chapter 1, the primary goal of the global justice system should be crime prevention, particularly through deterrence and the expression of global norms. International sentencing practices should therefore aim both to deter

Shocking the Conscience of Humanity. Margaret M. deGuzman, Oxford University Press (2020). © Margaret M. deGuzman.
DOI: 10.1093/oso/9780198786153.001.0001

future crimes and to prevent crimes through the expression of global norms. Retribution should not be a central goal of international punishment because there is no global agreement concerning deserved punishment, nor is one likely to emerge. Nonetheless, courts should be careful not to impose punishment that they, or others, view as undeserved. Punishment that is more severe than deserved violates the human rights of the offender. International courts should therefore err on the side of leniency, preferring the risk of ineffective punishment over that of violating rights. The goal should be to achieve the most deterrence and expressive prevention possible at the lowest cost.

Gravity's role in the sentencing process should be two-fold: to ensure that punishment is not undeserved, and to help judges determine the minimum punishment necessary for deterrence and expressive prevention. Judges should not use the concept as a proxy for retributive proportionality. The goal should not be to determine precisely what punishment an offender deserves—an impossible task—but rather, to identify the lowest effective punishment, while seeking to ensure it does not exceed anyone's likely intuition about what the offender deserves. In light of these goals, international courts should not adopt sentencing guidelines, but should instead preserve broad judicial discretion. Although guidelines may be useful in systems aimed at ensuring retributive proportionality, they hamper judges' ability to tailor sentences in ways that maximize utility.

I. Gravity in International Sentencing Decisions

The legal instruments governing sentencing at international criminal courts and tribunals all require judges to consider gravity in allocating punishment, but provide limited guidance regarding how such determinations should be made. The judges of the International Criminal Tribunal for the Former Yugoslavia (ICTY) and International Criminal Tribunal for Rwanda (ICTR) were simply instructed to "take into account such factors as the gravity of the offense and the individual circumstances of the convicted person"[1] in determining sentences, which could be terms of up to life imprisonment. Those courts were also required to "have recourse to the general practice regarding prison sentences in the courts of the Former Yugoslavia,"[2] although it was left unclear how gravity assessments in local courts ought to be factored in, if at all.

The Statute and Rules of the ICC provide somewhat more guidance. First, life sentences are only permitted when "justified by the extreme gravity of the crime and

---

[1] Statute of the ICTY (adopted on May 25, 1993) UN Doc. S/RES/827 art. 24(2); Statute of the ICTR (adopted on November 8, 1994) UN Doc. S/RES/955 art. 23(2).
[2] ICTY Statute (n. 1) art. 24(1). See also ICTR Statute (n. 1) art. 23(1).

the individual circumstances of the convicted person."[3] These factors must be "evidenced by the existence of one or more aggravating circumstances."[4] Aggravating circumstances include prior convictions for international crimes, abuse of power, crimes involving particularly defenseless victims, particular cruelty, multiple victims, discriminatory motives, and other similar circumstances.[5] Sentences other than life terms are capped at thirty years and, as at the *ad hoc* tribunals, determination of sentence requires consideration of gravity and the offender's individual circumstances.[6] The ICC Rules of Procedure and Evidence require the court to ensure proportionality, asserting that "the totality of any sentence of imprisonment and fine ... must reflect the culpability of the convicted person."[7] The Rules further instruct the judges to "[b]alance all the relevant factors, including any mitigating and aggravating factors and consider the circumstances both of the convicted person and of the crime."[8]

The Rules contribute to confusion about the meaning of gravity by asking judges to take separate account of various factors that are usually considered part of the gravity analysis. The Rules state that, *in addition* to considering the gravity of the crime and the circumstances of the offender, the Court should:

> give consideration, *inter alia*, to the extent of the damage caused, in particular the harm caused to the victims and their families, the nature of the unlawful behaviour and the means employed to execute the crime; the degree of participation of the convicted person; the degree of intent; the circumstances of manner, time and location; and the age, education, social and economic condition of the convicted person.[9]

Moreover, *in addition to these factors*, the Court must take account of mitigating circumstances, such as diminished capacity and cooperation, as well as the aggravating circumstances listed above.[10] By listing all of these factors as outside the gravity analysis, the Rules raise the question: what is left of gravity itself? The Appeals Chamber has thus far answered the question essentially by suggesting, somewhat contrary to the language of the text, that the factors in the Rules are intended to elaborate on the requirements of the Statute, including gravity.[11] Finally,

---

[3] Rome Statute of the ICC (adopted on July 17, 1998, entered into force on July 1, 2001) art. 77(1)(b).
[4] ICC Rules of Procedure and Evidence (2002) r. 145(3).
[5] Ibid. r. 145(2)(b).
[6] Rome Statute (n. 3) art. 78(1).
[7] ICC Rules (n. 4) r. 145(1)(a).
[8] Ibid. r. 145(1)(b).
[9] Ibid. r. 145(1)(c).
[10] Ibid. r. 145(2).
[11] *Prosecutor v. Lubanga Dyilo* (Judgment on the appeals of the Prosecutor and Mr. Thomas Lubanga Dyilo against the "Decision on Sentence pursuant to Article 76 of the Statute") ICC-01/04-01/06 A 4 A 6 (December 1, 2014) nn. 66–7; *Prosecutor v. Bemba Gombo et al.* (Sentencing Appeal) ICC-01/05-01/13 A6 A7 A8 A9 (March 8, 2018) para. 112.

the ICC Statute allows for an appeal from a sentencing decision only on the ground that the sentence is disproportionate to the gravity of the crime, not for other kinds of errors.[12] This provision differs from those in the Statutes of some other international courts and tribunals, which provide for broader grounds of appeal.[13]

The legal instruments governing the SCSL and ECCC likewise position gravity as an important factor in sentencing. Following the example of the *ad hoc* tribunals, the Statute of the SCSL states that judges "should take into account such factors as the gravity of the offence and the individual circumstances of the convicted person."[14] However, they must also consider, "as appropriate," the sentencing practice of the ICTR and of the national courts of Sierra Leone.[15] The law governing the ECCC does not explicitly require consideration of gravity, directing the court instead to apply Cambodian law and, in the absence of applicable Cambodian law, to seek guidance in international law.[16] However, the ECCC's Appellate Chamber, the Supreme Court Chamber, interpreted these directives to require that gravity play a central role in sentencing decisions.[17]

In fact, each of the international courts and tribunals has interpreted their governing law as requiring judges to give particular attention to gravity in determining sentences. The Appeals Chambers of the *ad hoc* tribunals held that the gravity of the offense is "the primary consideration when imposing a sentence and is the 'litmus test' for determining the appropriate sentence."[18] In the ICC's first sentencing judgment, the Trial Chamber declared the gravity of the crime to be "one of the principal factors to be considered in the determination of the sentence, which should be in proportion to the crime, ... and it should reflect the culpability of the convicted person . . . ."[19] The Supreme Court Chamber of the ECCC concluded that "[i]t is well-established in international jurisprudence that the primary factor at sentencing is the gravity of the convicted person's crimes . . . ."[20]

Some courts also consider gravity in determining whether to grant pardons or commute sentences. At the *ad hoc* tribunals, such decisions are made in part by

[12]   Rome Statute (n. 3) art. 81(2)(a).
[13]   See, e.g., ICTY Statute (n. 1) art. 25; ICTR Statute (n. 1) art. 24; *see also* Statute of the SCSL (signed on January 16, 2002) art. 20.
[14]   SCSL Statute (n. 13) art. 19(2).
[15]   Ibid. art. 19(1).
[16]   Agreement Between the United Nations and the Royal Government of Cambodia Concerning the Prosecution Under Cambodian Law of Crimes Committed During the Period of Democratic Kampuchea (established on June 6, 2003, entered into force on April 29, 2005) art. 12.
[17]   *Prosecutor v. KAING Guek Eav* (Appeals Judgment) 001/18-07-2007/ECCC/SC (February 3, 2012) para. 375.
[18]   *Prosecutor v. Nikolić* (Sentencing Appeal) IT-02-60/1-A (March 8, 2006) para. 11. See also *Prosecutor v. Bikindi* (Appeals Judgment) ICTR-01-72-A (March 18, 2010) para. 145 ("In determining a sentence, the deciding factor is the gravity of the offense committed, bearing in mind the particular circumstances surrounding the case and the form and degree of the accused's participation in the crime.").
[19]   *Prosecutor v. Lubanga Dyilo* (Decision on Sentence pursuant to Article 76 of the Statute) ICC-01/04-01/06 (July 10, 2012) para. 36.
[20]   *KAING Guek Eav* (Appeals Judgment) (n. 17) para. 375.

considering the gravity of the crimes committed, along with rehabilitation, cooperation, and treatment of similarly-situated prisoners.[21] At the ICC, on the other hand, decisions regarding sentence reductions do not take account of the gravity of the crimes committed, but rather require consideration of such factors as the convicted persons' cooperation and assistance in other cases,[22] their ability to reintegrate into society, and the impact their release would have on victims of their crimes.[23] Gravity is considered at the ICC in deciding whether to grant release pending appeal after an acquittal.[24] Judgments of acquittal generally require immediate release unless exceptional circumstances exist justifying detention. In making such determinations, the Trial Chamber must consider, inter alia, the seriousness of the offense charged, risk of flight, and probability the verdict will be overturned on appeal.[25]

Despite the importance of gravity to the allocation of punishment at all international courts and tribunals, none of the instruments discussed earlier explain how the judges ought to link their gravity assessments to particular sentences. There are no guidelines indicating sentencing ranges for particular international crimes or suggesting the kinds of influence various factors should have on sentences. Nonetheless, some broad parameters for assessing gravity for sentencing purposes have emerged in the jurisprudence. First, like in other contexts, gravity is usually viewed as including both qualitative and quantitative aspects.[26] Courts do not focus exclusively on the amount of harm a crime produced, but also on the nature of the harm, the vulnerability of the victims, and other qualitative factors. Second, gravity generally encompasses both the harm the crime caused and the offender's level of culpability, although the latter is sometimes discussed under a separate heading.[27] These categories mirror the understanding of sentencing gravity in many national systems.[28] Third, international courts and tribunals

---

[21] ICTY Statute (n. 1) r. 125, ICTR Statute (n. 1) r. 126; *Prosecutor v. Serushago* (Decision of the President on the application for early release) ICTR-98-39-S (May 12, 2005) para 7. For a discussion of the practice at the *ad hoc* tribunals, see Barbora Hola and Joris van Wijk, 'Life After Conviction at International Criminal Tribunals: An Empirical Overview' (2014) 12 J. Intl. Crim. Justice 109, 123–4 (noting that "gravity of crimes is often emphasized as the countervailing factor against early release").

[22] Rome Statute (n. 3) art. 110(4)(a–b).

[23] ICC Rules (n. 4) r. 223.

[24] Rome Statute (n. 3) art. 81(3)(c).

[25] Ibid.

[26] See, e.g., *Prosecutor v. Katanga* (Sentencing Judgment) ICC-01/04-01/07 (May 23, 2014) para. 43.

[27] Compare *Prosecutor v. Taylor* (Sentencing Judgment) SCSL-03-01-T (May 30, 2012) paras. 70–6 (considering together the underlying gravity of Taylor's offense and the nature and degree of his participation), with *Prosecutor v. Blaškić* (Trial Judgment) IT-95-14-T (March 3, 2000) paras. 783–7 and 790–2 (analyzing the scope of the crime, both how the crime was committed and the effects on the victims, separately from the degree of Blaškić's responsibility and his culpability).

[28] See, e.g., Franz Streng, 'Sentencing in Germany: Basic Questions and New Developments' (2007) 8 German L.J. 153, 156 (noting that the German discretionary mode of criminal sentencing requires that judges "must not act arbitrarily but must take heed of the gravity of the criminal act," including the "intensity of the criminal mind" and the "amount of damage"); Sentencing Guidelines Council, 'Overarching Principles: Seriousness' (December 16, 2004) 3 (stating that under English and Welsh sentencing guidelines there are two main components to the seriousness of a crime for purposes of criminal sentencing—the total harm caused by the criminal conduct and the culpability of the offender);

recognize that overlap exists among the factors affecting the gravity of crime and those pertinent to aggravating and mitigating circumstances.[29] They generally hold that the particular category under which a factor is considered is not important, as long as the courts do not double count factors as both increasing crime gravity and aggravating the sentence.[30]

Beyond these parameters, significant uncertainty remains regarding the appropriate content of sentencing gravity. International sentencing judgments are inconsistent as to whether they consider gravity *in abstracto, in concreto,* or both.[31] The gravity of a crime *in abstracto* depends on the gravity of its constitutive elements either in absolute terms or in relation to the gravity of the elements of other crimes. *In concreto* gravity analysis, on the other hand, focuses on the particular facts and circumstances of the crime of which a person is convicted, as well as those affecting the person's culpability for that crime. In some national criminal law systems, the *in abstracto* analysis is performed legislatively or administratively via sentencing guidelines.[32] For instance, the US Federal Sentencing Guidelines establish that murder is more serious than assault, assault with a deadly weapon is more severe than without, and so on. [33] Although such guidelines generally do not consider gravity *in concreto*—how the offense was committed in the particular case—they allow for departures from the usual guidelines in exceptional cases.[34]

As noted earlier, international courts do not have sentencing guidelines, and judges have different views as to whether international crimes can be ranked hierarchically in terms of their gravity. The ICTY Appeals Chamber endorsed a hierarchy of seriousness in the *Erdemović* sentencing judgment.[35] Erdemović was charged with war crimes and crimes against humanity, and pleaded guilty to the latter. On appeal, however, the majority found that his plea was uninformed

---

Law (1999:36) Swedish Penal Code, Chapter 29, s. 1 (stating that under Swedish law consideration should be given to "the damage, wrong or danger occasioned by the criminal act, what the accused realised about this, and the intentions or motives he may have had").

[29] See, e.g., *Prosecutor v. Al Mahdi* (Judgment and Sentence) ICC-01/12-01/15 (September 27, 2016) para. 74.

[30] *Katanga* (Sentencing Judgment) (n. 26) para. 35 (explaining that mitigating circumstances do not need to be analyzed under any particular heading but can be evaluated under gravity or mitigation and aggravation).

[31] Andrea Carcano, 'Sentencing and the Gravity of the Offence in International Criminal Law' (2002) 51 ICLQ 583, 607.

[32] Ibid. 590 (explaining how common law countries use the concept of gravity as a benchmark prepared by sentencing commissions while civil law countries typically add gravity into their criminal codes).

[33] United States Sentencing Commission, *Guidelines Manual*, ss. 2A1.1, 2A2.2, and 2A2.3 (November 2018).

[34] See, e.g., Ibid. ss. 5K2.8, 5K2.13, and 5K2.14, (p.s. listing permitted grounds for sentence departures, including "extreme conduct," "diminished capacity," and "public welfare").

[35] See *Prosecutor v. Erdemović* (Appeals Judgment) IT-96-22-A (October 7, 1997) para. 20; *Prosecutor v. Erdemović* (Joint Separate Opinion of Judge McDonald and Judge Vohrah) IT-96-22-A (October 7, 1997) para. 20–5.

because he was not aware that crimes against humanity are more serious than war crimes.[36] In later cases, however, the Appeals Chamber rejected the view that a hierarchy exists among international crimes. In the *Tadić* judgment, the Appeals Chamber asserted that "there is in law no distinction between the seriousness of a crime against humanity and that of war crimes."[37] Judge Cassese dissented from that decision, asserting that murder as a crime against humanity requires a more serious *mens rea* than murder as a war crime because the former "imperil[s] fundamental values of the international community to a greater extent than in the case [of war crimes]," and hence, "requir[es] a heavier penalty."[38] Although later decisions tended to reject the idea of a hierarchy, sufficient disagreement persisted for one observer to comment in 2005 that ICTY sentencing was "akin to a lottery system . . . because the penalty a particular defendant receives is entirely dependent on a particular judge, who may or may not be in favor of higher penalties for crimes against humanity vis-à-vis war crimes."[39]

The ICTR's judges also struggled with this question. In the *Kambanda* case, for instance, the Trial Chamber stated that war crimes are less serious than either genocide or crimes against humanity, but that it is more difficult to rank the latter crimes.[40] The Chamber noted that crimes against humanity "particularly shock the collective conscience" and genocide requires the specific intent to destroy a group.[41] However, the Chamber also called genocide "the crime of crimes," implying that it is more serious than crimes against humanity.[42] Indeed, many of the ICTR's early sentencing judgments use this phrase or similar language that seems to put genocide at the top of a hierarchy.[43] Like the ICTY, however, the ICTR moved away from recognizing a hierarchy in later judgments.[44] When the defendant in the *Kayishema* case appealed based on the use of the "crime of crimes" language, the Appeals Chamber denied that genocide is the most serious for sentencing purposes, noting that all crimes in the Statute are "capable of attracting the same sentence" and that this language is simply meant to indicate that genocide is "extremely grave."[45]

The ICC has not endorsed an abstract hierarchy of international crimes, but, like the other courts and tribunals, it has sometimes hinted at the existence of such

---

[36] *Prosecutor v. Erdemović* (Appeals Judgment) (n. 35) para. 20.

[37] *Prosecutor v. Tadić* (Sentencing Appeal) IT-94-1A and IT-94-1-A *bis* (January 26, 2000) para. 69.

[38] *Prosecutor v. Tadić* (Separate Opinion of Judge Cassese) IT-94-1A (January 26, 2000) para. 15.

[39] Olaoluwa Olusanya, *Sentencing War Crimes and Crimes Against Humanity Under the International Criminal Tribunal for the Former Yugoslavia* (Europa Law Publishing 2005) 139.

[40] *Prosecutor v. Kambanda* (Judgment and Sentence) ICTR 97-23-S (September 4, 1998) para 14.

[41] Ibid. paras. 14 and 16.

[42] Ibid. para. 16.

[43] See, e.g., *Prosecutor v. Serushago* (Sentence) ICTR-98-39-S (February 5, 1999) para. 15; *Prosecutor v. Rutaganda* (Judgment and Sentence) ICTR-96-3-T (December 6, 1999) para. 451.

[44] See Barbora Hola et al., 'Punishment for Genocide—Exploratory Analysis of ICTR Sentencing' (2011) 11 Intl. Crim. L. Rev. 745, 751.

[45] *Prosecutor v. Kayishema & Ruzindana* (Appeals Judgment) ICTR-95-1-A (June 1, 2001) para. 367.

distinctions. In the *Al Mahdi* Judgment, for instance, the ICC Trial Chamber noted that despite the generally high level of gravity of ICC crimes, not all such crimes are of equal gravity. It gave as an example the lesser gravity of crimes against property compared to those against persons.[46] The ECCC Supreme Court Chamber also articulated an *in concreto* approach.[47]

Interestingly, despite the general trend toward rejecting a hierarchy of crimes and taking an *in concreto* approach to gravity analysis, an empirical analysis of international sentencing decisions shows that, in practice, the sentences international courts impose reflect a hierarchy of crimes.[48] Courts tend to award the longest sentences for genocide, awarding a median of thirty-four years; followed by crimes against humanity, with a median of twenty years; and then grave breaches of the Geneva Conventions, with a median of eighteen years.[49]

International courts have also been inconsistent as to whether they consider levels of authority and degrees of participation as part of an abstract hierarchy for sentencing purposes, or only *in concreto*. In the *Musema* appeals judgment, for instance, the ICTR endorsed a hierarchy, asserting "the existence of a general principle that sentences should be graduated, that is, that the most senior levels of the command structure should attract the severest sentences, with less severe sentences for those lower down the structure."[50] The SCSL also held that the responsibility of superiors for failing to stop crimes is graver than that of direct perpetrators.[51]

Generally, however, the tribunals have focused on abuse of authority rather than on the position itself as aggravating sentences.[52] In other words, they have taken an *in concreto* approach to levels of authority as well as to the gravity of the crime. The

---

[46] See *Al Mahdi* (Judgment and Sentence) (n. 29) para. 72.

[47] *Co-Prosecutors v. Khieu & Nuon* (Appeals Judgment) 002/19-09-2007-ECCC/SC (November 23, 2016) para. 1112 ("As to the purported principle that the harshest punishment must be reserved for those bearing the highest responsibility for the crimes, the Supreme Court Chamber considers that the appropriate sentence will always have to be determined based on the facts of the specific case and the level of culpability of the individual accused.").

[48] Joseph W. Doherty and Richard H. Steinberg, 'Punishment and Policy in International Criminal Sentencing: An Empirical Study' (2016) 110 AJIL 49, 72.

[49] Ibid. 70 (displaying a table stating the median sentence lengths based on the presence of certain sentencing factors).

[50] *Prosecutor v. Musema* (Appeals Judgment) ICTR-96-13 (November 16, 2001) para. 382. See also *Prosecutor v. Tadic*, (Sentencing Appeals Judgment) IT-94-1-A and IT 94-1-A*bis* (January 26, 2000) paras. 56–7 ("Although the criminal conduct underlying the charges of which the Appellant now stands convicted was incontestably heinous, his level in the command structure, when compared to that of his superiors, i.e. commanders, or the very architects of the strategy of ethnic cleansing, was low. In the circumstances of the case, the Appeals Chamber considers that a sentence of more than 20 years' imprisonment for any count of the Indictment on which the Appellant stands convicted is excessive and cannot stand.").

[51] *Prosecutor v. Fofana & Kondewa* (Appeals Judgment) SCSL-04-14-14-A-829 (May 28, 2008) para 558. See also Barbora Hola, 'Sentencing of International Crimes at the ICTY and ICTR' (2002) 4 Amsterdam L.F. 3, 10 (stating that "a general principle evolved in the ICTY and ICTR case law that sentences should be gradated relative to the authority of a defendant in the state structure and the significance of his/her role in the crimes").

[52] *Prosecutor v. Hadžihasanović & Kubura* (Appeals Judgment) IT-01-47-A (April 22, 2008) para. 320.

ICC has likewise rejected a hierarchy that would place direct perpetrators above accessories. In the *Katanga* case, the Court held that:

> [T]he proposed distinction between the liability of a perpetrator of a crime and that of an accessory to a crime does not in any way amount to a hierarchy of blameworthiness, let alone prescribe, even by implication, a scale of punishments. The convicted person's degree of participation and intent must therefore be assessed *in concreto*, on the basis of the Chamber's factual and legal findings in its Judgment.[53]

However, as with the hierarchy of crimes, in practice, the sentences courts impose tend to reflect an *in abstracto* hierarchy of responsibility. At the ICTY, the highest sentences were imposed on offenders who planned, instigated, or ordered others to commit crimes; direct perpetrators and participants in joint criminal enterprises tended to receive the next highest sentences, followed by those convicted of aiding and abetting. [54] Offenders held liable on the basis of superior responsibility tended to receive the shortest sentences, probably because they generally are not considered guilty of the underlying offense, but rather of failing to prevent or punish it.[55] Even superiors who failed to stop or punish crimes as serious as torture and murder received relatively lenient sentences.[56] At the ICTR, the pattern was somewhat different, with order-givers and superiors generally receiving the longest sentences, followed by direct perpetrators, planners, and aiders and abettors, and finally by participants in joint criminal enterprises.[57]

In sum, the jurisprudence is inconsistent as to how the gravity analysis is conducted, although there is a trend toward *in concreto* analysis of the various aspects of sentencing gravity. Additionally, it is often difficult to discern how the gravity analysis relates to the sentence imposed.[58] ICC judgments, for instance, usually

---

[53] *Katanga* (Sentencing Judgment) (n. 26) para. 61. See also *Bemba Gombo et al.* (Sentencing Appeal) (n. 11) paras. 59 (rejecting the idea that "as a matter of law, a person who commits a crime within the meaning of article 25 (3) (a) of the Statute is automatically more blameworthy—and thus deserves a higher punishment—than the person who contributes to it").

[54] Barbora Hola et al., 'International Sentencing Facts and Figures: Sentencing Practices at the ICTY and ICTR' (2011) 9 J. Intl. Crim. Justice 411, 429.

[55] Ibid. See also Olaoluwa Olusanya (ed.), *Rethinking International Criminal Law: The Substantive Part* (Europa Law Publishing 2007) 147.

[56] Christine Bishai, 'Superior Responsibility, Inferior Sentencing: Sentencing Practices at the International Criminal Tribunals' (2013) 11 Northwestern J. Intl. Human Rights 83, 84.

[57] Hola et al, 'International Sentencing Facts and Figures' (n. 54) 429.

[58] See Jens David Ohlin, 'Proportional Sentences at the ICTY' in Bert Swart, Göran Sluiter, and Alexander Zahar (eds.), *The Legacy Of The International Criminal Tribunal For The Former Yugoslavia* (Oxford University Press 2011) 325 (arguing that despite the "carefully choreographed" factors noted in most sentencing decisions, there are usually "[v]ery few reasons ... offered to explain the actual trajectory from [the factors] to the final prison sentence"); but see Barbora Hola et al., 'Consistency of International Sentencing: ICTY and ICTR Case Study' (2012) 9 Eur. J. Criminology 539, 548 (finding that 70 percent of sentencing variation could be accounted for with traditional gravity factors, as well as factors related to aggravating and mitigating circumstances, leaving 30 percent unaccounted for).

start by noting that the crimes over which the Court has jurisdiction include only "the most serious crimes of concern to the international community as a whole."[59] They then discuss various factors related to the gravity of the particular crimes at issue, including the number of victims, the nature of the harm caused, the defendant's role, and so on, as well as aggravating and mitigating circumstances. At the end of the judgment, the judges impose a sentence—generally a number of years imprisonment—without explaining why that particular sentence is appropriate in light of the factors discussed. The absence of justificatory analysis often leaves the impression that the sentence is more a matter of the particular judges' intuition than of reasoned decision-making.[60]

Some international sentencing decisions focus on one or a small number of gravity factors, usually without justifying the selection. For instance, in the *Erdemović* sentencing judgment, the Tribunal spent just one paragraph on gravity, discussing only two criteria: the scale of the crimes and the defendant's role.[61] The *Babić* sentencing judgment's discussion of gravity is limited to the discriminatory nature of the crimes.[62] In *Al Mahdi*, the ICC focused almost exclusively on the cultural significance of the monuments destroyed;[63] and in *Lubanga*, the Court's gravity discussion pertained largely to the effects of the crimes on their victims.[64] In such cases, it is easier to understand what aspects of gravity motivated the outcome. However, because the judges rarely explain their selection of criteria, the justification for the sentence imposed remains unclear.

The subjective nature of the gravity analysis, combined with the high degree of discretion generally afforded to Trial Chambers in sentencing, means that gravity determinations are rarely reversed on appeal.[65] Although prosecutors frequently argue on appeal that sentences are inadequate to reflect the gravity of the crime, and defendants sometimes argue gravity was over-valued, Appeals Chambers usually reject such arguments.[66] Reversing a sentence at the ICC required "discernible

---

[59] *Katanga* (Sentencing Judgment) (n. 26) para. 42. See also *Al Mahdi* (Judgment and Sentence) (n. 29) para. 72.

[60] Uwe Ewald argues that international sentencing decisions are "predictably irrational" in that an institution's early decisions are a matter of the judges' intuitions and those decisions provide an anchor for subsequent decisions. 'Predictably Irrational—International Sentencing and its Discourse against the Backdrop of Preliminary Empirical Findings on ICTY Sentencing Practices' (2010) 10. Intl. Crim. L. Rev. 365, 384–7. The ICC Statute improves upon the sentencing process compared to earlier courts and tribunals, by requiring a separate sentence for each count of conviction. See Rome Statute (n. 3) art. 78(3).

[61] *Prosecutor v. Erdemović* (Sentencing Judgment) IT-96-22-T (November 29, 1996) para. 85.

[62] *Prosecutor v. Babić* (Sentencing Judgment) IT-03-72-S (June 29, 2004) paras. 50–3.

[63] *Al Mahdi* (Judgment and Sentence) (n. 29) paras. 78–81 (explaining the cultural and religious motives behind the property destruction in assessing the gravity of the offense).

[64] *Lubanga* (Decision on Sentence pursuant to Article 76 of the Statute) (n. 19) paras. 37–44.

[65] See Mark B. Harmon and Fergal Gaynor, 'Ordinary Sentences for Extraordinary Crimes' (2007) 5 J. Intl. Crim. Justice 683, 691.

[66] See, e.g., *Bikindi* (Appeals Judgment) (n. 18) paras. 6, 208–9 (finding that Bikindi's sentence was not manifestly inadequate without giving reasons); *Prosecutor v. Prlić et al.* (Appeals Judgment) IT-04-74 (November 29, 2017) paras. 1339–43 (holding that the sentences imposed were not manifestly inadequate because the Trial Chamber considered the factors the prosecution raised on appeal). For

error."[67] Given the subjectivity of the gravity calculation, it is difficult to demonstrate such error. Although an error could be found when the sentence was "so unreasonable as to constitute an abuse of discretion,"[68] showing such unreasonableness is difficult given the lack of specificity in many gravity analyses. For instance, Trial Chambers are not required to discuss each piece of evidence relevant to the gravity determination,[69] making it difficult to argue that they unreasonably failed to consider particular evidence. Nor must Trial Chambers explain clearly how they weighed gravity factors,[70] which makes it difficult to show error in balancing.

The *Đorđević* appeal at the ICTY demonstrates the imprecise analysis typical of sentencing appeals based on gravity. The defendant was sentenced to twenty-seven years imprisonment for his participation in a campaign of ethnic cleansing that killed hundreds of people. The Prosecutor appealed and requested a life sentence, arguing that twenty-seven years was "manifestly inadequate" in light of the gravity of Đorđević's crimes and the role he played.[71] Among other things, the Prosecutor asserted that the defendant's crimes "were particularly heinous because they were based on ethnic intolerance and, moreover, were committed in an 'exceptionally cruel' manner."[72] This included "the murders of 724 unarmed men, women, and children."[73] The Prosecutor also noted that the Trial Chamber had considered the sentence imposed in a different case in arriving at Đorđević's sentence, and that if the Appeals Chamber increased that sentence, it should also increase Đorđević's.[74] The Appeals Chamber rejected this ground of appeal in a few short paragraphs. It noted that the Trial Chamber had considered the fact that the purpose of the common plan at issue was to alter the ethnic balance of Kosovo and that the crimes involved violent and systematic attacks on Kosovo Albanian villages.[75] The Appeals Chamber went no further, however, in addressing the claims that the motives and exceptional cruelty of the crimes rendered the sentence manifestly inadequate. It also rejected the notion that a sentence increase in a different case would require an increase for Đorđević, noting that "each case is to be examined on its own facts."[76]

---

discussion of the few cases where sentences have been modified on appeal due to inadequate consideration of gravity, see nn. 92–100 and accompanying text.

[67] Lubanga (Judgment on the appeals of the Prosecutor and Mr. Thomas Lubanga Dyilo against the "Decision on Sentence pursuant to Article 76 of the Statute") (n. 11) para. 46.

[68] Ibid. para. 44.

[69] Ibid. para. 73.

[70] Ibid.

[71] *Prosecutor v. Đorđević* (Appeals Judgment) IT-05-87/1 (January 27, 2014) paras. 968–75 (dismissing the prosecutor's appeal arguing that the Trial Chamber's sentence was manifestly inadequate).

[72] Ibid. para. 960.

[73] Ibid.

[74] Ibid. para. 962.

[75] Ibid. para. 970.

[76] Ibid. para. 973.

Ultimately, it seems the Appeals Chamber simply disagreed with the Prosecutor that twenty-seven years is an inadequate sentence for an ethnic cleansing campaign that kills hundreds of innocent people. The Appeals Chamber concluded its analysis by agreeing with the Trial Chamber that the sentence reflects the gravity of Đorđević's crimes and indeed "mirrors the outrage of the international community and is sufficient to act as a deterrent for other similar crimes in the future."[77]

The Appeals Chamber was similarly cursory in its dismissal of a gravity-based appeal in the *Muvunyi* case. Muvunyi was sentenced to fifteen years imprisonment for direct and public incitement to genocide.[78] The prosecutor appealed the sentence, arguing that it did not reflect the severity of the crime, which is comparable in gravity to perpetrating genocide. The Appeals Chamber rejected the appeal in a few sentences, noting that the Trial Chamber had "briefly recalled the factual and legal basis of Muvunyi's crime," and had stated that incitement is of similar gravity to genocide.[79] The Appeals Chamber did not address the fact that the Tribunal's sentences for genocide have generally been much higher than fifteen years.[80]

Although parties sometimes appeal sentences on the grounds that they are disproportionate relative to sentences granted to other similarly situated perpetrators, such claims are usually dismissed.[81] In addressing such claims, Appeals Chambers tend to emphasize the Trial Chambers' obligation to tailor sentences to individual perpetrators, and they have little difficulty identifying factors that differentiate perpetrators in terms of gravity.[82] As the ICTR Appeals Chamber stated:

> As repeatedly held, any given case may contain a multitude of variables, ranging from the number and type of crimes committed to the personal circumstances of the individual, and often the differences are more significant than the similarities, and the mitigating and aggravating factors dictate different results for every individual.[83]

The ICC Appeals Chamber likewise noted in the *Lubanga* case that although previous sentencing practice is a relevant factor in determining sentences, it is of limited value in light of the obligation to tailor sentences to the gravity of each crime and the individual circumstances of each defendant.[84] It further noted that

---

[77]   Ibid. para. 974.

[78]   *Prosecutor v. Muvunyi* (Sentencing Judgment) ICTR-00-55A-T (February 11, 2010) para. 153.

[79]   *Prosecutor v. Muvunyi* (Appeals Judgment) ICTR-2000-55A-A (April 1, 2011) para. 66.

[80]   James Meernik, 'Proving and punishing genocide at the International Criminal Tribunal for Rwanda' 4 Intl. Crim. L. Rev. 65, 74 ("[T]hose convicted of genocide charges generally receive life sentences....").

[81]   Hola, 'Sentencing of International Crimes at the ICTY and ICTR' (n. 51) n. 32.

[82]   Jennifer Clark, 'Zero to Life: Sentencing Appeals at the International Criminal Tribunals for the Former Yugoslavia and Rwanda' (2008) 96 Georgetown L.J. 1685, 1698–9.

[83]   *Prosecutor v. Nyiramasuhuko et al.* (Appeals Judgment) ICTR-98-42 (December 14, 2015) para. 3400.

[84]   *Lubanga* (Judgment on the appeals of the Prosecutor and Mr. Thomas Lubanga Dyilo against the "Decision on Sentence pursuant to Article 76 of the Statute") (n. 11) para. 76.

the precedential value of sentences at other international tribunals is limited in light of the ICC's obligation to apply its Statute.[85] The Chamber thus rejected the Prosecutor's claim that Lubanga's sentence was disproportionately lenient compared to sentences the SCSL granted for recruiting and using child soldiers.[86]

Appeals Chambers have occasionally cited a complete failure to mention a particular gravity factor as a basis to overturn sentencing decisions. For instance, the ICTY Appeals Chamber overturned a sentencing decision wherein the Trial Chamber had failed to make any reference to the defendant's responsibility as a superior in its explanation for the sentence.[87] However, as long as a gravity factor was mentioned somewhere in the judgment, the Appeals Chamber will usually assume the Trial Chamber took it into consideration, even if the factor was not discussed in the gravity analysis.[88] The minimal gravity analysis in many sentencing judgments thus rarely provides the basis for a successful appeal. In the *Stanišić* case, for instance, the ICTY Appeals Chamber held that:

> despite the brevity of the Trial Chamber's reasoning in the sentencing section with respect to the gravity of Stanišić's conduct, the Appeals Chamber finds no merit in Stanišić's assertion that the Trial Chamber failed to adequately assess the form and degree of his participation ... in determining his sentence.[89]

The ICC Appeals Chamber has also asserted that a Trial Chamber's failure to mention particular evidence in its sentencing decision does not mean it did not consider the evidence in awarding a sentence.[90]

On the relatively rare occasions that Appeals Chambers reverse sentences on the grounds that they are insufficient to reflect the gravity of the offense, the analysis is often spare, leaving the impression the judges are simply substituting their intuitions about appropriate sentences for those of the judges below. For instance, in the case of Kaing Guek Eav, commonly known as *Duch*, the Supreme Court Chamber of the ECCC substituted a sentence of life imprisonment for the original thirty-five-year sentence, holding, with limited explanation, that the Trial Chamber had undervalued the gravity of Duch's crimes and overvalued the mitigating circumstances.[91] The Supreme Court Chamber found that the mitigating impact of Duch's

---

[85] Ibid. para. 77.

[86] Ibid. paras. 74–7.

[87] *Prosecutor v. Prlić et al.* (Appeals Judgment) (n. 66) paras. 32389.

[88] See, e.g., *Prosecutor v. Munyakazi* (Appeals Judgment) ICTR-97-36A-A (September 28, 2011) para. 174 (holding that "[a] Trial Chamber is not required to expressly reference and comment upon every piece of evidence admitted onto the record").

[89] *Prosecutor v. Stanišić & Župljanin* (Appeals Judgment) IT-08-91-A (June 30, 2016) para. 1108.

[90] *Lubanga* (Judgment on the appeals of the Prosecutor and Mr. Thomas Lubanga Dyilo against the "Decision on Sentence pursuant to Article 76 of the Statute") (n. 11) para. 7.

[91] See *KAING Guek Eav* (Appeals Judgment) (n. 17) paras. 376–83.

subordinate role and cooperation was "limited at best" in light of the aggravating circumstances and "exceptional magnitude" of Duch's crimes.[92]

In a decision with similarly slim analysis, the ICTY Appeals Chamber increased Veselin Šljivančanin's sentence for aiding and abetting torture from five to seventeen years based essentially on its disagreement with the Trial Chamber's assessment of the objective gravity of the crime.[93] According to the Appeals Chamber, the five-year sentence was "so unreasonable that it can be inferred that the Trial Chamber must have failed to exercise its discretion properly."[94] In the *Gacumbitsi* sentence appeal, the prosecutor argued that a life sentence is required for genocide absent mitigating circumstances.[95] Without specifically agreeing with this point, the Appeals Chamber reversed the lower court and imposed a life sentence.[96] The ICTY Appeals Chamber reduced Dusko Tadić's sentence from twenty-five to twenty years, essentially on the grounds that the additional five years was excessive in light of Tadić's role in the crimes.[97] The Chamber did not explain why twenty-five years was inappropriate in light of the serious harm the crimes caused or other gravity factors the Trial Chamber had considered.[98] Indeed, in the *Galić* case, the ICTY Appeals Chamber seemed essentially to admit that it simply disagreed with the Trial Chamber's intuition about the right punishment for the crime, asserting:

> Although the Trial Chamber did not err in its factual finding and correctly noted the principles governing sentencing, it committed an error in finding that the sentence imposed adequately reflects the level of gravity of the crimes committed by Galić and his degree of participation. The sentence rendered was taken from the wrong shelf. Galić's crimes were characterized by exceptional brutality and cruelty, his participation was systematic, prolonged and premeditated and he abused his senior position of VRS Corps commander .... The Appeals Chamber considers that the sentence of only 20 years was so unreasonable and plainly unjust, in that it underestimated the gravity of Galić's criminal conduct, that it is able to infer that the Trial Chamber failed to exercise its discretion properly.[99]

Accordingly, the Appeals Chamber changed the sentence from twenty years to life imprisonment.[100]

---

[92] Ibid. para. 371.

[93] *Prosecutor v. Mrkšić & Šljivančanin* (Appeals Judgment) IT-95-13/1-A (May 5, 2009) para. 406 (holding the Trial Chamber's assessment was "*solely*" in relation to the killings" and did not consider the impact on the victims' families).

[94] Ibid. para. 413.

[95] *Prosecutor v. Gacumbitsi* (Appeals Judgment) ICTR-2001-64-A (July 7, 2006) para. 188.

[96] See ibid. paras. 200–5.

[97] *Prosecutor v. Tadić* (Sentencing Appeal) (n. 37) paras 55–8.

[98] See ibid.

[99] *Prosecutor v. Galić* (Appeals Judgment) IT 98-29-A (November 30, 2006) para. 455.

[100] Ibid. para. 456.

In sum, while parameters for evaluating sentencing gravity are emerging, such as the trend toward rejecting rigid hierarchies, significant ambiguities and inconsistencies remain. Courts have difficulty justifying sentencing outcomes both in absolute terms and relative to sentences imposed on other defendants. While Trial and Appeals Chambers usually discuss a range of factors in their gravity analyses, they rarely tie those factors clearly to the sentences they impose. Instead, it seems that the intuitions of sentencing judges play an important role in international sentencing. The content of sentencing gravity and how it relates to international sentences thus remains unclear.

II. Ambiguous Sentencing Gravity Undermines the Legitimacy of International Sentences

Ambiguous interpretations of gravity undermine the normative and sociological legitimacy of international sentencing decisions. For sentencing decisions in any criminal justice system to have strong legitimacy, they must reflect the values of the relevant community or communities.[101] Those values relate to the goals of punishment and the amounts of punishment considered necessary to achieve them. Some communities are more retributive, while others focus more on deterrence, reform, or restoration. Likewise, norms about the appropriate nature and quantity of punishment vary tremendously around the world. In some systems, the death penalty is permitted, even for crimes involving harm to property,[102] while in others punishment for intentional murder can be as low as a few years in prison.[103] In democratic systems, these values are often reflected in binding legal norms, or at least they are communicated to judges via cultural and political processes. Judges have professional and reputational incentives to implement the community's values.

For international courts, in contrast, the task of identifying values relevant to sentencing is more complex and the incentives are less clear. As explained in Chapter 1, international courts generally view themselves as promoting the values of two communities: the global community and the national communities most affected by the crimes they adjudicate. Yet the values of these communities are often unclear to the judges. Global justice values are in the early stages of development and are thus hard to identify; and it is difficult for the judges, who hail from around the world, to ascertain and implement the values of the most affected

---

[101] For discussion see Chapter 1, section IV.

[102] See, e.g., Hong Lu and Lening Zhang, 'Death Penalty in China: The Law and The Practice' (2005) 33 J. Crim. Justice 367, 370 (discussing offenses punishable by death under Chinese law, including "forty-one property offenses").

[103] See, e.g., Ville Hinkkanen and Tapio Lappi-Seppälä, 'Sentencing Theory, Policy, and Research in the Nordic Countries' (2011) 50 Crime & Justice 349, 384 (noting that in Finland the median sentence for attempted homicide is forty-six months incarceration and the median sentence length for attempted murder is ninety months).

national communities. Additionally, even when the values of national communities and the global community can be identified, they are sometimes in tension. For
instance, Rwandan norms concerning the length and conditions of incarceration
are considerably harsher than the norms that are emerging in the global justice
arena.[104] The ICTR's judges thus faced challenges related to the absence of clarity
about which norms to apply, as well as how to navigate the tensions between potentially applicable norms.

The difficulties that international judges face in identifying and applying sentencing values are evident in their decisions. Those decisions usually mention sentencing goals toward the beginning, but then make little attempt to explain the
relationships among goals, or how those goals relate to the sentence imposed.[105]
For instance, in the ICC's first sentencing decision in the *Lubanga* case, the Trial
Chamber's attention to the purposes of punishment consisted merely in citing
the Rome Statute's preambular language, which asserts that international crimes
should not go unpunished and that the ICC was established to end impunity and
prevent international crimes.[106] The Appeals Chamber reiterated the same language without any further discussion of the relationship among these purposes.[107]
In the *Al Mahdi* case, an ICC Trial Chamber extrapolated from the Rome Statute's
preamble to conclude that the primary purposes of punishment at the ICC are
retribution and deterrence.[108] However, the Chamber also asserted that "a proportionate sentence acknowledges the harm to the victims of these crimes and promotes peace and reconciliation."[109] Nowhere did the Chamber explain the relative
importance of these goals or the priorities among them, let alone the relationship
between the goals and the sentence imposed in the case. ICC Chambers have also
cited rehabilitation as a relevant purpose, although they note that since they adjudicate "the most serious crimes of concern to the international community as a
whole, "rehabilitation should not be given undue weight."[110] Finally, ICC judges
have identified the "legitimate need for truth and justice" as a goal of sentencing,
again without explaining the importance of this goal or how it relates to sentences
imposed.[111]

In addition to the uncertainty about which norms ought to guide international
sentences, international sentencing judgments lack clarity regarding the meanings
of some key concepts—including, notably, that of retribution. Many international

---

[104] See Barbora Hola and Hollie Hyseth Brehm, 'Punishing Genocide: A Comparative Empirical
Analysis of Sentencing Laws and Practices at the International Criminal Tribunal for Rwanda (ICTR),
Rwandan Domestic Courts and Gacaca Courts' (2016) 10 Genocide Studies & Prevention 59, 77–8.

[105] Hola, 'Sentencing of International Crimes at the ICTY and ICTR' (2002) (n. 51) 7.

[106] See *Lubanga* (Decision on Sentence pursuant to Article 76 of the Statute) (n. 19) para 16.

[107] *Lubanga* (Judgment on the appeals of the Prosecutor and Mr. Thomas Lubanga Dyilo against the
"Decision on Sentence pursuant to Article 76 of the Statute") (n. 11) para. 16.

[108] *Al Mahdi* (Judgment and Sentence) (n. 29) paras. 66–7.

[109] Ibid. para. 67.

[110] *Prosecutor v. Bemba Gombo* (Sentencing Decision) ICC-01/05-01/08 (June 21, 2016) para. 11.

[111] *Katanga* (Sentencing Judgment) (n. 26) para. 38.

sentencing judgments assert deterrence and retribution as the primary purposes of punishment.[112] In the context of allocating punishment, criminal law theory generally views retribution as requiring that offenders be given the punishment they deserve.[113] Desert is typically conceptualized as a function of an offender's moral culpability and the harm they caused.[114] Some international sentencing decisions adopt this traditional understanding of retribution. For instance, in the *Krajišnik* case, the ICTY Appeals Chamber explained that retribution involves "an objective, reasoned and measured determination of an appropriate punishment which properly reflects the [...] culpability of the offender."[115] The Chamber went on to explain that culpability pertains to the offender's risk-taking, the harm they caused, and the character of their conduct.[116] This statement reflects factors typically associated with moral culpability.

Many international sentencing decisions, however, assert an understanding of retribution that sounds more like what is usually called "expressivism." Expressive theories of punishment view the purpose of punishment as expressing condemnation of the offense. In the *Aleksovski* judgment, the ICTY Appeals Chamber asserted:

[Retribution] is not to be understood as fulfilling a desire for revenge but as duly expressing the outrage of the international community at these crimes .... Accordingly, a sentence of the International Tribunal should make plain the condemnation of the international community of the behaviour in question and show "that the international community was not ready to tolerate serious violations of international humanitarian law and human rights."[117]

Some ICC judgments have also adopted this approach to retribution.[118]

Such statements are unclear about whether the global expression of condemnation is justified merely by the offender's desert (what has been called "expressive

---

[112] See, e.g., *Prosecutor v. Nahimana et al.* (Appeals Judgment) ICTR-99-52-A (November 28, 2007) para. 1057 ("[T]he two main purposes of sentencing are retribution and deterrence."); *Prosecutor v. Krajišnik* (Appeals Judgment) IT-00-39-A (March 17, 2009) paras. 775 ("It is well established that, at the Tribunal and at the ICTR, retribution and deterrence are the main objectives of sentencing"); *Taylor* (Sentencing Judgment) (n. 27) paras. 13–15 ("The SCSL Appeals Chamber has stated that, in relation to legitimate sentencing purposes, 'the primary objectives must be retribution and deterrence.' "); *Al Mahdi* (Judgment and Sentence) (n. 29) para. 66 ("Accordingly the [ICC] Chamber considers that the Preamble establishes retribution and deterrence as the primary objectives of punishment at the ICC.").

[113] See, e.g., Paul H. Robinson, 'Competing Conceptions of Modern Desert: Vengeful, Deontological, and Empirical' (2008) 67 Cambridge L.J. 145, 145.

[114] See Andrew Von Hirsch and Nils Jareborg, 'Gauging Criminal Harm: A Living Standard Analysis' (1991) 11 OJLS 1, 2–3.

[115] *Krajišnik* (Appeals Judgment) (n. 112) para. 775.

[116] Ibid.

[117] *Prosecutor v. Aleksovski* (Appeals Judgment) IT-95-14/1-A (March 24, 2000) para 185.

[118] See, e.g., *Bemba Gombo* (Sentencing Decision) (n. 110) para. 11 (citing *Katanga* (Sentencing Decision) (n. 26) para. 38); *Al Mahdi* (Judgment and Sentence) (n. 29) para. 67.

retributivism"),[119] or instead is related to crime prevention (a utilitarian version of the expressive rationale).[120] Although the courts frame their appeal to expression as an elaboration of retribution, the explanations they give often sound utilitarian. For instance, in the quote above, the idea that the international community cannot tolerate these crimes suggests that expression is aimed at crime prevention. In the *Nikolić* decision, the ICTY Trial Chamber distinguished the Tribunal's expressive approach from "classical retributive theory," which focuses on "just deserts" in light of the "purposes of the Tribunal and international humanitarian law generally ...."[121] Although this language is far from clear, the reference to the purposes of the Tribunal suggests that utilitarian goals, especially crime prevention, played an important role in the Chamber's approach to expression.

The difference between retributive and utilitarian expressivism is particularly important in cases where they suggest different results. The punishment that an offender deserves may not be the same as that which conveys the appropriate quantum of global condemnation to prevent future crimes. Take, for instance, a soldier who committed a horrible crime, such as the execution of 100 innocent civilians. Such an offender arguably deserves a harsh punishment, but the amount of punishment necessary to discourage other soldiers from committing similar crimes may be much lower.

Not only do international sentencing decisions reflect ambiguities about the goals of punishment, they rarely explain how the punishments they impose effectuate these goals. Indeed, some courts have gone so far as to reject the very idea that their sentencing analysis should be linked to the purposes of punishment. The ICTY Appeals Chamber asserted that the purposes of sentencing "should not be accorded undue prominence in the overall assessment of the sentences to be imposed."[122] Rather, according to the Appeals Chamber, the sentencing court's "duty remains to tailor the penalty to fit the individual circumstances of the accused and the gravity of the crime."[123] Yet it makes little sense to say that a sentence "fits" a crime without explaining that "fit" in terms of one or more purposes of punishment. The "fit" between crime and punishment, which is usually termed "proportionality," does not exist in a vacuum: legitimate proportionality requires anchoring values, in particular, those related to desert or utility, or both.[124]

International courts have sometimes declined to explain how the sentences they impose effectuate punishment goals even when a party to the case explicitly asks

[119] See, e.g., Jean Hampton, 'Correcting Harm versus Righting Wrongs: The Goal of Retribution' (1992) 39 UCLA L. Rev. 1659.
[120] Ibid.
[121] *Prosecutor v. Nikolić* (Sentencing Judgment) IT-02-60/1-S (December 2, 2003) para. 86.
[122] *Prosecutor v. Popović et al.* (Appeals Judgment) IT-05-88 (January 30, 2015) para. 1966.
[123] Ibid.
[124] I elaborate on this idea in Margaret M. deGuzman, 'Proportionate Sentencing at the ICC' in Carsten Stahn (ed.), *The Law and Practice of the International Criminal Court* (Oxford University Press 2015).

them to do so. In the *Šljivančanin* case, the prosecutor asked the Appeals Chamber to impose a sentence that promotes deterrence, arguing that the five-year sentence the Trial Chamber had imposed was insufficient in this regard.[125] The Appeals Chamber declined to establish such a link, holding instead that the Trial Chamber's mere mention of deterrence in the judgment was sufficient to show it had considered that value, despite the absence of any discussion of how the sentence would serve to deter.[126]

The absence of clarity about goals and the failure to link sentences to them undermines the normative legitimacy of international sentencing decisions: their legal legitimacy is weak because the norms the courts articulate are unclear; and at least some of them have weak moral legitimacy because they do not promote appropriate community values. Although sentences may reflect appropriate values even when those values are not clearly articulated and applied, the absence of clarity makes it highly likely that some sentences do not promote morally appropriate values.

Additionally, decisions with uncertain normative legitimacy tend to have weak sociological legitimacy. Strong sociological legitimacy requires relevant audiences to perceive that courts are adopting sentences that reflect the community's moral values. International courts have not only been unclear and inconsistent in their statements about the purposes of punishment and their relationship to proportionality, they have failed to clarify which communities' norms guide their decisions. Most international sentencing decisions implicitly adopt global community norms, but some, especially at the *ad hoc* tribunals, also acknowledge the importance of national community norms.[127]

By failing to explain which community norms they adopt and why, international courts leave themselves open to criticism from all quarters.[128] In particular, the communities most affected by the crimes at issue often feel that international sentences do not reflect their values and expectations. For instance, many people in the Former Yugoslavia believe the ICTY sentences were too lenient.[129] When Biljana Plavšić, who served in a key government position and participated in

---

[125] *Mrkšić & Šljivančanin* (Appeals Judgment) (n. 93) para. 393.

[126] Ibid. para. 416. See also *Prosecutor v. Mucić et al.* (Appeals Judgment) IT-96-21-A (February 20, 2001) para. 803.

[127] The *ad hoc* tribunals were required to "have recourse" to sentencing norms of the relevant national systems. See ICTY Statute (n. 1) art. 24(1); ICTR Statute (n. 1) art. 23(1).

[128] For an interesting related discussion, see Darryl Robinson, 'Inescapable Dyads: Why the International Criminal Court Cannot Win' (2015) 28 Leiden J. Intl. L. 323, 330 ("How is it possible that *opposite* criticisms can both be described as plausible? The reason is that each side of the dyad is based in *values that can be credibly argued as values underlying international criminal justice*.").

[129] Mirko Klarin, 'The Impact of the ICTY Trials on Public Opinion in the Former Yugoslavia' (2009) 7 J. Intl. Crim. Justice 89, 90. But see Diane F. Orentlicher, *That Someone Guilty Be Punished: The Impact of The ICTY in Bosnia* (Open Society Justice Initiative 2010) 54 ("Just as Bosniaks widely condemn ICTY sentences of Serb and Croat perpetrators on the grounds that they are too lenient, many Serbs say that the sentences the ICTY has imposed on 'Bosniaks are so small compared to [the penalty imposed] on Serbs' and that in general, the Tribunal has been overly harsh in sentencing Serb defendants.").

the planning of crimes against humanity, received an eleven-year sentence, one Bosnian observed that in the Former Yugoslavia: "you could get more years for killing someone in traffic."[130] Many Bosnian Muslims and Croats felt that Radovan Karadžić, the former President of Republika Srpska, should have been sentenced to life imprisonment, rather than forty years, for his central role in the conflict and associated atrocities.[131] After Radislav Krstić was sentenced to thirty-five years for aiding and abetting genocide, the President of the Srebrenica Women's Association remarked:

> Any sentence shorter than a life sentence for a criminal such as Krstić is un-acceptable for us. Of course, no-one listens to us. We are so disappointed with the Hague Tribunal and unhappy with their sentences. If a criminal who is being tried just admits that he committed crimes, he is forgiven for half [of what he did] and gets a minimum sentence. Thus, we really do not expect justice from them.[132]

Indeed, there is evidence that many, or perhaps even most, victims were dissatis-fied with the sentences the ICTY imposed.[133] Interviews with over 100 witnesses before the ICTY revealed that the tribunal's sentencing practices had "embit-tered" many of them.[134] Rwandans were similarly unhappy with many of the sen-tences the ICTR imposed.[135] Those sentences were generally less severe than the sentences national courts impose for similar offenses, and the conditions of im-prisonment for ICTR defendants were much better than those in national facil-ities.[136] Similar criticisms have been raised about sentencing at the SCSL[137] and at the ICC.[138]

---

[130] Orentlicher (n. 129) 51.

[131] Julien Borger and Owen Bowcott, ' "Is the Tribunal Not Ashamed?" Karadžić Sentence Angers Victims' *The Guardian* (March 24, 2016), available at https://www.theguardian.com/world/2016/mar/24/radovan-karadzic-hague-tribunal-sentence-survivors-victims-reaction (last accessed on June 14, 2019).

[132] Dan Saxon, 'Exporting Justice: Perceptions of the ICTY Among the Serbian, Croatian, and Muslim Communities in the Former Yugoslavia' (2005) 4 J. Human Rights 559, 564 (emphasis omitted).

[133] Janine Natalya Clark, 'Judging the ICTY: Has it Achieved its Objectives?' (2009) 9 Southeast European & Black Seas Studies 123, 130.

[134] Eric Stover, *The Witnesses: War Crimes and The Promise of Justice in The Hague* (University of Pennsylvania Press 2005) 142.

[135] See Klaus Bachmann and Aleksandar Fatic, *The U.N. Criminal Tribunals; Transition Without Justice?* (Routledge 2015) 94.

[136] Okechukwu Oko, 'The Challenges of International Criminal Prosecutions in Africa' (2008) 31 Fordham Intl. L.J. 343, 384–5.

[137] Nancy Amoury Combs, 'Seeking Inconsistency: Advancing Pluralism in International Criminal Sentencing' (2016) 41 Yale J. Intl. L. 1, 33.

[138] See Olivia Bueno, 'Reactions to the Sentencing of Germain Katanga: Some Comfort, Some Frustration,' *International Justice Monitor* (June 11, 2014), available at https://www.ijmonitor.org/2014/06/reactions-to-the-sentencing-of-germain-katanga-some-comfort-some-frustration/ (last accessed on June 14, 2019) (stating that some in Ituri, the eastern Democratic Republic of Congo province where Katanga's crimes took place, viewed the twelve-year sentence of Katanga as too lenient).

III. A Preventive Theory of Global Sentencing Gravity

To enhance the legitimacy of their sentencing decisions, international courts and tribunals should: (1) identify appropriate values and goals to promote through sentencing; and (2) explain how the sentences they impose advance those values and goals. As explained earlier, most international courts analyze gravity as independent of their sentencing objectives. As in the other contexts discussed in this book, gravity in sentencing is treated as a goal-independent concept that can be ascertained through the objective application of criteria. Sentences are assigned with little or no explanation of why the gravity of a particular crime requires, or even justifies, the level of punishment imposed.

This section argues that a better approach would be to interpret gravity in relation to the purposes of punishment: courts should explain why they believe a crime requires a particular sentence *in order to achieve the purposes the court ought to pursue*. It further argues that as agents of the global community, international courts should reject retribution as a goal. Although retribution should serve as a side-constraint to punishment, ensuring no offender receives more punishment than they deserve,[139] prevention should be the central sentencing objective of international courts. In particular, international courts should seek to prevent crimes through deterrence and norm expression—promoting global norms that shape global behavior. In light of the central goal of crime prevention, international courts should err on the side of leniency, expressing global norms at the lowest possible cost. Additionally, to best promote deterrence and norm expression, sentencing processes should be as transparent as possible, and should remain flexible, rather than restricted through guidelines or similar constraints.

Linking gravity to goals will support the normative legitimacy of international sentencing decisions because the gravity analyses and resulting sentences will be tied to appropriate moral norms. It should also support sociological legitimacy by clarifying the bases for sentencing decisions and thus enabling relevant audiences to provide feedback to decision-makers and, over time, to contribute to the process of developing global sentencing norms.

A. Sentencing Gravity as a Function of Punishment Goals

Assessing gravity in relation to punishment goals means using those goals to guide decisions about which gravity factors to emphasize. As this book has sought to demonstrate, there is no objective way to analyze gravity in the abstract. Instead, there are various factors that contribute to any gravity determination,

---

[139] Youngjae Lee, 'The Constitutional Right against Excessive Punishment' (2005) 91 Va. L. Rev. 677, 683–4.

and decision-makers must choose which factors to privilege in reaching decisions. Currently, most gravity-related decisions, whether in sentencing or other contexts, involve such prioritization with little or no attempt to justify the choices. This contributes to the legitimacy problems described earlier. To better promote the legitimacy of their decisions, sentencing courts should focus on the gravity factors that enable them to best effectuate the purposes of punishment they seek to pursue.

Under this approach, gravity would have different content depending on whether a court focuses primarily on retributive or utilitarian goals. Because inflicting retributively proportionate punishment requires identifying an offender's desert, a court focused on retribution would emphasize gravity factors related to the degree of an offender's culpability, as well as to the extent of harm they caused. Such an analysis would be primarily backward looking, seeking to evaluate the offender's moral culpability and to measure harm at the time the crime was committed. Gravity factors relevant to moral culpability include the offender's mental state, whether they abused a position of power, and their role in the offense. Gravity factors related to harm include the number of victims, the intensity of their suffering, their vulnerability to harm, and the temporal and geographic spread of the harm.

In contrast, a utilitarian court—one seeking to achieve social goods through sentencing—would highlight different gravity factors, depending on which goods the court privileges. The analysis would be forward-looking, seeking to identify the least costly punishment likely to effectuate the relevant goals in the future. For instance, a court pursuing general deterrence would focus more on measuring harm than on culpability. The extent of an offender's culpability generally has little bearing on whether others will offend in the future. In contrast, potential future offenders may take account of the nature and quantity of harm to victims, and sometimes corresponding "benefit" to themselves, in deciding whether to commit a crime. Moreover, the greater the harm, the more important it is to deter the conduct, justifying more punishment.

In rare cases, neither harm nor culpability will be very important to determining the utility of a punishment. For instance, if incapacitating an offender is the central goal, and the offender is very old or ill, neither the harm they caused, nor their culpability, will help determine efficient punishment. A short term of imprisonment may be all that is needed to achieve the goal regardless of these gravity factors. Additionally, factors that would be unimportant to most retributivists, such as post-offense conduct, may be central for some utilitarian goals. For specific deterrence, an offender's past reputation for good deeds may be relevant to sentencing gravity if it helps to predict the likelihood they will reoffend. A court seeking to promote prevention through rehabilitation or reconciliation might emphasize such factors as remorse, apologies, efforts at redress, and cooperation with the prosecution.

Identifying the most important sentencing goals, determining priorities among them, and assessing gravity accordingly, will help international courts enhance the normative legitimacy of their sentencing decisions. Gravity analyses will be more rational and clearly articulated. Over time, appropriate global norms of sentencing gravity will emerge. As in the contexts already discussed, the process of developing such norms should be a discursive one, with courts putting forth norms, communities providing feedback, courts adjusting, and so forth; and it will be particularly important to ensure that the voices of marginalized communities are heard.

To generate the most useful feedback, courts should articulate clearly both their goals and priorities, as well as how the sentences they award effectuate those goals and priorities. Observers may disagree with either of these determinations, or both. For instance, if a court awards a sentence of two years' incarceration for rape as a crime against humanity on the grounds that its primary objective is to rehabilitate the offender, observers may object both to the court's choice of priority, and to the quantum of punishment. If the same sentence is awarded for the primary purpose of deterrence, however, observers may agree with the goal, but nonetheless object that the sentence is insufficient to achieve that goal.

The global norms that develop for sentencing gravity are likely to be similar, but not identical, to those that develop in the context of case selection discussed in Chapter 4. That chapter argued that for purposes of legitimate case selection, gravity should be understood in relation to the global community's interest in adjudicating a given case relative to its interest in adjudicating other potential cases. The goals of adjudication and sentencing are related, although they are not always identical. For instance, if a case is selected for prosecution on the grounds that it will enable a court to express an important global norm, the sentence imposed on the offender must be one that sufficiently expresses that norm. Thus, the gravity analyses in both contexts should take account of the goal of norm expression. However, an additional goal at sentencing might be to rehabilitate the defendant, which could support a longer sentence than the minimum necessary to express the global norm, assuming appropriate conditions of incarceration.

As noted in Chapter 1, when gravity is understood as a function of goals, its importance as a unit of analysis diminishes; and it might even be considered superfluous.[140] Sentences could simply be explained by direct reference to the goals the court seeks to accomplish, rather than through the mediating concept of gravity. Nonetheless, the concept remains useful because it operates as a short-hand referent to a complex underlying analysis. For instance, once a court has performed the analysis necessary to determine appropriate sentences for two defendants, it can encapsulate any resulting sentencing differential by explaining that one case is of higher gravity than the other.

---

[140] See Chapter 1, section II.

B.   Global Sentencing Should be Preventive, Not Retributive

The central goal of global sentencing should mirror that of international criminal law generally: crime prevention. International courts should not seek to impose punishment that accurately reflects each offender's desert. Instead, retribution should serve only as a side-constraint, ensuring that courts impose no more punishment than an offender deserves.

This utilitarian approach to international punishment stands in contrast to that advocated in some of the scholarship on the topic. Jens Ohlin has written that retribution ought to be the central goal of international punishment, and has criticized international tribunals for imposing sentences he views as undeservedly lenient.[141] According to Ohlin, international crimes are categorically so grave that they require harsh punishment, even the death penalty in some cases.[142] In Ohlin's view, international judges ought to evaluate the gravity of international crimes in absolute terms and to allocate punishment that is retributively proportionate to each offender's desert.[143] Other scholars of international criminal law have espoused similar retributive views, either explicitly or implicitly.[144]

Adopting retribution as a goal of international sentencing is likely to undermine the legitimacy of the regime for several reasons. First, retribution is not a globally shared value, and punishing according to desert is therefore not a globally shared goal.[145] Retribution is difficult to distinguish from revenge because it arises from the same psychological source. As Neil Vidmar has written:

[141] See Jens David Ohlin, 'Applying the Death Penalty to Crimes of Genocide' (2005) 99 AJIL 747.

[142] Ibid. 765–7 (discussing the need for proportionality and the view of some countries that "mere imprisonment would not be a proportional response to genocide").

[143] Ibid.; Jens David Ohlin, 'Towards a Unique Theory of International Criminal Sentencing', in Goran Sluiter and Sergey Vasiliev (eds.), *International Criminal Procedure: Towards A Coherent Body of Law* (Cameron May Intl. L. and Policy 2009) 399; Ohlin, 'Proportional Sentences at the ICTY' (n. 58) 323.

[144] See Jean Galbraith, 'The Good Deeds of International Criminal Defendants' (2012) 25 Leiden J. Intl. L. 799, 810–11 (arguing that a certain amount of retribution is "due" both to the individual victims of international crimes and the groups to which they belong); Shahram Dana, 'The Limits of Judicial Idealism: Should the International Criminal Court Engage with Consequentialist Aspirations?' (2014) 3 Penn. State J.L. & Intl. Affairs 30, 110–11 (asserting that the punishment international courts have inflicted has often been too low to reflect adequately the offenders' culpability).

[145] Melanie Reid, 'Crime and Punishment, A Global Concern: Who Does It Best and Does Isolation Really Work?' (2014) 103 Kentucky L.J. 45, 74 (survey results of fifteen countries showing that retribution is not highlighted as a punishment goal in Argentina, Canada, China, Germany, Russia, and the United Kingdom); Richard J. Terrill, *World Criminal Justice Systems: A Survey* (Anderson Publishing Co. 1984) 65 (asserting that in the United Kingdom the retributive rationale "has largely been discredited, as modern perception has developed"); Stanley Yeo, 'India' in Kevin Jon Heller and Markus D. Dubber (eds.), *The Handbook of Comparative Criminal Law* (Stanford Law Books 2011) 289 (discussing the "utilitarian base" of Indian criminal code); John O. Haley, 'Japan' in Kevin Jon Heller and Markus D. Dubber (eds.), *The Handbook of Comparative Criminal Law* (Stanford Law Books 2011) 399 (stating that in Japanese law "[r]etribution is rejected as a socially beneficial response").

Legal and philosophical writings attempt to distinguish retribution from revenge in order to construct a rational system of punishment, but that distinction has been purposefully jettisoned [because] it distracts us from understanding the "moral and psychological appeal of retribution" ... [R]evenge and retribution arise out of the same basic psychological dynamics and structures.[146]

Many commentators reject retribution as a punishment goal for this reason.[147] This concern may explain why international judges sometimes seek to distinguish their version of retribution from revenge, an effort that leads them to adopt an expressive punishment philosophy as explained earlier.[148] Retributive scholars, particularly in the United States, have sought to articulate a retributive theory that distinguishes the infliction of harm for purposes of "justice" from retaliation.[149] Nonetheless, at least some significant portion of the global community believes that "just desert" is an insufficient reason to inflict harm on others.

Additionally, even if punishing according to desert were a shared global value, there is no global agreement about how to measure desert, nor is such agreement likely to emerge. Even supporters of retribution admit that desert is very difficult to gauge.[150] Desert can be measured in cardinal or ordinal terms. Cardinal measurement requires an objective rubric that aligns degrees of crime with degrees of punishment. Early retributivists like Immanuel Kant espoused cardinal measurements of desert whereby an offender should be made to suffer the same harm he or she inflicted on the victim: a murderer should be killed, a batterer beaten, and so on.[151] Today, most people consider this *lex talionis* approach to be inhumane.[152] Although some retributivists continue to endorse cardinal measurement, none has proposed a compelling alternative metric.[153] As Michael Dorf and Frederick

---

[146] See Neil Vidmar, 'Retribution and Revenge', in Joseph Sanders and V. Lee Hamilton (eds.), *Handbook of Justice Research in Law* (Kluwer Academic 2002) 56.

[147] See, e.g., William A. Schabas, 'Sentencing by International Tribunals: A Human Rights Approach' (1997) 7 Duke J. Comp. Intl. L. 461; Richard Lowell Nygaard, 'Crime, Pain, and Punishment: A Skeptic's View' (1998) 102 Dickinson L. Rev. 355, 363 (asserting: "[r]etribution is revenge plain and simple" and "I am opposed to any penological expression of revenge"); but see Susan Jacoby, *Wild Justice: The Evolution of Revenge* (Harper & Row 1983) 362 ("Dismissing the legitimate aspects of the human need for retribution only makes us more vulnerable to the illegitimate, murderous, wild impulses that always lie beneath the surface of civilization—beneath, but never so deep that they can be safely ignored.").

[148] See nn. 116–17 and accompanying text.

[149] Robert Nozick, *Philosophical Explanations* (Harvard University Press 1981) 366–8.

[150] See, e.g., Malcolm Thorburn and Allen Manson, 'The Sentencing Theory Debate: Convergence in Outcomes, Divergence in Reasoning' (2007) 10 New Crim. L. Rev. 278, 284–5 (reviewing Andrew von Hirsch and Andrew Ashcroft, *Proportionate Sentencing: Exploring the Principles* (Oxford University Press 2005)) (asserting that "[e]stablishing that it is even possible to determine sentence severity purely according to crime seriousness has proven to be a very difficult business").

[151] Immanuel Kant, *The Metaphysical Elements of Justice*, 2nd edn., John Ladd trans., (Hackett 1999) 138–9.

[152] Mark D. White, 'Lex Talionis' in Alain Marciano and Giovanni Battista Ramello (eds.), *Encyclopedia of Law and Economics* (Springer 2014) 1.

[153] See, e.g., Ohlin, 'Towards a Unique Theory of International Criminal Sentencing' (n. 143) 399; Nicola Lacey and Hanna Pickard, 'The Chimera of Proportionality: Institutionalizing Limits on Punishment in Contemporary Social and Political Systems' (2015) 78 Modern L. Rev. 216, 227.

Schauer explain, the fundamental problem is that the gravity of offenses and severity of punishment are "incommensurable: their degrees are determined on two different scales that cannot be either reduced to each other or translated into a common scale."[154] Others prefer an ordinal approach that seeks to punish offenders according to their desert in relation to the desert of other offenders.[155] The problem with this approach is that it requires anchoring values at the bottom, and perhaps top, of the scale, as well as increments between punishments. No theory convincingly establishes such anchors.

Some scholars attempt to avoid the measurement problem by arguing that humans share intuitions about deserved punishment.[156] The "utility of desert" theory asserts not only that such shared intuitions exist, but that courts must follow them in allocating punishment to preserve respect for the criminal justice system.[157] But the evidence of shared intuitions of desert is weak.[158] Moreover, even assuming some such intuitions exist within political communities, there is little reason to believe they reach across boundaries. Rather, punishment norms vary greatly around the world, suggesting that ideas about desert are socially constructed within communities.[159] For instance, in much of Europe and Latin America, terms of imprisonment are limited and must be accompanied by the possibility of parole.[160] In contrast, in the United States, China, and some Middle Eastern countries, life sentences are common, sometimes even for non-violent crimes.[161]

---

[154] Michael C. Dorf and Frederick Schauer, 'The Supreme Court 1997 Term' (1998) 122 Harv. L. Rev. 152, 158.

[155] See, e.g., Joseph L. Hoffman, 'On the Perils of Line-Drawing: Juveniles and the Death Penalty' (1989) 40 Hastings L.J. 229, 250 (arguing that ordinal proportionality allows more precise judgments about justice and injustice of punishment).

[156] See Robinson, 'Competing Conceptions of Modern Desert: Vengeful, Deontological, and Empirical' (n. 113) 165; John Darley, 'Realism on Change in Moral Intuitions' (2010) 77 U. Chi. L. Rev. 1643, 1644; J. L. Mackie, 'Morality and the Retributive Emotions' (1982) 1 Crim. Justice Ethics 3; Lawrence M. Solan, 'Cognitive Foundations of the Impulse to Blame' (2003) 68 Brooklyn L. Rev. 1003, 1004.

[157] Paul H. Robinson and John M. Daley, 'The Utility of Desert' (1997) 91 Northwestern University L. Rev. 453, 498.

[158] See Christopher Slobogin and Lauren Brinkley-Rubinstein, 'Putting Desert in its Place' (2013) 65 Stanford L. Rev. 77, 77; Donald Braman et al., 'Some Realism About Punishment Naturalism' (2010) 77 U. Chi. L. Rev. 1531, 1533; Terance D. Miethe, 'Public Consensus on Crime Seriousness: Normative Structure or Methodological Artifact?' (1982) 20 Criminology 515, 523; Francis T. Cullen et al., 'Consensus in Crime Seriousness: Empirical Reality or Methodological Artifact' (1985) 23 Criminology 99, 112.

[159] See V. Lee Hamilton and Steve Rytina, 'Social Consensus on Norms of Justice: Should the Punishment Fit the Crime?' (1980) 85 Am. J. Sociology 1117, 1139–40 (empirical study revealing differences in application of desert principles according to income and race).

[160] Dirk Van Zyl Smit, 'Outlawing Irreducible Life Sentences: Europe on the Brink' (2010) 23 Fed. Sentencing Rep. 39, 40.

[161] See, e.g., Bidish J. Sarma and Sophie Cull, 'The Emerging Eighth Amendment Consensus Against Life Without Parole Sentences for Nonviolent Offenses' (2015) 66 Case W. Res. L. Rev. 525, 535; Wei Luo, 'China' in Heller and Dubber (n. 145) 168–9 (stating that life sentences can be given to offenders who commit theft or fraud); 'Saudi Arabia: Executions for Drug Crimes,' Human Rights Watch, 25 April 2018, available at https://www.hrw.org/news/2018/04/25/saudi-arabia-executions-drug-crimes (last accessed 24 September 2019) (stating that over half of the forty-eight individuals executed in Saudi Arabia in the first four months of 2018 were for non-violent drug offenses).

Additionally, the nature of international crimes makes it particularly unlikely that shared intuitions regarding desert for international offenders will emerge.[162] Crimes like genocide, crimes against humanity, and war crimes include not only constitutive acts such as murder and rape, but also contextual elements, such as a nexus with armed conflict for war crimes, and a widespread or systematic attack for crimes against humanity. This more complex structure increases the difficulty of measuring harm and culpability. The harm of rape as a crime against humanity includes not only the harm to the immediate victims, but also to the entire population under attack. The offender's culpability relates not only to his mental state with regard to the immediate victim, but also regarding the attack as a whole.

Assessments of culpability at the international level are further complicated by the context of normalized violence in which international crimes often occur. Some scholars have argued that such normalization decreases culpability,[163] and have even questioned whether punishment is appropriate at all under such conditions.[164] Others disagree.[165] Scholars are likewise divided about the significance of the group nature of international crimes on assessments of individual culpability.[166] Moreover, even assuming an appropriate measure of desert could be found, the very limited resources international courts enjoy drastically impair their ability to achieve retributive goals, making them of comparatively little benefit in this regard.

In contrast to the disagreement about retribution, crime prevention is a widely accepted goal of criminal punishment. This goal is central in most national systems,[167] and is prominent in the sentencing jurisprudence of international

---

[162] Andrew K. Woods, 'Moral Judgments & International Crimes: The Disutility of Desert' (2012) 52 Va. J. Intl. L. 633, 681 ("This retributivism has a behavioral justification: some scholars and policy-makers believe that a deserts-based criminal regime will produce the best consequences. However, the behavioral arguments that justify such a 'utility of desert' view at the domestic level may not hold at the international level.").

[163] See Ziv Bohrer, 'Is the Prosecution of War Crimes Just and Effective? Rethinking the Lessons from Sociology and Psychology' (2012) 33 Michigan J. Intl. L. 749, 783–6; Mark A. Drumbl, 'Punishment, Postgenocide: From Guilt to Shame to Civis in Rwanda' (2000) 75 NYU L. Rev. 1221, 1252.

[164] See Woods, 'Moral Judgments' (n. 162) 654–5 (noting that "[g]iven the overwhelming evidence that people determine what is right or wrong by looking to the behavior of those around them, it may not make much sense to punish an individual for the immorality of acting on the moral authority of his peer group").

[165] Saira Mohamed, 'Deviance, Aspiration, and the Stories We Tell: Reconciling Mass Atrocity and the Criminal Law' (2015) 124 Yale L.J. 1628, 1637 (arguing that the normalcy of violence is what makes that violence an even more appropriate target for criminal law).

[166] Compare Antonio Cassese, 'The Proper Limits of Individual Responsibility under the Doctrine of Joint Criminal Enterprise' (2007) 5 J. Intl. Crim. Justice 109, 111 ("[I]n the case of collective criminality ... all participants in this common plan or design may be held criminally liable for the perpetration of the criminal act, even if they have not materially participated in the commission of said act."), with Allison Marston Danner and Jenny S. Martinez, 'Guilty Associations: Joint Criminal Enterprise, Command Responsibility, and the Development of International Criminal Law' (2005) 93 California L. Rev. 75, 167 (arguing that the overuse of Joint Criminal Enterprise (JCE) in criminal convictions will result in many of the most culpable offenders escaping liability because of JCE's focus on the broader perspective instead of individual culpability).

[167] See Heller and Dubber (n. 145) (providing an overview of comparative criminal law internationally and showing that many countries, including Germany, India, Iran, Russia, and South Africa

courts and tribunals.[168] Crime prevention can be pursued in various ways, with the most important methods being deterrence and norm expression. Although specific deterrence—discouraging an offender from reoffending—may be important in some cases, general deterrence should often be the primary focus of global sentencing. Global courts should seek to impose sentences that are likely to cause potential future offenders to view the costs of offending as greater than the benefits.

Although evidence is emerging suggesting that international punishment sometimes has deterrent effects,[169] the low likelihood of apprehension, combined with the political incentives driving many international offenders, reduces the deterrent value of punishment for many potential offenders. For that reason, norm expression should be considered an equally, or even more important goal of international punishment. International courts are particularly well-suited to the task of expressing global norms. This is especially true of the ICC, to which more than 120 states are parties, and which therefore has a global platform, as well as access to global media, and the stature to speak on behalf of the globe.

That international courts should privilege global prevention through deterrence and norm expression does not mean they should ignore all other goals. However, such goals should be pursued only when they are compatible with the courts' central preventive mission, and only to the extent that they can be pursued without undue cost to the institution. The ICC should not, for instance, decline to punish an offender on the grounds that a different form of justice, such as restorative justice, would better serve the goal of national reconciliation. Although national reconciliation may sometimes be an appropriate goal of international punishment, it should only be pursued when it is compatible with the primary goal of global prevention. Assuming that failing to punish a convicted offender would detract from the ICC's central goal of global prevention, such a result would undermine the institution's legitimacy and should be avoided. As explained in Chapter 4, the ICC can legitimately choose not to prosecute a situation or case when the interests of the local community outweigh those of the global community, but once it prosecutes an offender it should impose punishment in line with the goal of global prevention.

Privileging prevention has important implications for how international courts should assess gravity, and thus for the amount of punishment they should

consider deterrence and crime prevention among their top sentencing goals); Michael Tonry, 'Purposes and Functions of Sentencing' (2006) 34 Crime & Justice 1, 11 (asserting that "[m]ost people ... believe that prevention and diminution of crime, fear of crime, and their consequences are important and legitimate functions of sentencing").

[168] See *Prosecutor v. Brima* (Sentencing Judgment) SCSL-04-16-T (July 19, 2007) para. 16; *Prosecutor v. Popović et al.* (Trial Judgment) IT-05-88-T (June 10, 2010) paras. 2128–9; *Prosecutor v. Kambanda* (Judgment and Sentence) ICTR-97-23-S (September 4, 1998) para. 28.
[169] See Chapter 4, section II.B.

impose. In particular, it means that the gravity analysis should focus primarily on the harm a crime causes, rather than on the offender's culpability. It is the nature and quantity of harm that primarily determine the amount of punishment necessary to prevent future crimes. The offender's culpability relates more to desert, which is generally not important for determining the amount of punishment needed for preventive purposes. International courts should thus assess sentencing gravity primarily by considering factors related to harm, such as the number of victims, their vulnerability, the nature of the crime, the geographic and temporal spread of the harm, and so on. The extent of the offender's depravity should be considered only to the extent that it increases the harm to victims or the broader community. For instance, an offender's discriminatory animus may increase the harm of a crime when it is known to the victim or to the broader community the crime targets.

C. Necessary Punishment, Not Harsh Justice

Privileging global prevention also means that international courts should impose punishments that are sufficient, but no greater than necessary, to prevent future crimes. Numerous commentators have asserted that the gravity of international crimes requires harsh punishment of those who perpetrate them.[170] The ICC's first Prosecutor argued that the Court should apply a presumptive minimum sentence of twenty-four years' incarceration for all offenders in light of the gravity of the crimes within the Court's jurisdiction.[171] Such calls for harsh justice for international crimes are misplaced.[172] They result from the misleading narrative critiqued throughout this book that international crimes categorically surpass an unspecified gravity threshold.

Instead, international judges should respect the principle of parsimony, imposing only the minimum punishments they believe will serve to prevent future crimes.[173] This will usually mean they should impose the lowest punishments needed to deter and express relevant global norms adequately. In some cases, however, sentencing judges may impose additional punishment to pursue a subsidiary preventive objective such as incapacitation or community restoration. For instance, if an offender is particularly dangerous, additional incarceration beyond that needed to deter others and express condemnation may be necessary to prevent the offender from causing further harm. Likewise, it may sometimes be

---

[170] See generally, Ohlin, 'Towards a Unique Theory of International Criminal Sentencing' (n. 143) 390; Dana (n. 144) 38; Harmon and Gaynor, (n. 65) 711.

[171] *Lubanga* (Decision on Sentence Pursuant to Article 76 of the Statute) (n. 19) paras. 92–3.

[172] I elaborate on this point in Margaret M. deGuzman, 'Harsh Justice for International Crimes?' (2014) 39 Yale J. Intl. L. 1.

[173] See Norval Morris, *The Future of Imprisonment* (University of Chicago Press 1974) 60–1.

appropriate to impose additional punishment to facilitate restoration of victim and offender relationships—for instance, because national punishment norms dictate higher sentences. In no case, however, should international courts increase punishment merely on the grounds that preventive punishment is insufficient to reflect the offender's desert.

Although international sentences should not seek to reflect desert, retribution should play a limited role in international sentencing: it should serve as a constraint, preventing judges from imposing undeserved punishment. Adopting this "negative retributivism" is essential to avoiding injustice, as many utilitarian punishment theorists recognize.[174] A purely utilitarian approach to punishment could result in punishment of even an innocent person who is widely believed to have committed a crime. Such punishment might promote deterrence or other preventive objectives, but it would violate the fundamental moral principle of fairness.[175] Respecting the human dignity of each individual requires that people not be used merely as a means to a utilitarian end.[176]

Determining that a punishment is not undeserved, although challenging, is not as difficult as ascertaining precisely deserved punishment. Rather than requiring specific measurements of harm and culpability on the one hand, and a corresponding measurement of punishment's effects on the other, negative retribution merely requires that courts identify a ceiling above which punishment would not be deserved.[177] If international courts implement the principle of parsimony, the punishments they impose are unlikely ever to approach this ceiling. Nonetheless, negative retribution does require courts to take some account of culpability in assessing gravity. When an offender's culpability is very low, such as in a case of diminished mental capacity, even a great harm should not lead to significant punishment. In sum, adopting global crime prevention as the central purpose of punishment at international courts requires a gravity analysis focused on harm; and results in parsimonious punishment that, while no greater than deserved, serves to deter future crimes and promote global norms.

---

[174] Michael Tonry, 'Punishment and Human Dignity: Sentencing Principles for Twenty-First-Century America' (2018) 47 Crime & Justice 119, 131.

[175] Dirk van Zyl Smit and Andrew Ashworth, 'Disproportionate Sentences as Human Rights Violations' (2004) 67 Modern L. Rev. 541.

[176] Immanuel Kant, 'Groundwork of the Metaphysics of Morals', in Christine M. Korsgaard (ed.), *Kant: Groundwork of the Metaphysics of Morals* (Cambridge University Press 2012) 40.

[177] I am indebted to Tim Kelly for pointing out the relevance here of the Sorites Paradox, which notes that although people cannot agree how many grains of wheat constitute a "heap," at some point there is general agreement that a heap exists. See Dominic Hyde and Diana Raffman, 'Sorites Paradox' in Edward N. Zalta (ed.), *Stanford Encyclopedia of Philosophy*, (Stanford University 2018), available at https://plato.stanford.edu/entries/sorites-paradox/ (last accessed on September 10, 2019. Likewise, people cannot agree about precisely how much punishment an offender deserves, but can more easily agree to a ceiling of punishment that is undeserved.

D. Transparent and Flexible Procedures

To best promote legitimacy, international sentencing procedures should be transparent and flexible. Transparency is important because, as in the other contexts discussed in this book, courts are seeking to build a global justice community. To do so, they must articulate global norms clearly and openly, promoting conditions for constructive dialogue with other members of the global community. Sentencing decisions should thus link gravity analysis to goals and priorities explicitly, and courts should incorporate the feedback they receive about their analysis into future sentencing decisions.

The dialogue needed to develop global sentencing norms over time requires that sentencing procedures remain flexible. Some scholars have called for international sentencing guidelines to promote uniformity in sentencing.[178] Such uniformity may be desirable for some purposes, particularly to enhance perceptions of legitimacy. However, uniformity is less important to normative legitimacy than is the development of globally accepted norms about the purposes of punishment and how best to achieve them. At this stage, any effort to develop guidelines suggesting particular sentences for particular crimes would lack normative foundation because the global community has yet to determine its sentencing goals and priorities. At least until this occurs, international sentencing procedures should therefore remain flexible, enabling judges to articulate various visions of global sentencing, and inviting responses.

Conclusion

To enhance the legitimacy of international sentencing decisions, international criminal courts should end the practice of deploying gravity as a central sentencing factor without reference to the goals and values at stake in such decisions. Instead, they should express sentencing gravity as a function of the central goals of global punishment. Among those goals, the most important is crime prevention, which should be achieved principally through deterrence and norm expression. Sentencing procedures should remain transparent and flexible to promote the gradual development of global sentencing norms over time.

---

[178] See Guénaël Mettraux, *International Crimes and the Ad Hoc Tribunals* (Oxford University Press 2006) 347, 357 ("[T]he Judges have thus far refrained from adopting sentencing guidelines which would have provided some needed predictability in sentencing and would have somewhat constrained the almost absolute discretion which Judges have in regard to this matter."); Andrew N. Keller, 'Punishment for Violations of International Criminal Law: An Analysis of Sentencing at the ICTY and ICTR' (2001) 12 Indiana Intl. & Comp. L. Rev. 53, 66 ("General sentencing guidelines, which place certain limits on a Trial Chamber's discretion with regard to aggravating and mitigating circumstances, can help Trial Chambers make more appropriate sentencing determinations in the future.").

7

Conclusion

The concept of gravity plays a central role in determining the normative and socio-logical legitimacy of the international criminal law regime. This centrality was not a foregone conclusion at the regime's inception. International criminal law could have been crafted, like many other international regimes, around the need for inter-state coordination to address problems that cross borders. The jurisdictions of international criminal courts might then have focused on such transnational crimes as trafficking, damage to the environment, and terrorism, rather than on crimes defined significantly in terms of their gravity.

Gravity came to occupy the central justificatory role that it does today for several reasons. First, after World War II, and again in response to the conflicts in the Former Yugoslavia and Rwanda, powerful international actors decided to establish international tribunals to adjudicate crimes that were universally regarded as some of the worst in human history. These moves promoted a growing global consensus that particularly serious crimes can legitimately be punished at the international level. Indeed, by the early 1990s, that consensus, rooted in a post-Cold War environment, was strong enough that the ICTY and ICTR faced much less sovereignty-based resistance than had their post-World War II predecessors. Moreover, the extreme levels of harm suffered in each of those situations seems to have obviated the need to examine in any detail what makes crimes sufficiently serious to merit international adjudication.

The landscape changed with the advent of the ICC. The ICC's potentially global reach—it can adjudicate any situation in the world with the Security Council's blessing—made it important for the Rome Statute to limit more clearly the Court's prescriptive scope and adjudicative authority. The drafters of the Rome Statute relied significantly on the concept of gravity for these purposes: The crimes proscribed in the Statute are limited to "the most serious crimes of concern to the international community as a whole," and the Court's admissibility regime restricts its reach to cases that are of sufficient gravity to merit the Court's attention. In adopting these limits to the ICC's authority, the international community entrenched gravity as the basis for legitimate global prescriptive and adjudicative authority.

International courts and tribunals, including the ICC, also rely on gravity to justify limitations on defendants' rights and available defenses. International judges disregard immunities and amnesties on the basis of the extreme gravity of international crimes, and reject defenses based in the principle of legality and statutory

Shocking the Conscience of Humanity. Margaret M. deGuzman, Oxford University Press (2020). © Margaret M. deGuzman.
DOI: 10.1093/oso/9780198786153.001.0001

limitations on the same grounds. An interesting exception is the availability of the superior orders defense for war crimes at the ICC—an indication that at least that category of crimes is not always considered so grave that offenders are presumed to know of their illegality in all cases. Courts and tribunals also reference gravity to justify limiting defendants' rights by applying presumptions of pre-trial detention, lowering burdens of proof, and permitting lengthy trials. Finally, the sentences international courts and tribunals award are usually justified largely by the gravity of the cases.

Gravity is thus the central concept used to justify the existence and authority of the international criminal law regime, as well as many of its most important decisions. As such, gravity is crucial to the regime's normative and sociological legitimacy. Strong normative legitimacy requires a regime to implement appropriate moral values, and to pursue appropriate goals; and strong sociological legitimacy requires it to be perceived as doing so. Thus, for the regime's reliance on gravity to bolster its legitimacy, the concept must be used in ways that promote the values and goals that are most appropriate for the regime to pursue.

Yet despite the importance of gravity to the regime's legitimacy, the concept has received remarkably little attention. The Rome Statute's drafters did not explain what they meant by "sufficient gravity" for admissibility before the Court, and the definitions of crimes within the Court's jurisdiction leave many unanswered questions about what makes them "serious crimes of concern to the international community as a whole." It remains unclear, for instance, how "widespread" crimes must be to qualify as crimes against humanity under that prong of the definition, and what "part" of a group an offender must intend to destroy to commit genocide. Such ambiguities affect the legitimacy of all international courts and tribunals, and even jeopardize the legitimacy of decisions by national courts to exercise universal jurisdiction.

The failure of international criminal law's supporters, judges, and advocates to endow the concept of gravity with greater content stems in part from the difficulty of the task. Citing an ambiguous notion of gravity to justify a decision is far easier than identifying the values and goals that undergird an outcome. Indeed, such identification entails a significant risk for the decision-maker: it requires them to expose their normative framework, and potentially to have that framework critiqued by those who disagree with their decision.

Another explanation for the relative lack of attention to gravity is that people often believe they recognize gravity intuitively, even if they cannot articulate reasons for their intuitions. But, like US Supreme Court Justice Potter Stewart's famous claim that he knows pornography when he sees it, this rationale fails empirically. There may be agreement at the margins: virtually everyone acknowledges that the Holocaust was very grave, and most people would hesitate to attach that label to a single soldier's act of verbally abusing a civilian. Yet in the vast middle where most crimes reside there is plenty of room for disagreement. Not only do people disagree about whether crimes are grave in an abstract sense, once the question is posed in the context of a particular decision, such as whether an international court should exercise jurisdiction, significant divergences of opinion emerge.

The hesitation of many regime actors to engage more deeply with the concept of gravity probably also relates to the constructive role that gravity's ambiguity has played in the regime's development. Leaving gravity vague helped to ensure the adoption of the Rome Statute, and encouraged political actors in the world's capitals to join the regime. Indeed, gravity's ambiguity continues to facilitate "incompletely theorized agreements"[1] around regime decisions. For some audiences, in some contexts, the explanation that a crime is grave enough to justify an outcome is sufficient to garner their agreement.

To play this kind of constructive role, gravity must remain vague enough to mask tensions and disagreements among competing values and goals. By agreeing that international adjudication is appropriate for "atrocities," state actors can avoid difficult conversations about when international goals such as global deterrence and norm promotion should be given priority over conflicting national goals such as peace and reconciliation. By invoking gravity, decision-makers purport to provide a goal-neutral explanation for selection decisions that in fact require them to prioritize some goals over others. Likewise, in citing gravity to justify punishment decisions, international judges avoid deep inquiry into how the punishments they impose relate to the goals of international criminal adjudication.

However, as the practice of international criminal law expands, it is becoming increasingly problematic for regime actors to seek to legitimize decisions by relying on vague notions of gravity. From a normative perspective, such reliance is undesirable because it detracts from the important process of identifying global values and goals upon which to build the global justice community, thereby jeopardizing the regime's long-term normative legitimacy. Additionally, as gravity's ambiguity is exposed, observers of international criminal justice increasingly question whether the true motivations for some gravity-related decisions are improperly political or otherwise inappropriate. Such charges harm the sociological legitimacy of the regime.

The normative theories that have been advanced to justify international prescriptive and adjudicative authority have largely failed to notice, let alone solve, this problem. Virtually every theory of what makes a crime "international" includes a gravity component, but most pay scant attention, if any, to what that component entails. Likewise, the theories seeking to explain the moral legitimacy of international and universal adjudication mostly rely on a gravity threshold without identifying the location of that threshold.

---

[1] Cass Sunstein, 'Incompletely Theorized Agreements' (1995) 108 Harv. L. Rev. 1733, 1735.

This book has set forth proposals to operationalize gravity in both the theory and practice of international criminal law. These proposals foreground the relationship between gravity-based authority and decisions on the one hand, and the values and goals that motivate the international criminal law regime on the other. With regard to global prescriptive authority, the core value the regime seeks to promote is the protection of human dignity. It does so through the adjudication of crimes that threaten or harm human dignity in an effort to prevent such harms in the future. In light of this broad core value, it is important that any gravity threshold for legitimate global prescriptive authority be a very low one. Such a threshold should exclude only harms to human dignity that arguably do not qualify for criminal punishment at all.

Gravity's more important work in the context of legitimizing global prescriptive authority is to justify the global community's choices about how to allocate scarce resources. To do so, gravity must be understood in relation to the global community's goals and priorities at a given time. A crime is especially grave for purposes of being included in an international convention or court Statute when its prevention reflects an appropriate priority of the global community. Thus, for instance, aggression might be considered grave because the global community has a strong interest in its prevention both because it tends to produce large-scale harms to human dignity, and because it threatens the underlying structure of the global legal order. But greater specificity is needed beyond this general statement. For instance, how do the requirements of "character, gravity and scale" in the Rome Statute's definition of aggression reflect particular global interests? The interests underlying crimes against humanity are perhaps even less clear. Are such crimes of particular interest to the global community because of the scale of harm they produce, the involvement of state actors, the harms they inflict on groups, or for other reasons? Such issues must be addressed for the regime to have strong long-term legitimacy.

Legitimate decisions to adjudicate situations and cases also require an understanding of gravity linked to the global interests in such adjudication. In this context, gravity should again serve as a threshold, excluding from adjudication cases of international crimes that, although they involve the kinds of harms that meet the minimal gravity threshold for prescription, nonetheless fail to warrant criminal adjudication because the harm they cause or the offender's culpability is negligible. Under such circumstances, there is no global interest in adjudication, and adjudication would therefore be illegitimate.

Likewise, for global adjudication to be legitimate, the global interest must be sufficiently strong to overcome any competing interests in non-adjudication, particularly of relevant national communities. This requires decision-makers to balance the gravity of situations and cases, understood in terms of the extent of global interest in adjudication, against whatever values are in tension with that interest. The global interest in adjudication depends on both the importance of the goals at stake in a situation or case to the global community, and the likelihood of achieving those goals. Because the most important goal of global adjudication is crime prevention, the second question generally involves an evaluation of the likelihood adjudication will prevent future crimes. Thus, for instance, global adjudication would be illegitimate in a situation in which such adjudication is unlikely to contribute greatly to preventing future crimes and a national community has a strong interest in non-adjudication in service of national goals, such as peace or reconciliation.

A final role gravity can productively play in legitimizing global adjudication is to guide decision-makers in their allocation of scarce resources. This role parallels that described earlier regarding the allocation of limited prescriptive resources. Here, gravity is a relative consideration that can serve to identify the situations and cases in which the global community has the greatest interest in adjudication from among those it may legitimately adjudicate. That is, gravity can help decision-makers select the situations and cases that present the highest likelihood of promoting the regime's most important goals. By selecting such situations and cases, international courts and tribunals can increase their effectiveness, and thus promote regime legitimacy.

The ICC Prosecutor has made progress toward implementing a goal-based understanding of gravity with regard to case selection decisions. Her policy on case selection identifies priorities to guide application of the gravity factors, such as the prevention of crimes that particularly affect women and children, and the protection of the environment; and she has justified some of her case selection decisions by reference to such goals. The Court should take a similar approach to selecting situations from among the potentially admissible situations. The Prosecutor and judges should seek to allocate resources to the situations that will best promote the institution's most important goals. Contrary to the Prosecutor's current interpretation of the Rome Statute, the discretion to select among admissible situations can be found in the "interests of justice" provision governing the initiation of investigations.

Gravity should also be operationalized in relation to goals and values in resolving questions related to defendants' rights and defenses, and in allocating punishment. When decision-makers face choices between the values associated with accountability and those related to defendants' rights, they should never resolve them with unexamined and ambiguous claims about gravity. Instead, they should interrogate the purposes accountability would serve in the circumstances and determine whether those goals are sufficiently important to warrant the restrictions in question. Of course, they should never adopt restrictions that violate defendants' fundamental human rights. In sentencing defendants, judges should likewise avoid justifications that purport to determine gravity based on lists of factors unrelated to the purposes of punishment. Rather, they should determine which punishment goals are most appropriate for global institutions and align their gravity analyses with those goals.

To operationalize gravity in these ways will require the regime's decision-makers to identify the regime's values and goals, and to establish priorities among them when they conflict. This is a daunting task, particularly for a regime that was built in part by fostering ambiguity about its values and goals. Ideally, this task will be undertaken significantly by the regime's equivalents to a legislature—the Assembly of States Parties for the ICC, and the United Nations for courts created under the auspices of that body. Political actors in such bodies are best placed to articulate and debate values and to implement policies aimed at establishing goals and priorities. For instance, states have an opportunity to clarify the goals they seek to further through global prescription when they consider the proposed convention on crimes against humanity. Likewise, the ICC's Assembly of States Parties could, for instance, provide guidance to the Court regarding how to allocate its resources among competing goals, and could amend the Rome Statute to include more specific criteria for various kinds of gravity-related decisions.

However, because global norms continually evolve and international political bodies are even less nimble than national ones, it is important for political actors to avoid imposing stringent limits on international courts. As such, the task of identifying and applying global norms will inevitably fall significantly to institutional actors. To ask prosecutors and judges to articulate institutional goals and priorities through their decisions is to ask them to expose themselves to potential criticism and even to legitimacy challenges in the short term. This is particularly challenging at this early stage in the regime's development when little consensus has emerged around regime norms. Nonetheless, unless regime actors rise to this challenge, it will be difficult for the regime to build strong long-term legitimacy.

Regardless of which decision-makers are involved in identifying global norms, it is essential that the process be a dialogic and inclusive one. Decision-makers should express their views clearly and disseminate them broadly, inviting responses from diverse audiences and incorporating the feedback they receive into future decisions. Decision-makers should, whenever possible, make special efforts to solicit feedback from community members removed from sources of political and economic power; and they should actively seek to ensure that their decisions do not promote or reinforce structures of repression and domination. Such dynamic dialogue will help the regime to evolve in ways that best promote global well-being.

In the short term, engaging in this dialogue about regime values and goals may actually harm perceptions of the regime's legitimacy by exposing a fragile foundation. The undertheorized notion of gravity may mask deep and broad disagreements about the appropriate role of international criminal law in the world. Once the mask is removed, regime critics may gain traction. Alternatively, the relative success the regime has enjoyed in the past few decades may reflect strong basic agreements that have yet to be recognized, partly because the regime has worked fairly well. In that case, increased dialogue about goals and values will simply continue to build on a strong foundation.

Regardless of the short-term legitimacy consequences, engaging in this process is essential because the regime's long-term legitimacy depends upon it. Over time, a global regime that fails to articulate and pursue values that are widely accepted by the global community is destined to fail. Replacing the current undertheorized version of gravity with one tied to global values and goals will promote the regime's normative and sociological legitimacy, enabling it to serve as a more effective tool to prevent crimes that "shock the conscience of humanity."

Selected Bibliography

Adeno Addis, 'Imagining the International Community: The Constitutive Dimension of Universal Jurisdiction' (2009) 31 Human Rights Q. 129.

Adeno Addis, 'Genocide and Belonging: Processes of Imagining Communities' (2017) 38 U. Pa. J. Intl. L. 1041.

Adeno Addis, 'The Role of Human Dignity in a World of Plural Values and Ethical Commitments' (2013) 31 Netherlands Q. of Human Rights 403.

Akira Iriye, *Global Community: The Role of International Organizations in the Making of the Contemporary World* (University of California Press 2002).

Alain Pellet, 'Internationalized Courts; Better than Nothing … ' in Cesare P.R. Romano, et al. (eds.), *Internationalized Criminal Courts: Sierra Leone, East Timor, Kosovo, and Cambodia* (Oxford University Press 2004).

Alejandro Chehtman, *The Philosophical Foundations of Extraterritorial Jurisdiction* (Oxford University Press 2010).

Allen Buchanan and Robert O. Keohane, 'The Legitimacy of Global Governance Institutions' (2006) 20 Ethics & Intl. Affairs 405.

Allison Marston Danner, 'Constructing a Hierarchy of Crimes in International Criminal Law Sentencing' (2001) 87 Va. L. Rev. 415.

Andrea Carcano, 'Sentencing and the Gravity of the Offence in International Criminal Law' (2002) 51 ICLQ 583.

Andrew Altman and Christopher Heath Wellman, 'A Defense of International Criminal Law' (2004) 115 Ethics 35.

Andrew K. Woods, 'Moral Judgments & International Crimes: The Disutility of Desert' (2012) 52 Va. J. Intl. L. 633.

Anthony D'Amato, 'Is International Law a Part of Natural Law?' (1989) 9 Vera Lex 8.

Antony Duff, 'Authority and Responsibility in International Criminal Law' in Samantha Besson and John Tasioulas (eds.), *The Philosophy of International Law* (Oxford University Press 2010).

Asher Alkoby, 'Three Images of "Global Community": Theorizing Law and Community in a Multicultural World' (2010) 12 Intl. Community L. Rev. 35.

Barbora Hola, et al., 'Consistency of International Sentencing: ICTY and ICTR Case Study' (2012) 9 Eur. J. Criminology 539.

Barbora Hola, et al., 'International Sentencing Facts and Figures: Sentencing Practices at the ICTY and ICTR' (2011) 9 J. Intl. Crim. Justice 411.

Beth Van Schaack, 'The Principle of Legality in International Criminal Law' (2009) 103 ASIL Proc. 101.

Bruce Broomhall, *International Justice and the International Criminal Court: Between Sovereignty and the Rule of Law* (Oxford University Press 2004).

Caroline Davidson, 'No Shortcuts on Human Rights: Bail and the International Criminal Trial' (2010) 60 Am. U. L. Rev. 1.

Cass Sunstein, 'Incompletely Theorized Agreements' (1995) 108 Harv. L. Rev. 1733.

Charles Beitz, *The Idea of Human Rights* (Oxford University Press 2009).

Charles Jalloh, 'Immunity from Prosecution for International Crimes: The Case of Charles Taylor at the Special Court for Sierra Leone' 8(21) ASIL Insights, available at www.asil.org/insights/volume/8/issue/21/immunity-prosecution-international-crimes-case-charles-taylor-special (last accessed on September 14, 2019).

Christopher A. Thomas, 'The Uses and Abuses of Legitimacy in International Law' (2014) 34 OJLS 729.

Daniel Bodansky, 'The Legitimacy of International Governance: A Coming Challenge for International Environmental Law?' (1999) 93 AJIL 596.

Daniel Bodansky, 'Legitimacy in International Law and International Relations' in Jeffrey L. Dunoff and Mark A. Pollack (eds.), *Interdisciplinary Perspectives on International Law and International Relations: The State of the Art* (Cambridge University Press 2013).

Darryl Robinson, 'The Identity Crisis of International Criminal Law' (2008) 21 Leiden J. Intl. L. 925.

Darryl Robinson, 'Serving the Interests of Justice: Amnesties, Truth Commissions and the International Criminal Court' (2003) 14 Eur. J. Intl. L. 481.

David Alonzo-Maizlish, 'In Whole or In Part: Group Rights, The Intent Element of Genocide, and the "Quantitative Criterion"' (2002) 77 NYU. L. Rev. 1369.

David Beetham, *The Legitimation of Power*, 2nd edn., (Palgrave 1990).

David Kennedy, 'The Mystery of Global Governance' (2008) 34 Ohio Northern Univ. L. Rev. 827.

David Luban, 'A Theory of Crimes Against Humanity' (2004) 29 Yale J. Intl. L. 85.

David Scheffer, 'Genocide and Atrocity Crimes' (2006) 1 Genocide Stud. & Prevention 229.

Dirk van Zyl Smit and Andrew Ashworth, 'Disproportionate Sentences as Human Rights Violations' (2004) 67 Modern L. Rev. 541.

Dragana Radosavljevic, 'Mala Captus Bene Detentus and the Right to Challenge the Legality of Arrests Under the ICC Statute' (2008) 29 Liverpool L. Rev. 269.

Egon Schwelb, 'Crimes Against Humanity' (1946) 23 Brit. Y.B. Intl. L. 178.

Eugene Kontorovich, 'The Piracy Analogy: Modern Universal Jurisdiction's Hollow Foundation' (2004) 45 Harv. Intl. L.J. 183.

Gillian Brock and Harry Brighouse (eds.), *The Political Philosophy of Cosmopolitanism* (Cambridge University Press 2005).

Giuliana Ziccardi Capaldo, 'Global Constitutionalism and Global Governance: Towards a UN-Driven Global Constitutional Governance Model' in M. Cherif Bassiouni (ed.), *Globalization and its Impact on the Future of Human Rights and International Criminal Justice* (Intersentia 2015).

Hugo Grotius, *Hugonis Grotii De Jure Belli Et Pacis Libri Tres: Accompanied by an Abridged Translation*, William Whewell (trans.), (J.W. Parker 1853).

Human Rights Watch, 'Policy Paper: The Meaning of "The Interests of Justice" in Article 53 of the Rome Statute' (2005).

Immanuel Kant, 'Groundwork of the Metaphysics of Morals' in Christine M. Korsgaard (ed.), *Kant: Groundwork of the Metaphysics of Morals* (Cambridge University Press 2012).

Immanuel Kant, *The Metaphysical Elements of Justice*, 2nd edn., John Ladd (trans.), (Hackett 1999).

J. Benton Heath, 'Mapping Extensive Uses of Human Dignity in International Criminal Law' in Siljia Vöneky (ed.), *Ethics and Law: The Ethicalization of Law* (Springer Press 2013).

Jenia Turner, 'Policing International Prosecutors' (2012) 45 Intl. L. & Politics 175.

Jennifer Clark, 'Zero to Life: Sentencing Appeals at the International Criminal Tribunals for the Former Yugoslavia and Rwanda' (2008) 96 Georgetown L.J. 1685.

Jens David Ohlin, 'Applying the Death Penalty to Crimes of Genocide' (2005) 99 AJIL 747.

Jens David Ohlin, 'Proportional Sentences at the ICTY' in Bert Swart, Göran Sluiter, and Alexander Zahar (eds.), *The Legacy of the International Criminal Tribunal for the Former Yugoslavia* (Oxford University Press 2011).

Jens David Ohlin, 'Towards a Unique Theory of International Criminal Sentencing' in Goran Sluiter and Sergey Vasiliev (eds.), *International Criminal Procedure: Towards a Coherent Body of Law* (Cameron May Intl. L. and Policy 2009).

Johanna Herman, 'Realities of Victim Participation: The Civil Party System in Practice at the Extraordinary Chambers in the Courts of Cambodia (ECCC)' (2013) 16 Contemporary Justice Rev. 461.

Joseph B. Keenan and Brendan F. Brown, *Crimes Against International Law* (Public Affairs Press 1950).

Joseph W. Doherty and Richard H. Steinberg, 'Punishment and Policy in International Criminal Sentencing: An Empirical Study' (2016) 110 AJIL 49.

Jürgen Habermas, 'The Concept of Human Dignity and the Realistic Utopia of Human Rights' (2010) 41 Metaphilosophy 464.

Jürgen Habermas, *Structural Transformation of the Public Sphere*, Thomas Burger (trans.), (MIT Press 1989).

Kai Ambos, 'Punishment without a Sovereign?: The *Ius Puniendi* Issue of International Criminal Law: A First Contribution towards a Consistent Theory of International Criminal Law' (2013) 33 OJLS 293.

Kai Ambos, 'The Overall Function of International Criminal Law: Striking the Right Balance Between the Rechtsgut and the Harm Principles' (2015) 9 Crim. L. & Philosophy 301.

Kirsten Fisher, *Moral Accountability and International Criminal Law: Holding Agents of Atrocity Accountable to the World* (Routledge 2013).

Larry May, *Crimes Against Humanity: A Normative Account* (Cambridge University Press 2004).

M. Cherif Bassiouni, *Crimes Against Humanity in International Criminal Law* (Kluwer Law International 1999).

M. Cherif Bassiouni, 'International Crimes: The *Ratione Materiae* of International Criminal Law' in M. Cherif Bassiouni (ed.), *International Criminal Law: Sources, Subjects and Content*, Vol. 1, 3rd edn. (Martinus Nijhoff 2008).

Mahnoush H. Arsanjani and W. Michael Reisman, 'The Law-in-Action of the International Criminal Court' (2005) 99 AJIL 2.

Makua Mutua, 'What is TWAIL?' (2000) 94 ASIL Proc. 31.

Mark B. Harmon and Fergal Gaynor, 'Ordinary Sentences for Extraordinary Crimes' (2007) 5 J. Intl. Crim. Justice 683.

Markus Benzing, 'Community Interests in the Procedure of International Courts and Tribunals' (2006) 5 L. & Practice Intl. Courts & Tribunals 369.

Massimo Renzo, 'A Criticism of the International Harm Principle' (2010) 4 Crim. L. & Philosophy 267.

Massimo Renzo, 'Crimes Against Humanity and the Limits of International Criminal Law' (2012) 31 L. & Philosophy 443.

Micaela Frulli, 'Are Crimes against Humanity More Serious than War Crimes?' (2001) 12 Eur. J. Intl. L. 329.

Michael C. Dorf and Frederick Schauer, 'The Supreme Court 1997 Term' (1998) 122 Harv. L. Rev. 152.

Mirjan Damaska, 'Reflections on Fairness in International Criminal Justice' (2012) 10 J. Intl. Crim. Justice 611.

Myres S. McDougal and W. Michael Reisman, 'Rhodesia and the United Nations: The Lawfulness of International Concern' (1968) 62 AJIL 1.

Nancy A. Combs, *Fact-Finding Without Facts: The Uncertain Evidentiary Foundations of International Criminal Convictions* (Cambridge University Press 2010).

Nancy A. Combs, 'Seeking Inconsistency: Advancing Pluralism in International Criminal Sentencing' (2016) 41 Yale J. Intl. L. 1.

Neil Vidmar, 'Retribution and Revenge' in Joseph Sanders and V. Lee Hamilton (eds.), *Handbook of Justice Research in Law* (Kluwer Academic 2002).

Olaoluwa Olusanya, *Sentencing War Crimes and Crimes Against Humanity Under the International Criminal Tribunal for the Former Yugoslavia* (Europa Law Publishing 2005).

Otto Triffterer, 'The Preventive and Repressive Function of the International Criminal Court' in Mauro Politi and Guiseppe Nesi (eds.), *The Rome Statute of the International Criminal Court* (Routledge 2001).

Paolo G. Carozza, 'Human Dignity and Judicial Interpretation of Human Rights: A Reply' (2008) 19 Eur. J. Intl. L. 931.

Patricia M. Wald, 'Genocide and Crimes Against Humanity' (2007) 6 Wash. U. Global Studies L. Rev. 621.

Paul H. Robinson, 'Competing Conceptions of Modern Desert: Vengeful, Deontological, and Empirical' (2008) 67 Cambridge L.J. 145.

Paul H. Robinson and John M. Darley, 'The Utility of Desert' (1997) 91 Northwestern U. L. Rev. 453.

Quincy Wright, 'The Law of the Nuremberg Trial' (1947) 41 AJIL 38.

Rafael Domingo, 'The New Global Human Community' (2012) 12 Chi. J. Intl. L. 563.

Raphael Lemkin, 'Genocide as a Crime Under International Law' (1947) 41 AJIL 145.

Richard Vernon, *Cosmopolitan Regard: Political Membership and Global Justice* (Cambridge University Press 2010).

Richard Vernon, 'Crimes Against Humanity: A Defense of the "Subsidiarity" View' (2013) 26 Canadian J.L. & Jurisprudence 229.

Richard Vernon, 'What is Crime Against Humanity?' (2003) 10 J. Political Philosophy 231.

Roy S. K. Lee (ed.), *The International Criminal Court: The Making of the Rome Statute* (Martinus Nijhoff 1999).

Ruti G. Teitel, *Humanity's Law* (Oxford University Press 2011).

Salvatore Zappala, 'Do Heads of State in Office Enjoy Immunity from Jurisdiction for International Crimes? The Ghaddafi Case Before the French Cour de Cassation' (2001) 12 Eur. J. Intl. L. 595.

Sarah M. Nouwen, *Complementarity in the Line of Fire: The Catalysing Effect of the International Criminal Court in Uganda and Sudan* (Cambridge University Press 2013).

Shane Darcy, 'The Principle of Legality at the Crossroads of Human Rights and International Criminal Law' in Margaret M. deGuzman and Diane Marie Amann (eds.), *Arcs of Global Justice: Essays in Honour of William A. Schabas* (Oxford University Press 2018).

Stephen D. Krasner, 'Structural Causes and Regime Consequences: Regimes as Intervening Variables' (1982) 36 Intl. Org. 185.

Stephen Macedo (ed.), *The Princeton Principles on Universal Jurisdiction* (Princeton Project on Universal Jurisdiction 2001).

Steven D. Roper and Lillian A. Barria, *Designing Criminal Tribunals: Sovereignty and International Concerns in the Protection of Human Rights* (Ashgate 2006).

William A. Schabas, *An Introduction to the International Criminal Court* (Cambridge University Press 2007).

William A. Schabas, *Genocide in International Law: The Crime of Crimes* (Cambridge University Press 2009).

William A. Schabas, *The International Criminal Court: A Commentary on the Rome Statute* (Oxford University Press 2010).

William A. Schabas, 'Sentencing by International Tribunals: A Human Rights Approach' (1997) 7 Duke J. Comp. Intl. L. 461.

William A. Schabas, 'State Policy as an Element of International Crimes' (2007) 98 J. Crim. L. & Criminology 953.

Uwe Ewald, 'Predictably Irrational—International Sentencing and its Discourse against the Backdrop of Preliminary Empirical Findings on ICTY Sentencing Practices' (2010) 10 Intl. Crim. L. Rev. 365.

Win-chiat Lee, 'International Law and Universal Jurisdiction' in Larry May and Zachary Hoskins (eds.), *International Criminal Law and Philosophy* (Cambridge University Press 2010).

Yuval Shany, 'Assessing the Effectiveness of International Courts: A Goal-Based Approach' (2012) 106 AJIL 225.

Yuval Shany, 'Stronger Together? Legitimacy and Effectiveness of International Courts as Mutually Reinforcing or Undermining Notions' in Nienke Grossman et al. (eds.), *Legitimacy and International Courts* (Cambridge University Press 2018).

Index

Note: *For the benefit of digital users, indexed terms that span two pages (e.g., 52–53) may, on occasion, appear on only one of those pages.*

Printed and bound by CPI Group (UK) Ltd, Croydon, CR0 4YY